READ NGEMENT

Julia Kristeva

Readings of Exile and Estrangement

Anna Smith
Lecturer in English, University of Canterbury
New Zealand

St. Martin's Press
New York

JULIA KRISTEVA

For information, address:

St. Martin's Press, Scholarly and Reference Division,
175 Fifth Avenue, New York, N.Y. 10010

First published in the United States of America in 1996

Printed in Great Britain

ISBN 0–312–16432–7 (cloth)
ISBN 0–312–16434–3 (paperback)

Library of Congress Cataloging-in-Publication Data
Smith, Anna, 1952–
Julia Kristeva : readings of exile and estrangement / Anna Smith.
p. cm.
Includes bibliographical references and index.
ISBN 0–312–16432–7 (cloth). — ISBN 0–312–16434–3 (pbk.)
1. Kristeva, Julia, 1941– 2. Feminist literary criticism.
3. Psychoanalysis and literature. I. Title.
PN75.K75S64 1996
801'.95'092—dc20 96–24147
CIP

'No one escapes it. Except perhaps the saint, the mystic, or the writer who, through the power of language ... [identifies] with love itself and what he is in fact – a fire of tongues, an exit from representation.'

Julia Kristeva

Contents

Acknowledgements

Many people have helped me in the preparation of this book. I would especially like to thank Pauline Brook and Keren Smith who advised me on points of translation; Alan Clarke from the French Department, University of Canterbury; Annabel Cooper and Chris Prentice, whose encouragement at different times was invaluable; Patrick Fuery, a stimulating colleague and good friend; Lucy Holmes, whose attraction to Kristeva matches my own; George Hook, Malcolm Macfarlane and Kate Trevella, who generously gave of their time to assist me with formatting; Ken Bragan, Rosey Mabin, Keren and Allan Smith for good conversation; Howard McNaughton, Leonard Wilcox, Jane Jones and Mary Sullivan, for their help with preparing the bibliography. Devon Sinclair from the Canterbury School of Fine Arts and Jonathan Smart provided me with valuable resources on Julia Morison. I am grateful for their interest in this project. I would also like to acknowledge the continuing interest and loving support offered by Patrick Evans, Sarah, Frances and Jacob Hook, George Hook, Jennifer Smith, Lydia and Richard Gardiner and my parents, Jean and Bryan Smith.

Denis Walker ably supervised the early stages of my research on Kristeva, and I would like to thank him for his careful reading and thoughtful responses. John Lechte read this manuscript when it was nearing completion and gave me a greater clarity in approaching the idea of 'foreignness'. I have appreciated his enthusiasm and advice. My thanks also to Charmian Hearne and her editorial staff at Macmillan.

Finally I must acknowledge the support provided by the staff and students of the English Departments of Canterbury and Otago Universities during the past seven years. Without their encouragement, and without a scholarship from the University Grants Committee, this book would never have been completed.

Abbreviations

KRISTEVA

More extensive details are to be found in the bibliography

English texts

ACW	*About Chinese Women*
'ANT'	'A New Type of Intellectual: the Dissident'
BS	*Black Sun*
Desire	*Desire in Language*
LtU	*Language the Unknown*
'MMH'	'My Memory's Hyperbole'
'Oscillation'	'Oscillation Between Power and Denial'
Powers	*Powers of Horror*
'PatP'	'Psychoanalysis and the Polis'
PatS	*Proust and the Sense of Time*
RPL	*Revolution in Poetic Language*
'SN'	'Say Nothing'
Tales	*Tales of Love*
'Talking'	'Talking About Polylogue'
'TLW'	'The Last Word of this Adventure'
TOM	*The Old Man and the Wolves*
'WT'	'Women's Time'

French texts

'DINY'	'D'Ithaca à New York'
'ER'	'Evenément et révélation'
Etrangers	*Etrangers à nous-mêmes*
LS	*Les Samouraïs*
LVH	*Le Vieil Homme et les Loups*
Pouvoirs	*Pouvoirs de l'horreur*
RLP	*Révolution du langage poétique*
Sém	*Séméiotiké*

FREUD

SE followed by volume number
Unless otherwise indicated, all references to Freud are from the *Standard Edition of the Complete Psychological Works of Sigmund Freud*, trans. and ed. James Strachey (London: The Hogarth Press, 1951–73).

Part I
Introducing the Subject

Introduction

Schopenhauer once wrote of how the common mass of people lived existence as if surrounded by the smells of a perfume shop – so engendered were they by its environment, that they were unable to recognise its distinctive beauty. Anyone who has taken the trouble to reflect on the nature of perception will agree with Schopenhauer that the means we have for registering information about the world that surrounds us is constrained and filtered through the screen of habit. From the rituals of daily routine to the paradigms that construct our experiences of reality, perception does indeed have a regularised quality which if we notice it at all, we find profoundly comforting. One of the distinctive aspects to creative thought is the conviction that perception could (and should) be something quite different. Curious inquiry, so the assumption goes, re-presents the heady sensations of experience, or at least the means to understand them. Through prising off the carapace of routine, criticism allows the intellectual to extend the boundaries of what can be said about an experience. In different ways, philosophy and literature have sought procedures that would estrange the object of perception in order to render it paradoxically more beautiful, more knowable, or both. It is not an exaggeration to assert that estrangement of some kind, in fact, is presupposed by all forms of critical analysis.

What do we understand by the word, *estrangement*? Is it best reflected by the Russian formalists' concept of 'defamiliarisation' (*ostranenie*) that sought to counter automatised perception and stale overused poetic conventions by making language (and reading) strange? Is it closer to 'alienation' (*Entfremdung*) which Hegel used to describe the self-estrangement of mind into matter, and which Marx instinctively acknowledged when he spoke of the alienating relations under capitalism: 'all that is solid melts into air'?[1] Is it the instantaneous flash of recognition, somewhat in the manner of an epiphany, that tells us something for which we had been seeking was present all along, and which Hegel expresses as the Absolute revealing itself to the subject as 'from the outset in and for itself beside us and [who] wants to be beside us'?[2] Or does Julia Kristeva's reading of abjection which puts the subject beside himself with horror come closest to estrangement?[3] The *Oxford English Dictionary* lists at least nine entries for estrangement including: to remove something from its familiar place; to make someone a stranger to a condition or place; to withhold from a person's perception or knowledge; to render alien; to alienate in feeling or affection; to make unlike oneself; to render strange or unfamiliar in appearance; to be astonished (*obs.*). Each of these cases, however apparently diverse, arises out of a shift of perception. There is a change in a state of affairs that the consciousness registers as a form of loss or difference, as the habitual suddenly or by degrees is transformed into the site of exile, discomfort, and sometimes novelty, astonishment, or awe.

When the Russian formalist Victor Shklovsky wrote that 'art exists that one may recover the sensation of life; it exists to make one feel things, to make the stone *stony*',[4] it was precisely this latter experience of novel perception that he was reaching for. Although Shklovsky was concerned that habitual perception devoured our appreciation for the daily activities of life, including those we loved, his preoccupation with defamiliarisation was directed towards estranging perception as an end in itself. Unlike the scientist, the writer seeks to make his representation of perception dense: formal texture in literature works not to produce knowledge but to elevate the aesthetic function, and accordingly its characteristics must be 'roughened', 'difficult' and 'impeded'. The work carried out by the formalists into the nature of poetic language and the autonomy of the aesthetic function[5] is an invaluable beginning to a study of estrangement, but also a limited one. Some of Julia Kristeva's earliest essays indicate a debt to such thinking but moved far beyond its limitations.

In 'The Ethics of Linguistics', Kristeva congratulated the linguist Roman Jakobson for his sensitive listening to the phonic textures of language. Despite his inability to make of this texture a function which would radically challenge the linguist's preference for lucid models, Kristeva saw that the scope of what she termed 'poetic language' could be enlarged to incorporate 'a heterogeneous, destructive causality'.[6] Poetic language could then be seen as an entity that challenged linguistic paradigms without acceding to them. From this early essay arises the claim that the new theorist of poetic language will depart from the strict rigours of science and pass across 'whole geographic and discursive continents as an impertinent traveller, a "faun in the house"' (*faune au logis / phonologie*). (*Desire*: 32) He or she would be a stranger to language, at home with no single model or theory. The new theorist would be an inventive traveller borrowing from numerous discourses, always sensitive to the estranging nature of rhythm and its violent clash with history. Such impertinence was the only means, she insisted, whereby the subject might redraw the boundaries that define the nature of his existence. For Kristeva, poetic language was the key to estranging perception and, more ambitiously, all thought, because it introduced a heterogeneous space into signifying structures and subjective identity. Poetic language transmuted the ecstasy of the visionary or mystic experience *outside* language into an ecstatic experience *within* language: '*a fire of tongues*, an exit from representation.' (*Tales*: 253) Thus language already contains the potential for its own Pentecostal renewal: what she terms the fire of tongues. When language became dense with phonic textures and semantic associations, that is, when it became *poetic*, it acted as an entry-point for the drives to transfer their psychic imprints from the unconscious directly into signification, causing it to falter and renew itself. The subject of poetic language is the product of this discharge into signification. But to speak of a subject as if it were both familiar and stable is misleading. The identity and space of Kristeva's subject are simultaneously destroyed and recreated by the pressures exerted on language from an affect-driven body. Neither at home with himself nor his speech, he is restless wherever he finds himself; an exile to all origins and habitual pursuits, he is the perfect example of the stranger who never settles in.

Much of Kristeva's writing gives the impression that the language of exile is the only language worth knowing, especially for intellectuals and, perhaps, most especially for her own discourse as a woman. 'How can one avoid sinking into the mire of common sense,' she asks, 'if not by becoming a stranger to one's own country, language, sex and identity? Writing is impossible without some kind of exile.'[7] This brief statement encapsulates the many different forms of thought which will be challenged and estranged by her readings of semiotics and psychoanalysis. For Kristeva, the call of writing demands that the exile refuses to take comfort in narcissistic regression to maternal origins or in clinging to a singular identity. Subjectivity is heterogeneous, and the exile is most at home with an intolerable excess in language that leads away from the representation of one's sexual identity, for instance, to effect 'multiple sublations of the unnameable, the unrepresentable, the void.' ('ANT': 300) In an effort to represent the universally alienated quality of existence, her subject is always expressed in the masculine, but as we shall discover, for some critics this strategy may lead the female reader into a double exile. For all subjects however, male or female, alterity founds questions of origin and identity, and provides the grounds for reading differently.

The heterogeneity that is a product of constant creativity and loss within language and the subject rejects a transcendent form of incarnation. There can thus be no external source for Pentecost, no 'big bang' theory able to generate the kind of revolutionary poetics that explicitly rejects a First Cause outside of language. Nevertheless Kristeva appeals to the visionary language of epiphany and apocalypse to elaborate the earth shaking nature of those borderline states of language and human experience which continue to fascinate her. Poetic language is revolutionary because it redefines the subject as a 'man-process' recognising not the linear time of history, but time as rupture and discontinuity: Apocalypse Now. That time when the mountains smoked and the gods descended is over, but the notion of an estranging intervention in history that *rearranges space* is still repeatedly invoked in Kristeva's texts. From the 'flash' of conception in 'Stabat Mater'[8] to the 'flash' of forgiveness in *Black Sun*,[9] she finds a new place for the language of origin in a discourse that now *plays* with origins but appears not to believe in them.

As a consequence, if language plays with origins, there can be no privileging of one form of identity. The subject is multiple, not singular, and identity is at least double, as her reading of Lautréamont shows in *Revolution in Poetic Language*.[10] The author's enunciation is at once product and a continuous production, dissected by the voices of others and always already oriented to the Other (culture, language, the unconscious). Kristeva is a female writer, but seems to suggest that we should not allocate a permanently privileged position in the language of the text for women, since this would merely affirm a rigidity of meaning which she wishes to displace. There are periods in her writing when femininity is linked to the destabilising qualities of poetic language (the 'semiotic') but these instances equally ensure that there is no room here for a female subject to take up permanent residence. However, it does appear that while the quest for estrangement in one sense dissolves sexual identities, at other times she has granted women exemplary status as strangers and exiles, whose place on the margins of public discourse potentially gives them a special indifference to 'the mire of common sense'.

Estrangement therefore lies at the heart of subjectivity just as it problematises our relation to a transcendent Other. Yet perhaps it has an even more profound effect on the nature of the reading contract. Speech and writing presuppose an interlocutor to whom I address my desires. I constrain my aggression and my need to devour by constructing subjectivity in loving relation to an other. My sense of space is redefined. In so doing, I am subject to constant change and renewal, for as I enter into conversation, 'my' speech, 'my' opinions become 'ours', and meaning becomes pluralised, enriched. We leave each contract permanently altered but hopefully, not absolute masters. What is meaning, then? As Heidegger reminds us, 'every metaphysical question can be asked only in such a way that the questioner as such is present together with the question, that is, is placed in question'.[11] In reading and writing on strangeness, I am constructed and deconstructed, formed and re-formed when my own thinking, my own questions, intersect with the texts of others. This recognition to my mind lies at the centre of Kristeva's writing, which sets out the limits of subjectivity even as it explores the means to exceed those limits.

In the chapters that follow I intend to bring into relation the variables of exile, estrangement, and the female intellectual or writer, and I shall ask what kind of a relationship is established between criticism, identity, and alterity in a selection of her texts. Kristeva's thought has a confessed anti-phenomenological cast but it cannot abandon notions of presence and identity altogether. For this reason, despite the fact that a concept like the female intellectual never gains absolute hold, its problematic nature can still be read in the silences and ellipses of her discourse as much as in those places where the question is under explicit discussion.

To give my investigation of exile and estrangement a tighter focus, my readings of Kristeva in Part II of this book will be organised around metaphors of dwelling and inhabiting. I will examine the dual nature of the dilemma that confronts the theorist when she deconstructs the exterior space assumed by a metaphysics of presence. While taking on the status of an exile who wanders from place to place, the subject must also face moments when he or she cannot escape being crushed by space. As Kristeva tells us, to write on melancholy, one has to be a melancholic (*BS*: 3); to write on exile, one must be one; yet such an intense identification with the object of analysis exposes thought and the psyche to the threat of dissolution. Exile presupposes a certain distance from the intimate spaces of home; its preferred spaces are disfigured dwellings, and strange hostile places outside 'common sense'. When all notions of exteriority are discredited however, the ensuing *lack* of space becomes a problem for the subject (and the reader). In this sense, strangeness is an affect imaginatively experienced by the reader and strategically produced by Kristeva's language as much as it is a recurring theme for reflection. I pay particular attention to the literary element of my chosen texts in the emphasis I give to the estranging affective world they create and the intuitive associations I bring to this world. Paul de Man, speaking of the presence of a 'critical element' within literature observed that:

> the critical and the poetic components are so closely intertwined that it is impossible to touch the one without coming into contact with the other. It can be said of these works that they carry a constitutive critical element within themselves, exactly as Friedrich Schlegel, at the onset of the nineteenth century, characterized all 'modern' literature by the ineluctable presence of a critical dimension. If this is true, then the opposite is just as likely, and critics can be granted the full authority of literary authorship.[12]

Although wishing to make a distinction between literature and criticism, I am nevertheless sensitive to the aesthetic function of critical texts, and my analysis attempts to bring this function into play. However, I equally endorse the injunction that criticism involves mastery as well as play, which entails a position that involves 'resting on the brink of fiction without ever completely toppling over into it'. (*Desire*: ix) Criticism calls for analytical distance as well as recognising excess and play. In this I am merely echoing Kristeva's own judgement that distinguishes theoretical discourse from fiction in the former's emphasis on logical argument and the Law.[13]

Chapter 1 presents a study of estrangement. It provides a history of the term, and looks at the cluster of associations or modulations which surround the experience of exile. I pay particular attention to the apparent opposition between the space of exile outside language on the one hand, and the space of exile within language on the other. I argue that while Kristeva affirms that we are all subject to loss and estrangement within language, and offers the phenomenon of the *mother-tongue* as a kind of compensation for our exile, she has a fascination for moments when language fails and when another enigmatic kind of identification takes over. This gives her work an intriguing complexity and ambiguity.

In Chapter 2 I introduce the persona of the female voyager as a figure for Kristeva herself: the 'female intellectual', and for myself as reader: another female intellectual. I am interested here in assessing the extent to which Kristeva as intellectual has made an identification with femininity in her writing, and more generally, to what extent any woman who becomes an intellectual is able to identify with being female. I argue that the experience of reading estrangement is one of both fascination and critique, love and distaste: abjection, as Kristeva terms it, but in any case, another form of *identification* which draws the reader as voyager into and through the text. I invite the reader, then, on a voyage with me across Kristeva's textual landscape only to discover once more that exile does not always mean separation and loss.

Chapter 3 offers a reading of *Revolution in Poetic Language* that explores the unsettling effects of its thought on (female) identity as well as intellectual inquiry. Concept and style are read as mutually reinforcing functions of an estranging textual universe with a distinctive topography. In this unfamiliar place, the subject of language is not at home with himself or his speech; instead he discovers himself to be in an ambivalent environment that wavers between destruction and jouissance. Kristeva's challenge to Hegel and humanism are reflected in the construction of the semiotic's negativity as 'feminine', which although an aestheticisation of female experience, nonetheless enables the theorist to remind us that there are personal implications impossible to finally remove from abstract thought. As Michèle le Doeuff observes, there is always something of the philosopher in philosophy.

Chapter 4 again takes up the two variables of home and exile as they appear in the most archaic site of home: the mother's body. In this chapter I argue that when Kristeva begins to approach such an intimate but unhomely place, abjection appears on the scene: a terrifying form of estrangement that can only be lifted with the intervention of a loving third term. This chapter in particular attempts to map the interventions of a discourse in the text that interrogates feminine subjectivity. I offer close and extensive readings of 'Stabat Mater', *Powers of Horror* and *Tales of Love* that consider the form of privilege accorded to subjectivity, and ask to what extent it is overridden by the style of other questions.

The final chapter is an evaluation of Kristeva's contribution to postmodernity, literature and, to a lesser extent, feminism. It suggests that Kristeva is an intellectual who appropriates a postmodern critique of meaning but who equally wishes to retrieve an investment in human particularity. To which end she advances the idea of the 'reversible space' traversed by a female detective in her latest novel, *The Old Man and the Wolves*.[14] This complex, problematic relationship between performance and judgement, *énoncé* and *énonciation*, is further developed in a reading of her book on Proust,[15] where I look more closely at the implicit opposition between inside and outside, private and collective modes of experience elaborated by Proust and endorsed by Kristeva. I conclude the chapter by focusing more closely on the potential capacity of the psyche, whether it inhabits male or female bodies, to transform events and experiences into fiery-tongued 'revelations'.

Throughout the book I have made consistent reference to the subject of language in the masculine, and have usually referred to the reader as plural or feminine. The decision to do so reflects in part a desire to align myself with Kristeva's own enunciative strategies in this regard, and partly a feeling that such a division between 'he' and 'she' reflects both textual tidiness and a primitive kind of fairness. I have consciously opted for a strategy that does not fully concur with recent conventions of reading and writing where an inclusive subject is used as a matter of course.

1

'Strangers to Ourselves'

THE 'FIRE OF TONGUES': AN APOSTROPHE TO THE WORD

Literature brings us to the brink of existence. Its imaginary landscapes invite the reader to be a voyager filled with wonder, but the prospect of the marvellous that dazzles the eye may also open on to a dark world of terror and despair. Literature, like dreams, cannot be controlled, and disrupts the hold we have on habitual experience. When we read or write, we inevitably follow the traveller's impulse and steer a course across unknown countries with the help of a map, yet language, and literary language most especially, creates its own ephemeral universe resistant to all that is familiar. Something in this shifting landscape escapes and alienates our travelling eye. The most intense forms of estrangement experienced by the subject, according to Julia Kristeva, are those produced by poetic language. For while its origins are implicated in the origins of subjectivity, poetic language is a *fire of tongues*. It has an infinite, ecstatic quality that eludes the mastery of human consciousness. The landscape of literature then, is inhabited by a foreignness that deflects the traveller and divides us from ourselves. We become, in other words, exiles.

To take pleasure in literature, as Kristeva reminds us, the subject must be reduced to a state of crisis where speech fails. Familiar and habitual supports are pared away as the subject confronts the unpredictable world of the imagination. Thus writing begins when the traveller has lost his or her bearings. But this loss is not the loss staged in order merely to confess oneself intrigued by the strange and bizarre. Rather Kristeva would argue that literature causes the subject to be reinhabited by a strangeness that is powerfully affective. It exalts and casts down, promotes ungovernable impulses, creates fantasies of horror and delight. Its language produces an intensity of experience akin to those states of psychic extremity that have been termed 'borderline'.[1] For literature and language raise vast invisible walls which dazzle with scintillating shadows and against which we can stumble and fall. Here we find revived our most ancient and vulnerable memories, played on, made to vibrate, and projected, so that momentarily we take them for real. Language and the imagination can give us the impression that the space between our bodies and the outside world is inhabited by peculiar sensations. The invisible takes on qualities of plasticity: the nose, the skin, the mouth, the eyes become permeable receptors to indescribable impulses with strange textures and contours. The air swarms with invisible shapes, the eye strains to contain them. We see the movement of imagination in the light that is more intense around an object, its shadows sharp as glass; in a familiar odour now become dense and enigmatic; in a sound whose vibrations make the air replete with coloured shapes massed and pressing against the body. Words themselves become weighty bodies, folded over our own. From the lacy bread of the page they can metamorphose into stones, warm and comfortingly solid, or heavy and malignant burdens crushing and grinding, making us break and bleed. Letters slide off the surface of the page and inhabit the jellied surface of the eye, transfixing and segmenting it into grids of steel. And isn't it on account of this transmutation of the word into the body and the body into the word that the borderline person who experiences a similar confusion between the space of the body and the space of the word can believe in tongues of fire, where the 'as if' of the metaphor is drowned in the seething of the real? In the landscape of what is often called psychosis, its sufferers fail to clearly distinguish between themselves and the outside world. They manifest a difficulty in differentiating *space*, and so to speak of an object is also to call up its hallucination. Thus the object is not an object to be ingested by the consciousness, but one whose hallucinatory vividness resists domestication. It persists outside of the subject, exterior to the consciousness. Perceived as inexplicable yet somehow present, such an event gives the borderline a shock, a sense of physical invasion. Yet literature to a greater or lesser extent frequently activates in every reader what Kristeva calls our 'psychotic latencies'.[2] The separation between subject and object in any individual is never complete, and when a literary text assumes a subjective crisis, it reactivates those latencies. Our universal exile within language is suddenly overshadowed by the peculiar sensation of a more profound form of estrangement where language seems to fail altogether. The reader as well as the writer then may confuse the imaginary with the real. (The real, Lacan says, is an impossible place outside language.) But what is to prevent the crisis invoked by literature from becoming permanent?

Following Lacan, Kristeva argues that to become a subject and belong to language, we must separate from our first object, the mother. Through this primary separation we can begin to distinguish between self and other, and between what is inside the self and the world outside. Separation paves the way to acquire speech. But just as the word intrudes into the world of infancy signifying a loss of polymorphous pleasure, Kristeva believes that language can compensate for what it takes away by causing us to delight in its own pleasurable body. The maternal space englobing the infant is replaced by the nurturing space of language. To remain permanently wounded by an original loss or separation from the mother is in a sense to refuse to grow up. Maturity comes from recognising that to *speak* of objects and experiences or to write about them enriches the psyche. The sophistication of the psychic structures at our disposal allows us to integrate perceptions into our speech, thereby enabling the encounter with the real to be imaginatively symbolised. The outside – the real world outside writing – then becomes mysteriously incorporated within the inside of language and the psyche. Thus in transforming these blinding 'shocks' into psychic 'revelations', the encounter with literature literally enlarges the compass of the mind.[3] Through passing the estranging effects of the unsayable and the incredible through the membrane of imaginative speech, literature effects an extension of both. In fact, alongside its capacity to record human distress, the potentially renewing effects of literature make it a transformative register of contemporary life.

Language renews the subject and turns crisis into a pretext for innovation. And so to read is also to hear one's name called across space. If I have lost language and language has lost me, the Word solicits me and comforts me. In that soliciting, in that calling, I return from exile into the name. Literature then functions as the giving of a gift. I am summoned to a movable feast where Love invites me to sit and eat. I feel the extension of my psyche, my inner boundaries that had been assailed by an overwhelming outside now unfold and warm themselves as at a celebratory banquet. To be fully attendant to these cathartic qualities of language without losing a certain scepticism may well lie beyond the reach of most intellectuals today. Contemporary literary theory has frequently celebrated the play of meaning implicit in language while denying there is an exterior metaphysical reality. There is nothing outside the text, we read, but words and more words. Rather than meeting at a celebratory banquet however, often readers of theory have encountered a terrible dryness or experienced a sense of constriction, where language as text and only text, turns into a prison. Kristeva has always been sensitive to this dilemma and has increasingly focused on the capacity of language to be endlessly transformed and renewed in such a way as to leave its subject extended, but not crushed. Writing of the generative powers of language, no theorist has been more inventive, yet more trenchantly atheistic than Kristeva.[4] Paradoxically, however, she has sought to irrigate the landscape of theory by drawing on figures from theology. Her passionate apostrophe to the word (and in one sense we could regard all her work as apostrophising language) evokes the discourse of mysticism which a prodigious intellectualising on the other hand, never quite dispels.

Other critics have echoed Kristeva. Similarly indebted to the speech of theology, Beryl Schlossman tells us that in Jewish rabinnical tradition, 'The voice aflame with infinite language, the luminous word, becomes a dream-image, a multiple illumination – in which language unfolds as kaleidoscopic theophany, as mystical vision ... an illumination of darkness: the jubilation of the ineffable *Verbum* is heard by the subject's infinite ear.'[5] She draws a parallel between this tradition and James Joyce's belief that art has 'the gift of tongues'.[6] Language in its infinite creative aspect causes the subject to experience bliss or *jouissance*. Jouissance can produce ecstasy and a sense of fainting into language. The subject, dissolved and falling, is ravished by the unending stream of words that speak their ineffable mysteries seemingly from an exterior. Jouissance can also open the subject to the space of the sonorous, material qualities of language: its *bruissement*, as Barthes would say. Many writers with an ear for the infinite apostrophise the mystery of transubstantiation. Joyce does, and so does the Chilean poet, Vicente Huidobro:

> I'm leaving my clothes behind
> My flesh is falling away on all sides
> And my skeleton's putting on bark
> I'm turning into a tree
> How often I've turned into other things ...
> It's painful and full of tenderness
> I could cry out but it would scare away the transubstantiation ...[7]

Huidobro's verse frequently resembles a Joycean play with language that celebrates the transforming power of the poetic word; a word that despite its power to transport remains readable. Likewise, Schlossman insists that Joyce speaks a jubilatory glossalia that nonetheless still manages to communicate. If mystery inhabits the letter, it does not overwhelm communication. The plurality of speech must be maintained as a sociable, conventional activity able to be read. Real mysticism (tongues of fire) transmutes into the fire of tongues, where the visionary impulse is translated into stunning languages of the imagination. Here is Huidobro again:

> Now I'm rosebush and speak in rosebush language
> And I say
> Rise rose rorosarose
> Rise rose to the day
> Rose ary arose to the sun ... [8]

The point of enunciation must therefore be given a limit, or as Kristeva terms it, 'guard rails', to keep us from being overwhelmed by the signifier's excess.[9] The fiery play of sounds has to be given a limit that retains at least a minimal form of sense. But if madness or death are risks that ensue when the visible limits of the subject and object are radically dissolved, too much form, or form as formula, functions as a depressant. Sensitive to the deadening effect of habit on language, Huidobro calls for 'Fires of laughter' to 'revive the languages' and 'Astral gymnastics for the numb tongues.'[10] Fresh ways of seeing and writing preserve us from becoming dead subjects of language. What revolutionises form therefore, also revolutionises literature (and us). Kristeva equates stylistic novelty with literary novelty and is particularly critical of writing by women which fails to access rhythmical and alliterative resources of language in an innovative way.[11] These '"feminine" attempts at writing' are unadventurous formally, and so either fall into banality, or are wordless when they should be engaged in producing new forms of thought. Kristeva believes that if the text is too silent and not immediately transformed by the imagination working on speech, we will be left with the illusion that a mysterious presence or origin exists *outside* language. So rather than maintaining a space of mystical contemplation or quietude, poetic words must dissect our fantasies of presence, or God. Kristeva admires Joyce because the luminous resonances of his prose did just that, whereas much writing by women, she believes, does not even begin to register this fiery atheistic struggle and transformation *within* the space of language.

I do not accept the universalising gestures of Kristeva's judgement which confines all women to a zone perilously close to psychosis, nor her atheism, for that matter, but I do maintain that women may have a different relation to the symbolic and the body which is capable of producing a *different* identification with language and thought. Mallarmé elevated the 'fibre' of the flesh into a poetic logic, celebrated by Kristeva. He wove the bodily desires and experiences *into* language and so transformed *both*. By contrast, in her terms, a feminine circumvention of poetic logic leaves us merely with fibre, or with events uninterpreted by the incandescent revelation that language, acting on the marvellous, can bring. Kristeva's own gestures however, as analyst and writer at times would appear to contradict her negative assessment of women who write. As we shall see, female intellectuals may be more favourably placed than men to explore the nature of the fragile skin of language that makes us speaking beings. While explicitly locating all subjects as exiles *in* language, Kristeva's fascination for moments when language *fails* suggests that the boundary between a real and metaphorical Pentecost – between tongues of fire and the fire of tongues – is less secure than it appears. It is even possible to suggest that when this form of empathic identification with the space of the real (or at least an imagined real) occurs, the writer is acknowledging a 'feminine' form of subjectivity which Kristeva sometimes links in a privileged way with her own writing as a woman who is an intellectual. This is a point which I will take up in later chapters.

For both men and women though, Kristeva believes that literature offers a resurrection, a kind of tropic medicine[12] or journeying mercy that revives aesthetic form and offers a catharsis to the psyche. It restores affects, connects impulsive and disconnected flashes, shocks or events. As if in a dream we can say with Blake, 'And did the Countenance Divine/Shine forth upon our clouded hills?' Here the distinction between wonder and delight in the world and wonder and delight in the word is impossible to maintain. Freshness overtakes habitual perception. There seems to be a literal peeling of the eye, a literal pouring of light on to the landscape. The cloud is pierced, its sullen blanket thins and dissolves. The inner world reaches out and meets the reaching out of the outer world. The shining on the hills and the shining on the eye engulf the watcher in flames of love. Symbolic capacity misses a beat, the real and the imaginary merge and fuse. Thus alchemical tongues weave their fiery thread through signifiers animated by an excess of energy while remaining perpetually open to the strangeness of the real, to the movements of the desiring body that looks for the flame to appear as a miraculous sign trembling, illuminated, in the upper room.

MEDITATIONS ON EXILE AND ESTRANGEMENT

Why does Kristeva connect the jouissance of tongues with estrangement? Why is the infinity of language celebrated though the persona of the exile? As readers of literature we still assume that texts are there to lead us to truth, beauty, or both. The enormous crises of the twentieth century notwithstanding, we most frequently teach the power of literature to effect an enlightened subjectivity, not an estranged one. The desire for a self at home with itself, even if it must like the prodigal wander, still drives our reading of texts. Yet Kristeva works to expose what is for her the profound unhomeliness of subjective existence today. And poetic language is the crucible in which this crisis both ignites and yet is also alleviated. It is precisely because the poetic word and literature take subjects beyond themselves that they simultaneously produce sculptures of anguish and excess, destitution and renewal. In so doing, they make us strangers to ourselves. This, Kristeva believes, is the essential human condition, where the riches of language compensate, but imperfectly, for an original loss that occurs to all human beings when they leave the amorphous world of childhood behind to become subjects of speech. The meditations that follow will provide a certain history of the nature of estrangement in order to understand exactly what a theorist like Kristeva means when she speaks of the loss that founds subjectivity and makes one an exile.

The majority of Kristeva's subjects lead a marginal existence on the edge of the community. The exile, the alien, the stranger, the eccentric are figures driven by unfulfilled desires and a longing for love. They frequently demonstrate a vitality of speech far beyond the ordinary. A similar marginality is to be found in the extreme psychic conditions and odd perceptual experiences that interest her. If the purpose of literature (and analysis) is to make the object vibrate oneirically, reviving a host of lost memories, the condition of exile is an archaeologically dense term replete with multiple associations from subjective and collective history. What theoretical discourse surrounds the word estrangement, for instance? And how do its various modulations of unhomeliness, alterity, epiphany, difference and *unheimlich*: (es)-trangement, function in Kristeva's texts?

The City of Lights

Firstly they reflect of course, the exigencies of history. 'We are today confronted by an obsession with the unnameable', we read in *Le texte du roman*.[13] Arriving in Paris from Bulgaria at the close of 1965, Kristeva's declared intention was to break open and recast old terminology in the light of the unnameable to bring a revolution to the very heart of conceptual thought. Her revolution was a reaction to the dominant discourse of the times. It set a subject at odds with itself and an unquantifiable object against the contemporary taste for rigid systems of thought (structuralism, Marxism, existentialism, for instance) that in different ways, Kristeva believed, propped up humanism. Now the subject she had in mind was clearly not a humanist subject, but one in the constant process of transformation. Endlessly generated and negated within discourse, this subject was a *stranger* to identity since it did not recognise the psychological ego. There was no 'I' who inhabited or owned language, she argued, rather the place where the ego was now came to be occupied by a thickening or accretion of language, the locus of a *generative space*. Kristeva's subject became a potentially infinite function but in order that this concept of the subject was embodied in a material practice and did not fly away into an abstract world of ideas, she linked it to the Freudian psychic drives.[14] As we know, the drives are primitive energy flows that move across the body, connecting it to sites of pleasure and desire. They are impossible to fully register but nonetheless as Kristeva argued, when understood as infinite processes, were able to constantly renew language. The transformation and renewal of language by the drives, she concluded, was most apparent in the literary text. Kristeva's reading turned the literary text into a strange non-object which she named an unthinkable 'alterity' or 'outside' (*altérité, dehors*). Because the text was the exemplary site of homelessness where meaning and the subject were constantly produced and erased, it could not be studied as a static object. Existentialism, structuralism and Marxism failed to grasp its unrepresentable nature. Unorthodox procedures which turn customary terminology on its head, Kristeva concluded, must then be used to provide a model for a generative signifying practice. Radical semiotics would thus supply the new context for the appropriation of old terminology, a linguistic appropriation which Louis Althusser had named 'the novelty of non-novelty'.[15]

This kind of displacing and recontextualising of worn material recalls the Russian formalists' *ostranenie* or defamiliarisation. In keeping with her intention to turn thought upside down and add revolutionary new resonances to old, Kristeva borrowed vocabulary from a vast range of disciplines and synthesised them into an estranging dialectics. Not surprisingly, symptomatic of the new synthetic vocabulary was her estrangement of 'estrangement', and we should touch briefly on its history. The term estrangement goes at least as far back as Hegel who, like most philosophers, was fascinated with the relationship between the mind and the world. He began with the assumption that the mind was estranged from itself; man was estranged from nature, and the subject from the object: 'Nature is Spirit estranged from itself', he wrote.[16] In order to lose its external and alien qualities, the object must be thought actively by the consciousness and not merely perceived or intuited. Otherwise objects remained products of the alienation of the subject or the spirit, unable to bring enlightenment to the consciousness.[17] Hegel's analysis of the master/slave relationship displayed a similar indebtedness to the concept of estrangement or alienation (*Entfremdung*). Their mutual loss of independence produced the unhappy consciousness where the master becomes alienated from things by appropriating them as products while the slave is alienated because he is continually trapped within the mode of production. Marx by contrast, who also made use of the term estrangement or alienation, argued that the object in capitalist society was an estranged and alienated product. Through alienated labour, man was alienated from himself, from nature and from his fellow man.[18] A point of difference: with Marx, the process of objectification was inhuman, whereas with Hegel the objectification was a necessary distinction between man and abstract thought: while its objective character alienated self-consciousness, it was a necessary step on the path to Spirit and therefore must be successively transcended.[19] Both men, while attributing alienation to different sources however, affirmed that a divided man estranged from himself inhabited a divided world.

Writing a century later, Marcuse pressed this popular notion of Marxism to its logical conclusion. If the free individual was the goal of the new Marxist society,[20] he stated, late capitalism strips away all possibilities for self-development through alienating man from the authentic exercise of his critical faculties. Marcuse humanised Marxism. The figure of thinking man occupied centre stage of his reading of history, but he saw this figure as emasculated and machine-like, incapable of truly radical or innovative thought. If man could only revolt against the estranging nature of contemporary society which had removed the inner space necessary for critical reflection, he would be free of alienation and would no longer need to behave like a machine. He would be able to reason with himself, and so realise himself more fully: 'The idea of "inner freedom" here has its reality: it designates the private space in which man may become and remain "himself." ... The loss of this dimension, in which the power of negative thinking – the critical power of reason – is at home', is alienation, *Entfremdung*.[21] Critical thought has lost its true home, concluded Marcuse, thus the unique space of reflection which made man truly man – which humanised him – had vanished from contemporary life.

By contrast, communist philosopher Louis Althusser who rejected Hegel's absolute subject and supported Lacan's critique of ego psychology, criticised Marx for precisely the same reasons that drew Marxist humanists like Marcuse to his work. Althusser was especially critical of Marx's thought prior to *Capital*. As he notes, the early Marx had believed that man had merely to reclaim 'as subject his own essence alienated in property, religion and the State to become total man, true man'.[22] Althusser believed that the Marx of *The German Ideology* stayed too close to idealism, his reading of history finally resting on a notion of the essence of man. Althusser was an anti-essentialist. His anti-humanism led him to state that '"man" has no history since there is no such thing as "man"'.[23] Thus he approved when Marx later abandoned the concepts of alienation [*Entäusserung*] and estrangement [*Entfremdung*] and rooted human practice in what Althusser called 'historico-dialectical materialism'.[24] The forces of history that arose out of materialism were generated by economic and political discursive structures, not human behaviour, a conclusion that made sense to a new generation of thinkers already making waves in Paris.

Under the influence of Althusser, avant-garde writers and critics like Philippe Sollers and Kristeva recognised in the late 1960s that the new textual economy enacted by modern literature was on a par with the political economy studied by Marx after his break with humanism.[25] The subject of writing was swept up in the many-levelled processes of the text's generative economy and lost its singular boundaries. Constantly in the process of becoming, it thereby took part in the dialectics of history. A mature Marxist-Leninist science, they believed, would assist in a revolutionary reading of literature because it cut across bourgeois idealising which attempted to mystify history in placing concepts like humanism and commitment at the centre of discourse. Since there was no longer any room for an intentioned work or an identity named 'author', a revolutionary poetics went out of its way to dislocate and estrange the subject of thought. Clearly this appropriation of estrangement was not at all the same as Hegel's, nor Marcuse's; nor indeed did it correspond precisely to Althusser's re-reading of Marx.

Why then does Kristeva use terminology with such a powerful history? Why in turn have I chosen an overdetermined concept to bear the weight of my reading of her poetics? Does estrangement really bear sufficiently on language to warrant the attention it gets? To respond to our first question, to renew thought, Kristeva believed that one must renew terminology; this is how to break out of the restrictive habits prescribed by the old definitions, for these terms used in new contexts come to have other meanings, possessing an alterity or novelty. Just as the term author was no longer to be understood as the effects of man's subjectivity or essence, so the concept of estrangement escapes its Marxist and idealist moorings, explodes, and becomes an excessive textual expenditure, a radical transformation of identities, bodies and speech. Linked to Kristeva's discourse of exile, it will take on resonances of the failure and subsequent renewal of identity and language. And so without entirely eliminating its intertextual associations, in this chapter I will examine the difference between an estrangement caused when language fails, when the subject is exiled *from* language and consequently may become a visionary, and the estrangement that ensues for all subjects *within* language. I will additionally suggest that there are moments and states when such a division is impossible to sustain. Thus estrangement can equally express the confusion that arises for the subject when he no longer recognises whether he is within the space of language or in a space outside it. A similar confusion arises when we attempt to separate the speaker from what is spoken, the *énoncé* from the *énonciation*. As Yeats reminds us, 'How can we tell the dancer from the dance?' Perhaps one of postmodernity's most characteristic moments as well as its weakest point, the involution of space opens our eyes to a world rich in correspondences but limited in its ethical reach. Because Kristeva is at times engaged in procedures that emphasise a separation of spaces and at others endorses the collapse of one space into another, I have found it impossible, indeed undesirable, to completely eliminate the multiple resonances of estrangement. So in the chapters that follow, I will also examine the term as an alienation of the subject, comprehending both psychic anguish or ecstasy, and the sense of homelessness induced as an effect of the reading process.

Reading and Foreignness

One of the most striking of Kristeva's personal and theoretical emphases has been the experience of being an outsider, an exile. Her preoccupation with linguistic anomalies and borderline patients has been increasingly matched with relatively frequent allusions to personal alienation and a highly wrought style which attempts to reproduce the condition it describes. Concluding her essay on Samuel Beckett, she envisages the most visceral of responses as coming from an intellectual who is marginal and dispossessed, commenting: 'Such a text necessarily attracts a certain number of admirers or even accomplices from among the "others," the "dissimilar," the strange, foreigners, and exiles.' (*Desire*: 158) The reader is, then, actually drawn into the estranging effects produced by Kristeva's representation of exile. Through empathic identification, she too becomes a fellow-sufferer, *une étrangère*.[26] Now this sense of homelessness which the reader shares is not an isolated phenomenon, but recurs in various forms in all Kristeva's writing. Thus in *Etrangers à nous-mêmes* she gives the experience of estrangement as it assails fixed entities of space and time vivid thematic life:

> ... a stranger inhabits us: it is the hidden face of our identity, the space that ruins our resting place, the moment where understanding and instinctive fellow feeling become swallowed up. Recognising the stranger within ourselves, we are spared from hating him in himself. A symptom which renders precisely the 'we' problematic, perhaps impossible, the stranger begins when the awareness of my difference arises and reaches its completion when we acknowledge ourselves all to be strangers, rebels from ties and communities. (*Etrangers*: 9)

The stranger suffers from a perpetual loss of identity which makes him abject, unable to clearly differentiate between a threatening outside and his own body which now appears repugnant to him. This personal depletion may be eased, she argues, through recognising and loving his own alterity. Furthermore, in accepting that there is never a fixed dwelling or 'chez soi', he may come to accept the strangeness of others. For the sole support that enables us to live with strangers is knowing that we are strangers to ourselves. (*Etrangers*: 250) Knowledge then, is produced through *identification*, through an enigmatic performance on the very site of our investigation. We can only respect incompatible differences within communities if we confront the fact that we too are split subjects: desiring and desirable, mortal and death-bearing [*mortifières*], (*Etrangers*: 269) subject to the Law, but by the same token to abjection: the corrupt lining of the Law.

The intensity of the problem of the stranger or foreigner stems, Kristeva believes, from a crisis of Western religion, and not primarily from the historical presence of the post-colonial other in the First World: 'one becomes a foreigner in another country because one is already a foreigner within' (*Etrangers*: 26), although clearly the experience of being an immigrant herself has directed the production of this text.[27] Despite her personal identification with the state of exile however, the problem we face today can be attributed, she suggests, to a failure of a term strong enough to accommodate difference without becoming oppressive. In the past, Kristeva argues, religious and ethical sanctions to be found in Stoicism, Judaism, Christianity and humanism until the time of the Enlightenment afforded a certain number of safeguards, even if weak and imperfect ones, that made some provision for the outsider. These discourses each managed to calm the universal suspicion which greeted those outside the privileged group. The modern world lacks these safeguards unfortunately, because any sense of collective or transcendent values has collapsed, and yet we are at the same time being pushed closer together through more extensive political and economic ties. We can now find no single moral code to integrate and transcend the space of our particularities. (*Etrangers*: 195) How then, Kristeva asks, can we learn to live together without wishing to retreat into subjectivism or self-preserving nationhood on the one hand and a levelling kind of universalism on the other? How can we live as foreigners today without becoming permanently locked in abjection?

For the experience of strangeness is, like abjection, the sign of incomplete separation from our first home – the mother's body – where the drives do not remain housed securely in the unconscious, but return in estranging bodily symptoms and affects. Metaphors of indigestion and incomplete introjection dominate this borderline condition: the stranger feels an 'unappeased hunger', (*Etrangers*: 37) 'a burning taste' (*Etrangers*: 12) and a 'strangled rage at the back of ... his throat'. (*Etrangers*: 9) Ambivalence founds his social relations, for although a foreigner to his mother and to the land of his birth, a 'cold orphan' whose only passion is 'an insipid rapture' (*Etrangers*: 15) in the face of death, underneath this indifferent carapace lies a 'flayed animal'. (*Etrangers*: 25) Bearing hatred and antagonism towards himself and others, which is the most primitive reaction to the outside world a body can display according to Freud,[28] the stranger's sense of ego is precarious, and at times prompts him to make a direct identification with the Other (the Law), becoming either paranoid or psychotic.

The stranger has no soul, Kristeva tells us. This is because the condition of exile is a 'space that ruins our resting place'. Exile deprives people of a sense of possessing an interior space from which to reflect, to love themselves, and to project themselves out towards an exterior through loving others. The exile's sense of space is so dislocated that he can no longer affirm either the security of a psychic interior or the comforts of a normatising, 'transcendent' exterior (the father, the Law, God). There is no place that offers itself as home. Exiled from the community, the foreigner becomes an eccentric anti-humanist, probably an atheist, and in that sense his strangeness as difference is a threat to the social fabric. In fact, the a-*lien* is a rebel against 'all bonds and communities' ('*aux liens* et aux communautés', my emphasis). (*Etrangers*: 9) Equally, we cannot escape the stranger (the unconscious) that lives within, for we are *bound* to it. Similar to the real foreigner, our alien status makes us abject, asocial creatures stuck within 'polymorphic mutism'. (*Etrangers*: 28) So the space of reflection in the abject person or foreigner is foreshortened to such an extent, Kristeva believes, that the shock of displacement into a new language foreign to our mother-tongue condemns us to partial silence. The foreigner can get involved in projects, but cannot reflect on his status. He expends himself but cannot find any sustenance in speech to replace that expenditure.

If this is a feminising position, it is also reminiscent of psychosis. Kristeva suggests that where the body has not been fully caught up in language, psychic contents properly belonging to the unconscious impose themselves on, and reify signs. Where fantasy rules, commonsense reality fades, and the sign drops its arbitrary importance to assume a real one. Words develop object-like qualities; objects resonate with divine messages. Paradoxically therefore, even though the stranger has no soul he may have visions. And isn't the visionary who desires an encounter with a force of presence somehow outside language a stranger? When writers describe their thirst for a blinding revelation of presence, they are seeking one of the most intense forms of estrangement, where representation is eclipsed by the flash of an epiphany.

Revelation and the Intellectual

From the Greek 'to manifest, to show', the term epiphany has traditionally been used to designate the revelation of some divine or superhuman being, although it has recently acquired currency as a figurative or secularised equivalent to account for moments of striking perception.[29] When speech fails, the visionary person may find himself caught up in the flames of ecstasy. Yet the writer seeks to reproduce ecstasy too. His impulse to make familiar forms unfamiliar through estranging language can have an effect as seductive as the visionary's refulgent optics. Heidegger and Schopenhauer recognised this, as in a different way did the Russian formalists. Along with writers such as Joyce and Huidobro they aimed to transform perception. When repetitive forms encrust language and perception with a petrifying speech that makes us indifferent to change, literature and thought suffer. We need the whirlwind of an apocalypse to bring our dry tongues to life and irradiate our syntax. Undoubtedly though, no matter how refreshing and exciting new poetic forms or ways of thought may be, the space of language has limits: it continues to be prosthetic. To the extent that we are all strangers, even our first language, our mother-tongue, opens a gap between being and representation, between language and the world of objects. Language speaks from the place of the Other, as Lacan reminds us, the place where 'we' are not. Language is at once our home and the agent of our homelessness, responsible for our separation from things. To be exiled outside of language, or without language on the other hand, solicits us with the prospect of remaining mute or becoming prophets, but these kinds of experiences, however fascinating, are not the rule. The reality is that we are always already within language, even if that 'within' is shaky and provisional. And despite the essential foreignness of all speech, remaining within language and refreshing it from within *does* offer a kind of compensation for aliens. It enables us to project our losses on to words and thus through the extension of our symbolising capacities, to experience regeneration.

Thus speaking about exile and performing an enigmatic identification with it, will help to alleviate its oppressive qualities. Identifying with that elusive foreigner of Nabokov's, Sebastian Knight, Kristeva has this to say: 'Let me suppose that the fact of speaking a foreign language, being exiled within language, is perhaps not alien to the interest that *I* bring to this particular case of the eclipsing of representation.'[30] Undoubtedly, we cannot ignore the personal investments being voiced here. As Kelly Oliver comments, Kristeva's own foreignness is invested in her analysis of the alien: 'the strangers speak her unconscious as well as theirs'.[31] Now Kristeva is a *legal* alien, a Bulgarian who married to remain in France, or so she tells us in 'Polylogue'.[32] In 1989 *Etrangers à nous-mêmes* was awarded the Prix Henri Hertz, and on the dust-jacket of the English translation, we read that Kristeva has received the honour of being named 'Chevalier de l'ordre des arts et des lettres'. Perhaps her privileged intellectual status has given her the means to articulate a condition that leaves *real* sufferers, bound to the brutal round of events in their lives, without the means of understanding, and therefore, without comfort. Perhaps too her remarkable powers of rationalising in order to understand psychic pain give her the confidence to proclaim the truth of modernity as non-transcendent. ('Postmodernism?': 141) Supplied with the language of analysis, then, the foreigner's angry indifference can evolve, according to Kristeva, into the thoughtful atheism of the intellectual.

For the intellectual too is not only an atheist, but an exile, living on the edge of comfortable structures. The life of thought and writing effects a constant sense of uneasiness and discomfort. Some years ago in a paper entitled 'A New Type of Intellectual: the Dissident', Kristeva maintained that the fundamental role of the intellectual was to exist as a subject who constantly put structures and meanings in question. This kind of a perspective worked against the natural grain of institutionalised intellectual life to engender a discomfort with the notion of 'home'. Domesticated habits of thought included all those forms of analysis that presupposed a common consensus and a fixed identity (author/critic; man/woman; meaning/non-meaning, for instance). By contrast, the intellectual in permanent dissent was exhorted to assume the language of exile as his most true, but most evasive, home: 'How can one avoid sinking into the mire of common sense, if not by becoming a stranger to one's own country, language, sex and identity? Writing is impossible without some kind of exile.' ('ANT': 298) The intellectual is not indifferent to his exile in language, recognising that men and women are uprooted beings; the *lack* of being, the *manque à être*, founding us all.

The *Unheimlich*

Unlike those foreigners who never manage to conquer their estrangement, the intellectual, according to Kristeva, has a wealth of language at his disposal to analyse his discomfort. Freud was one such intellectual who attempted to explore and articulate the *unhomeliness* at the heart of human experience. His reading of the uncanny[33] is central to Kristeva's reading of estrangement. Freud begins by defining the uncanny as being related to what is frightening, 'to what arouses dread and horror'.[34] Rendered in German, uncanny is *unheimlich*, literally 'unhomely'. Infinitely more powerful than any intellectual sensation of novelty, uncanniness has a more visceral quality capable of arousing irrational responses in the individual. The uncanny actually is not that which is alien or new, Freud believed, 'but something which is familiar and old-established in the mind and which has become alienated from it only through the process of repression'.[35] Repression which constructs the other and the strange in the shape of the unconscious is a thin shield, and when the contents of the unconscious (repressed emotional affects and ideas) return, Freud argued that they assert themselves in the individual's consciousness in all their primitive terror and glory. The uncanny occurs then when the imagination becomes indistinguishable from reality. For Freudian psychoanalysis, it is the quintessentially strange object because it is a horror of what was once familiar, and because within the etymology of the word *heimlich* or 'homely' lies the suggestion that something is being concealed and kept out of sight. Paradoxically, *unheimlich* has been defined as 'the name for everything that ought to have remained ... secret and hidden but has come to light'.[36] Playing on this ambiguity, Hélène Cixous describes *unheimlich(e)* as 'the baroque forest of the dictionary',[37] the fecundity at the centre of the text that covertly animates the whole and eludes the impulse to rationalise still present in psychoanalysis.

Freud's journey across that baroque forest of the unconscious led him to ask what happens when repressed ideas and affects move away from consciousness to the more primitive regions of the mind. His influential book *The Interpretation of Dreams* finds that the visual images activated by dreams arise in the body's perceptual system which does not have access to the motor or qualitative aspects of the psyche that are responsible for translating a perception into a series of recognisable ideas linked with affects.[38] Dreams are hallucinations that ignore symbolic logic, while tapping the most archaic areas of memory. I would argue that visions or waking hallucinations are the products of a similar process. A state of crisis triggers off the relaxing of the represssive shield and the regressive movement of an idea or wish towards the perception end of the nervous system. The 'body' takes over from language and one sees visions, experiences an epiphany. An intensely luminous event comes to indelibly mark the visionary's consciousness, just as the shock of exile scars the foreigner. Unintegrated within a more complex psychic system, these events and shocks can lead to delusions and madness. Freud's confidence in the benefits of analysis are, when it comes to so-called psychotic experiences, only implicit, and even when mentioned, not all developed,[39] but Kristeva is emphatic that to leave strange experiences unexplored by intellectual and/or therapeutic analysis is to ignore the possibilities for psychic growth, as well as to run the risk of being permanently estranged *from* language. Once however one allows for the passage of the body (visions, archaic memories, *jouissance*) into language, the human condition of uprootedness is eased. Thus when writing and thought draws on the infinite capacities of language for renewal through recognising the presence of the drives in speech, it finds another *mother-tongue*. This is the same creative reservoir that Joyce drew on when he 'spoke in tongues'. Of course, intellectuals are not creative writers, but in exploring extreme conditions of being, both share a common task, and affirm the same 'maternal' potentiality of speech.

The 'Mother-Tongue'

If intellectual thought for Kristeva recognises loss as universal, a loss that may be somehow compensated in the maternal qualities of language, it does seem to require an estrangement from sexual identity. The dissident is a stranger to his or her sex. Surprisingly though, in 'A New Type of Intellectual' we read of the privileged place Kristeva accords to women. They too, it would seem, find the rigidity of meaning frustrating. Like the writer's capacity for speaking in tongues and the intellectual's ability to analyse them, women's investment in maternity means that they are similarly able to link 'heterogeneous sites' in thought or creative acts. I shall explore the question of women and their relation to intellectual practice in subsequent chapters, but one of the ways in which women in general differ from intellectuals, Kristeva claims, is in their weaker symbolic capacities. Woman can *never* feel as at home in the symbolic as can man. She becomes the female exile:

> A woman is trapped within the frontiers of her body and even of her species, and consequently always feels *exiled* both by the general clichés that make up a common consensus and by the very powers

> of generalization intrinsic to language. This female exile in relation to the General and to Meaning is such that a woman is always singular, to the point where she comes to represent the singularity of the singular – the fragmentation, the drive, the unnameable. ('ANT': 296)

All women are female voyagers in perpetual transit over foreign lands in which they never quite feel at home. Kristeva represents women as foreigners unable to extricate themselves from abjection. In *Etrangers à nous-mêmes*, the experience of foreignness is *feminising*, inducing a despondent gaze like that 'of sorrowful women coiled up in some non-existent eternity.' (*Etrangers*: 29) Furthermore, estranged *from* language, writes Kristeva, women are *visionaries*, 'dancers who suffer as they speak'.[40]

A brilliant illustration of a woman's alienation from language occurs in Sylvia Plath's representation of Esther Greenwood. In Plath's novel *The Bell Jar*, Esther is reading Joyce's *Finnegan's Wake* and finds that 'the thick book made an unpleasant dent in my stomach'.[41] She pronounces Joyce's one hundred lettered word in the middle of the page: 'It sounded like a heavy wooden object falling downstairs ... The letters grew barbs and rams' horns. I watched them separate, each from the other, and jiggle up and down in a silly way. Then they associated themselves in fantastic, untranslatable shapes, like Arabic or Chinese.'[42] Esther's impending breakdown should not deter us from recognising that her sense of being *outside* language is symptomatic of an estrangement that can momentarily possess all subjects, activating their 'psychotic latencies', but it additionally dramatises the alienation women feel from the world of thought and culture in which they have rarely had an active part. This makes them exiles, but unfortunately their form of exile does not always seem to be one that Kristeva privileges. The scepticism women have at times for socially approved values gives them the dissident status she applauds, yet she also believes that their laudably ironic relation to clichés is undercut by a closeness to the drives which makes them unable to take advantage of scepticism, and ultimately in hostile opposition to Joycean prose! This lack of space for Kristeva means that their perspectival hold on language is weak. Like Esther Greenwood, they become derelicts outside of language. Inevitably, one is led to ask where this judgement places Kristeva herself. How does she deflect the threat of Esther Greenwood in her theorising? Do these deflections then lead her to develop strategies that might modify women's relation to language and culture so that they may claim an exile within language rather than remaining outside it? In the rest of the chapter I will further explore these two conditions of estrangement: that is, the distinction between being on the one hand subjects of loss inside language, and being on the other exiled to a space outside its borders. Of course, it is not only women who may be drawn to states of exile outside language, although even Maurice Blanchot who like Beckett is fascinated by silence, turns his fascination into a complex treatise on language and its failure. As we shall see however, women intellectuals like Luce Irigaray and Hélène Cixous, in claiming a strategic reinscription of the loss of language, have differently negotiated the distinction, privileging the textualised representation of the female body. I will close the chapter with another feminine performance different from theirs: an account of Kristeva's reading of the mother-tongue, a strategy she has evolved to make language and subjects 'maternal'.

ESTRANGEMENT: A 'DAZZLING OBSCURITY' OUTSIDE LANGUAGE

We spend a good deal of our lives living in what Heidegger took to be the blanched anaemia of the present. Humdrum reality sticks to us as *papier mâché* composes familiar shapes and forms. Daily the discourse of routine and habitual thought builds its accretions over and through us. It is almost as if we viewed reality through a transparent but resilient skin, or from the far side of a room filled with smoke. Kristeva has argued that this particular structure of perception is a turning away from or a mediation of what lies beyond and is indispensable for human survival: 'The love of death, the desire of death is the secret on which we close our eyes in order to be able to look without seeing, to sleep and to dream. If we were not to close our eyes, we would only see emptiness, dark, blanks and broken forms.'[43] Whether we conclude with Kristeva that to look beyond the commonplace reflects a desire for death, we can agree that desire longs for a less mediated reality. Any thoughtful response to the question of life and how we live it has always involved a recognition that the time of this world, the time taken up with attending to our human needs and demands, is furrowed with a longing for something else, for an inhabiting and in-dwelling that welcomes strangeness as a beloved guest.

How is the encounter with strangeness represented? Sometimes as an event that occurs all at once in a flash, dazzling us with its novelty, its sheer alterity. Hegel wrote of this dazzling in terms of a sunburst: 'The frivolity and boredom which unsettle the established order, the vague foreboding of something unknown, these are the heralds of approaching change. The gradual crumbling that left unaltered the face of the whole is cut short by a sunburst which, in one flash, illuminates the features of the new world.'[44] Illumination akin to an epiphany occurs in the twinkling of an eye, in an instant, flooding our vision with a sense of the unknown. It is a catastrophic movement from darkness to light that defies the limits of history and time. For a moment, the world and our perceptions seem rinsed and sparkle with clarity and we come face to face with a strangeness that is as much loving as it may be terrifying. In fact, joy rather than terror may be the more frequent response to an encounter with the unknown. Something has occurred – a hallucinatory vision? a radical shifting of the patterns we impose on reality? a transference of meaning from one place to another? In each case the event is momentous enough to cause us to return again and again to it through memory and to invoke it as foundational, or at the very least, germane to new ways of looking at things. Surprise is the hallmark of this form of strangeness, and joy its most frequent companion.

In modern literature the classic account of striking perception amounting to an epiphany is given by Proust in *Remembrance of Things Past*. As he is crossing the cobbled courtyard belonging to the Princesse de Guermantes, Proust trips and his unexpected fall triggers a radiant memory of the Venice of his past: 'a profound azure intoxicated my eyes, impressions of coolness, of dazzling light, swirled round me'.[45] Beckett eloquently recapitulates for us: 'His surroundings vanish ... he is stunned by waves of rapture, saturated in that same felicity that had irrigated so sparingly the desolation of his life. Drabness is obliterated in an intolerable brightness. And suddenly Venice emerges from the series of forgotten days ... lifted from its Adriatic shore and set down, a bright and vehement interloper, in the courtyard of the Princesse de Guermantes.'[46] Other such chance incidents before and following occur equally 'as if by magic', and usher in the same joy which is so powerful that it temporarily makes Proust indifferent to death and the passing of time.

The experience of estrangement as I have described it as epiphany, is *insistent*, 'vehement', and also paradoxically blinding. The intensity of light, Beckett tells us, is 'intolerable', yet its searing quality gives rise to illumination, even if this is transient. A particular everyday kind of clarity loses its moorings at the same moment as something else bursts into consciousness, leaving what had gone before in the dark. However as other writers have also noted, luminosity brings its own reserve, since the subject both can and cannot look in the face of this light. Maurice Blanchot links the fascination of writing as occurring outside the space of dialectics within a 'blinding light';[47] Freud writes of the 'sun-drenched face of the young Persian god [who] has remained incomprehensible to us'.[48] Mallarmé in more obscure fashion designates the work of 'the primitive thunderbolts of Logic'[49] as a 'distant reciprocity of fires'.[50] Too close to the maternal body, Georges Bataille fuses 'perfect darkness' with light, an impossible oxymoronic unity that produces 'a state of shock'. (*Tales*: 365)

Enigmatic, resistant to being named, these moments of perception involve an experience that however disturbing, presents itself to the consciousness as unique, unmediated, and foundational – an originary moment of presence as real as the Pentecostal tongues of fire. Beckett represents Proust's courtyard experience and the subsequent events as forms of a miracle occurring outside of the will. Some contingency unforeseen and unplanned by the subject gives rise to the return to consciousness of a memory, not in the form of an edited represented copy but 'the sensation itself, annihilating every spatial and temporal restriction, [which] comes in a rush to engulf the subject in all the beauty of its infallible proportion'.[51] This is the modernist moment at its most mysterious. For the point of this unpremeditated return, it is argued, is to reveal to us the power of Art to offer up through moments such as these its extratemporal, revivifying qualities to all who wish to 'breathe the true air of Paradise, ... the Paradise that has been lost'.[52] From outside language the real intrudes, a 'bright and vehement interloper'.

Clearly, we are dealing with the realm of mystical experience here, a realm that has been too quickly passed over as theological and always already nostalgic by contemporary criticism. Today, the insistence on the deconstruction of presence and hence extratemporality ('Paradise'), has produced a new and less romantic paradigm that would attribute all such mysteries to unreadable textual inscriptions, or to the return of the repressed.[53] If, as post-structuralism asserts, identity is only an endless weave of differences, any sense of mystery and conversely, enlightenment, must remain structured by the fabric of the text. Deconstruction argues that any direct and immediate founding moment is a domestication of a much harsher truth: that the Logos is the necessary exteriority that language both assumes and tears apart. Furthermore, Kristeva's atheistic and materialist understanding of psychoanalysis would regard the origins of epiphany as residing in the shocks and contradictions of matter in endless process across the body of a subject. Both grammatology and psychoanalysis, whatever their differences, would be equally insistent that transcendence in the way Proust may have understood it is impossible: all notions of exteriority are produced by, and remain within, language.

But can the notion of estrangement as at once illuminating and instantaneous still exist? Is there still a place for a blinding flash that would come from a space *outside* the system and thus be in a position to renew it? Thomas Kuhn once remarked that when 'paradigms change, the world itself changes with them'.[54] In a similar vein, Lacan wrote that 'the slightest alteration in the relation between man and the signifier, in this case the procedures of exegesis, changes the whole course of history by modifying the moorings that anchor his being'.[55] For change to be radically transformative rather than enacting an endless return, a passage needs to be preserved between inside and outside. How then in the light of contemporary scepticism, do we represent a strangeness that might come from the 'outside'? What is being strange about today? What is strange about being?

Beginning with the way strangeness impinges on subjectivity, on how we live life, I am led to conclude that its quality as perception rests on its *difference* from other kinds of perception. My pleasure of the 'now' in all its sensuous detail for instance, belongs neither to the terrors of death, nor the joys of luminous experience that we have observed above. When I take in the calm blocks of silence on a hot day interrupted occasionally by the sound of water in distant pipes and house timbers creaking in the sun, when I watch the play of light and shade on the floor and an iridescent begonia sweating on the window-sill, then catch the pungent smell of burnt dust, I am responding to what is called 'settled happiness', not 'momentary joy'.[56] The sense of rootedness and connection these pleasurable experiences give me enhances my life and comforts me. They affirm my status as a being of and in this world. They add to my facticity, my 'thisness', although they are more than purely instrumental, since in loving what is immediately outside of myself I am actively engaged in loving what is inside myself – the psyche. As Bachelard remarked in his marvellous book *The Poetics of Space*, 'Isn't the exterior an old intimacy lost in the shadow of memory?'[57] While not in themselves displacing reality, such pleasures in living and being are *enabling*: They sustain a venturing out of oneself in creative thought and, paradoxically, can provide the physical and psychic means to think loss, alterity and strangeness, since otherness is not necessarily dependent for its thinking on personal alienation. Quite the contrary, in fact, in Bachelard's text on poetry and space. On the other hand, when these simple and life-affirming comforts are absent, and when thought truly does in all of its aspects find itself in exile, the glowing interiors of home observed as if from outside a window stand as the objects of our longing. Loss presents itself to the consciousness as the absence of *something*. In this instance, it is the unattainable quality of the particular object that we have once known, or long to know that provides the means to think *beyond* the particular: to think differently.

Thinking differently does not of course usually resemble the entirely unpremeditated resurgence of exteriority or memory that Beckett finds in Proust There are forms and degrees of estrangement, from moments that threaten to sweep away our old worlds and our selves with them, to less apocalyptic forms that result in heightened perception or give us cause to read the texts of our experience in a new way. Nonetheless, to begin a study of estrangement by reflecting on the nature of an unpremeditated, instantaneous experience is a recognition of the strategic implications of this space for language. Thought needs the idea of an outside, an exterior in order to function. Admit the possibility of such a position or event occurring outside discourse, and a First Cause is restored to thought, which in turn ushers in notions of transcendence and, according to many contemporary theorists, fixed identity. Surprisingly though, while Julia Kristeva argues that the subject is *heterogeneous*, and affirms the eclipse of the Absolute Ideal (God), she continues to recognise the need for metaphysics, but redefines it as the incessant task of moving between a subjectivity shaped by the unconscious and an objectivity confirmed by relations with others. One's subjectivity then is constructed in relation to God or the Other; one's objectivity in relation to the Other and others. For this reason Kristeva believes that it is not possible in practice to think beyond language to an exterior space, but she also acknowledges that moments of creation or upheaval are the product of ruptures in the symbolic crust: *biology made manifest*. These strange threshold events on the border of nature and culture are the moments that intrigue her, and their time is one of crisis, which her language registers in strikingly apocalyptic, metaphysical terms. From the vantage point of semiotics for example, she has argued that 'Whether in the realm of metalanguage (mathematics, for example) or literature, what remodels the symbolic order is always the influx of the semiotic.' (*RPL*: 62) The emergence of the *semiotic* (the modality of language that our rational, communicative order of experience attempts to constrain) is always accompanied by violence and a loss of identity, but its end result is the radical transformation and renewal of thought. Kristevan semiotics wrenched concepts away from their traditional supports and synthesised them into an estranging dialectics. If God or Being were ruthlessly dethroned, these gestures were always accompanied by the exhilaration that an old order was giving way before a new: 'the *passage from one sign system to another* ... involves an altering of the thetic *position* – the destruction of an old position and the formation of a new one.' (*RPL*: 59) One way to read Kristeva's revolution in poetic language is as the correlative for a desacralised epiphany, since a language that estranges, that excavates categories of their denotational meaning and forges new syntagmatic chains of speech from traditionally hostile paradigms, is germane to revolutionary thought. While she would not support a Proustian extratemporality, the *desire* for the sudden presentation or return of a striking perception is unquestionably present in much of her work. Her determination approaches Mallarmé's: to summon and account for the production of the 'primitive lightning bolts of logic' dressed in the limpid structures of syntax.

To what degree then, is the concept of an unmediated position compatible with Kristeva's view of language? Undoubtedly for her there can be no question of a transcendent entity – God or Art – who would temporarily lift the subject out of time. And where heterogeneity is the precondition for subjectivity (we are, to repeat, strangers to ourselves), nor can there be a concession to perfect enlightenment or absolute knowledge. But in other respects, it appears that Kristeva still considers the mechanism of an interruption in time to be indispensable to establish language as a dialectical signifying structure capable of radical displacement. A closed system is not open to change. Innovation in language then, must maintain an investment in shocks, disturbances, and the opening of boundaries to an outside. In 'Stabat Mater' for example, epiphany receives explicit recognition in the account of conception as a 'flash', an 'instant of time or of dream without time ... folding in unimagineable spaces ... Flash on the unnameable, weavings of abstractions to be torn.' (*Tales*: 234–5) The relation between Word and Flesh established here prioritises the intrusion of the real (all that lies beyond representation) into discourse. Although speech breaks up visions, it remains in necessary relation with an invisible, unnamable exterior – a manifestation of the 'divine' perhaps? At the very least, an exterior whose always already existence estranges language and identity when it breaks through resistances weakened by social, individual, and aesthetic crises. Having deconstructed God, therefore, it seems Kristeva has reinvented the very structures that were supported by transcendence.

One could hardly imagine these flashes of the unnamable as represented by Kristeva to lead to the kind of reconciled happiness described by Proust. When the real shatters temporality and speech it can be profoundly disturbing, even terrifying. Rather than a lucidity that can be analysed, the affects aroused by the real lead to an impossible confrontation between abjection and the sublime: 'Not at all short of but always with and through perception and words, the sublime is a *something added* that expands us, overstrains us, and causes us to be both *here*, as dejects, and *there*, as others and sparkling.' (*Powers*: 12) The sublime is the limitless, the boundless, the absolutely great that overwhelms with awe or terror. Long before Kristeva, a whole tradition of imagination had thought of the sublime as something utterly alienating that impaired perception and even threatened to engulf the subject and deprive him of words. Edmund Burke for instance believed that the fundamental quality of the sublime lay in obscurity and a frustration of perception, not enlightenment.[58] But Burke averted the sublime's threat of wordlessness by locating alienation within language. Language was the medium which best achieved subliminity, because lacking access to visual representation, it naturally harboured an excess of confused perceptions in the way that 'extreme light, by overcoming the organs of sight, obliterates all objects, so as in its effect exactly to resemble darkness'.[59] In fact, Burke's linkage of darkness and light in the one perceptual experience represented his belief that the sublime presupposed a union of two mutually antagonistic concepts that intellectual discourse could name, but never master. If we were to scrutinise the representation of epiphany therefore, we would discover that its blinding light hides a mystery – the unnamable, as Kristeva terms it, but we could then press further towards a representation of this unnamable by giving it a linguistic context, which is precisely what Lacan does in his narrative of the mirror stage.

LANGUAGE AS LACK: EXILED BY LANGUAGE

Like Burke, Lacan found the prospect of visual eclipse seductive. Lacan linked both the *exaltation* that accompanies its perception and the *alienation* other writers have observed in the face of the sublime, to the experience that accompanies the mirror stage. Indeed, the 'jubilant assumption' which characterises the infant's reception of his first image of himself, his narcissistic ideal ego, bears all the qualities of exaltation and joy which we had earlier designated as belonging to that radically estranging form of perception experienced by Proust. Whereas Proust, however, viewed the perception as possessing miraculous and redemptive qualities, the identification that takes place in the mirror stage lends the infant an *imago* which it *misrecognises* as its own. Thus the heart of subjectivity lies in a *failure* of identification, since the child is both joyfully at home with his new found image and tragically alienated from the 'turbulent' activity that he feels actually composes his body.[60]

The mirror stage looks forward to the child's active entry into language at the end of the Oedipal phase, the stage of development that Freud described as occurring when the child became aware of the father's imposition in its own intimate relation with the mother. Turning the father's intervention into a constitutive metaphor, Lacan concludes that *le non du père/le nom de père* cuts us off forever from the world of things. Henceforth the child will be an exile *within* language, permanently bearing his 'castration' as a sign of initiation into a world of lack and desire. Claiming his image for his own, the child sustains its loss with imaginary fantasies of power and control. Unfolded in this Lacanian account of the alterity that lies at the heart of subjectivity we see two apparently opposed concepts of perception – jubilation and alienation, joy and estrangement – brought into relation on the obscure surfaces of speech. If light is cast on this scene, it is an illusory one, for when we imagine ourselves to be most informed about identity and meaning, we are actually locked within fantasy and childish narcissism. Lacan names narcissism's deceptive vision 'heliocentrism'.[61] Elsewhere he asks 'Is not the maximum of light also the source of all obscurity?'[62] Thus with Lacan, even more radically than in Burke, the image of visual clarity is simultaneously undercut by the presence of misrecognition and failed sight.

Psychoanalysis contained its own misrecognitions, however. Perhaps as jubilant as Proust's narrator sprawled on the cobblestones, Freud had celebrated the enlightening discovery of the unconscious as a new

Copernican revolution which would strip away the pretensions of the ego and the conscious mind in much the same way that Copernicus had revealed the earth travelled around the sun.[63] But Lacan, more sceptical, cautioned against a too easy identification with the 'centre' that merely became 'no more than the earth nodding its assent' to its own projected image.[64] Such identifications domesticated the unconscious and led to the practice of ego-centred psychology. The subject was never a subject of absolute knowledge, because truth only appeared as the repressed of the system, its signifier always intervening elsewhere. What the insights of religion or literature named as the subject's ineffable moment of truth, for Lacan was nothing other than a temporary upheaval in the orders of speech that ultimately served to displace presence, rather than revealing it. In this way, he argued that the subject was never the subject of revelation, being instead uncomfortably poised between an extinction 'still glowing' and a 'birth that is retarded'.[65]

Kristeva would by and large agree with the dangers of heliocentrism and would too, have an 'explanation' for Proust's visions,[66] but that did not prevent her in *Black Sun* from taking the figure of the sun as the governing trope for her text. In *Tales of Love*, infatuated by the sun as a dazzling agent, she maintained that all reflection reaches towards the solar source of light; her subsequent book illuminates the literally unthinkable nature of that light, for melancholia and depression acknowledge that at the heart of human experience lies an inconsolable grief over the perpetually estranged nature of existence. Separated from the wholeness we once belonged to, henceforth we will conduct our lives in the shadow of suffering and despair, she writes. If there is a place for ineffable experience here, like Lacan's imaginary jubilation it will be cast in anti-theological terms, which in *Black Sun* implies that the ecstatic moment is an *affect* following on the heels of a depressive or epileptic attack.[67] (*BS*: 177–184) In Kristeva's terms, the discomfort and separation of estrangement are foundational; unmediated joy and the intimation of its other-worldly qualities are merely after-shocks registered through the body's signifying system. And with Lacan, Kristeva presupposes the loss of the mother and the subsequent exile within language to be imperative for the formation of subjectivity.

Ecstasy, illumination, and a joy in the face of transcendent mysteries must therefore be modified according to the sceptical light of radical materialism. With Kristeva however, such a form of materialism does not set out to privilege rationality in assuming there is an Explanation for everything. While she repudiates a transcendent exterior and accepts the subject's exile within language, like the foreigner she is fascinated with moments when the real and the imaginary coincide, and when language appears as if a luminous body outside the subject. Unexpectedly, it seems that mystery has now been accommodated within the unreadable nature of affect to produce the ultimately unthinkable trope – a 'dazzling obscurity' – that estrangement is. What we have here, quite simply, is a shift of the source of the marvellous from a transcendent entity, God, to the site of the body. Yet that site is enigmatic, resistant to interpretation. Neither completely exterior to discourse nor determined by it, the most intense forms of estrangement involve a confusion of boundaries similar to those experienced by the immigrant. Visible or invisible? Inside me or outside? They disturb demarcations between interior and exterior space and unsettle the speaking subject in his customary dwelling-place. To write, to experience the time of dazzling obscurity, is to become a stranger to oneself and the familiar. At times exhilarating, at others encompassing a painful destitution of spirit, estrangement is a profoundly disquieting experience that turns the house of being upside down and presents its subject with new forms of speech and thought. Not that the renewal of language is easily acquired, for estrangement still demands a consciousness of separation. Blanchot pronounces a severe judgement on the place of writing as one of dissatisfied exile shut out in the cold, and 'the poet who belongs to it ... [as] always lost to himself, outside, far from home; he belongs to the foreign, to the outside which knows no intimacy or limit'.[68] Blanchot's position is an extreme one. More overtly preoccupied than Kristeva with the exile *from* language, his anonymous figures waiting silently without faces approach the mutism of beings permanently deprived of representation.

There could not be more of a contrast to Blanchot's time of exile or, on the other hand, Kristeva's revolutionary poetics, than a view which holds the ordinary with loving regard, or that looks towards an elsewhere without anxiety. The necessary exile within language need not be without its compensations. To return for a moment to Bachelard, we find that this philosopher discovered a private source of nourishment in his imagined worlds of the elements which he then translated into signs and symbols. For Bachelard, the nameless space of elsewhere that calls to the dreamer is not frightening or destructive but ultimately enlarging, because it allows him to redefine the protection offered by intimate space as one that both nurtures and permits movement away from its enclosure. In that way the dreamer may know the prospect of comfort in adversity: longing recognises the unhappy consciousness but does not have its permanent home there, constantly returning through dream to the places we know and love:

> To illustrate the metaphysics of consciousness we should have to wait for the experiences during which being is cast out, that is to say, thrown out, outside the being of the house, a circumstance in which the hostility of men and the universe accumulates. But a complete metaphysics, englobing both the conscious and the unconscious, would leave the privilege of its values within. Within the being, in the being of within, an enveloping warmth welcomes being ... It is as though in this material paradise, the human being were bathed in nourishment ...[69]

Obviously, there are alternative narratives one could compose about the terrain of writing and its call to the subject. The tone of Bachelard's text differs markedly from Blanchot's and Kristeva's; indeed I find it a refreshing change from what often appears to be a faddish mania for disavowing the pleasures of dwelling, an interpretive habit which our current social uncertainties have surely encouraged. Bachelard is no stranger to deprivation either though, and his passion for renewing the poetic image leads him to surrender the comforts of home for a journey marked by loss.

Common to all readings of estrangement and exile, then, is the notion of habitation and its interrogation: of the coupling of inside and outside, comfort and discomfort, resting and the journey. Deconstructing the mansion of presence and its oppositional forms, Jacques Derrida writes of voyages of creative and intellectual discovery as forms of positioning, rhetorical evasions in the face of an endlessly disseminated forest of significations. In which case Bachelard's comforting and upholding space would be a banal longing that in reality has lost its metaphysical 'woof'. Home as presence, even as presence going out of itself in daydream is an illusion, a pretence we maintain in the face of the failure of being and self-presence. One dwells thus only as through 'expropriation' in a 'borrowed dwelling ... outside of the self in itself ... This is the philosophical metaphor as a detour within (or in sight of) reappropriation, parousia [the second coming], the self-presence of the idea in its own light. The metaphorical trajectory [journey] from the Platonic *eidos* to the Hegelian Idea.'[70] The myth of self-presence is actually established through *différance*, a structured movement of deferral. There is no space outside the text, and no room for a moment without figure (or difference). Unwilling to relinquish the search for estrangement entirely though, Derrida redefines his own quest as to make 'enigmatic what one thinks one understands by the words "proximity," "immediacy," "presence"'.[71] By folding the unknown over the spaces with which we are most familiar, grammatology elides the intimate places of habitation and the external spaces of exile, and by this means effects its critique of structure in general. Structure as architecture, structure as topography, structure as body: all metaphors that are grounded on the distinction between exterior and interior space will be dismantled. Conventional notions of Home and Space now mutually imbricated, lose their oppositional character and become unreadable inscriptions.

Yet were we to dismiss such a relentless critique of presence and inhabiting, we would have to concede that the question of strangeness *tout court* involves being cast out or called forth. It is a leaving, a distancing, a spacing. Saint Augustine knew the discourse of exile when he called the people of God to dwell in 'no continuing city'. The redeemed dwelling was always viewed from outside, from the place of exile: 'For it is one thing,' he writes, 'to see the land of peace from a wooded ridge ... and another to tread the road that leads to it.'[72] All who actively engage with the creative processes of questioning, thinking and writing view the object of their goal as from a wooded ridge, that is, with longing from afar. This viewing is part of a quest; a quest for knowledge, 'truth', enlightenment – all of which may themselves be figures for a desire for the novelty of estrangement itself. But even though exile carries within its discourse the memory of a happier time when one was at home with oneself, or when it asserts a future time of reconciliation, thinking and writing about estrangement presuppose being conscious of loss and in exile from the beginning.

To think, one has to think already. (Blanchot said the same of writing.) Is exile the origin of writing and creative thought then? This opinion certainly seems to be widely held by intellectuals, and not only those who inhabit the late twentieth century. Disaffection and desire rather than a sense of quietude drive the quest for estrangement, which in turn may well be the universal symbolic form of which intellectual enterprise itself is but a particular variation. The nature of this disaffection and its journey of desire takes varied forms however. Speaking of the relation of inspiration to creativity, Blanchot mentions the example of Mallarmé whose sense of sterility and deprivation was a personal weakness and 'did not signify that he was deprived of the work, but announced his encounter with the work, the threatening intimacy of this encounter'.[73] Writing in these post-Romantic terms is an enabling founded on weakness, where loss and leaving the comforts of home are the first steps towards true creativity. And creativity, of course, extends far beyond the familiar notion of the poet searching for his muse to encompass all forms of thought, including that of asking a question.

When Heidegger asks 'what calls for thinking?',[74] his response is to reflect on the usefulness of the word 'call'. He at once makes language *unfamiliar* to us by restoring to it apprehensions of meaning which habitual use had obscured, as well as insisting that such a return can only enable us to live more vitally within the house of Being that language is. Unlike Blanchot, Heidegger investigates language from within. He assumes, in other words, that the human need for shelter can be most satisfied by discovering the unexpected in the familiar, in itself a recognition that involves 'leaving home'. In the 'Letter on Humanism' he turns to the Greek Sophists, and tells the story of Heraclitus who was keeping himself warm by a stove one day when visited by a group of strangers. They were immediately chagrined to see the great philosopher engaged in such a humble ritual.[75] Seeing their consternation, he encourages them to come in saying, 'For here too the gods are present.' Thus mysteries are to be found in the commonplace, riches in the most humble of dwellings, and so does thought entertain angels unawares. Heidegger reads Heraclitus' observation, *ēthos anthrōpōi daimōn* as the opening out of the familiar to the unfamiliar: 'The (familiar) abode is for man the open region for the presencing of god (the unfamiliar one).'[76]

In this sense, thinking the strangeness of exile is something joyful, because the unexpected turns out to house that which one had most sought elsewhere. Thought, in calling us out of our habitual enclosures, brings this advent of Being to language and enriches our understanding of what the words 'house' and 'to dwell' mean. But if there is a sense of epiphany in Heidegger it is always articulated as a blinding obscurity, as a sign that withdraws in the face of our turning towards it.[77] The truth of Being is concealed, and presence eludes us in the same way that the original source recedes when we approach it. It would appear therefore that any form of reflection on being, on the nature of things, must inevitably ground itself in loss, in the consciousness of distance between observer and observed, which Lacan would rewrite as the gap between signifier and signified. In recognising this gap, Heidegger does not take the step that grammatology does, and collapse the subject of thought into its object. Exile may be interior to the subject of thought, but it is also an 'exterior' that is approached through language as a refreshed kind of instrumentality. Nevertheless, it is true that for Heidegger too, authentic thought and existence ultimately submit to an unstoppable, anxiety-producing void.

What strikes me as a more or less universal feature of philosophy's attempts to think the nature of being and habitation as a form of exile within language is the insistence on a subject who begins his venture by a yearning for otherness that is most often accompanied by distress, anxiety, angst. Heidegger terms such anxiety as being 'ill at ease' ('*unheimlich*') in the face of Nothing.[78] The exile must forgo the pleasures of settled domesticity if he is to elaborate the essence of man, because man's essence is intimately connected to Being, which is the Nothing. Thus the 'more we turn toward beings in our preoccupations the less we let beings as a whole slip away as such and the more we turn away from the nothing.'[79] Anxiety then, not only signifies we are facing in the right direction, it itself induces the 'slipping away' of beings and of rootedness in the commonplace which imprisons perception in a succession of everyday trivialities. So it seems that a longing for elsewhere has the tendency to be accompanied by a turning away from the realities of this world. Heidegger's thinking man recognises the solitude and abandonment in which we find ourselves and from which we attempt to hide by sinking in an unreflective way into everyday existence. *Death is my eminent possibility*, and if I do not openly acknowledge death and finitude I cut myself off from Being and an authentic existence.[80] The place that Heidegger allows for a joy in the usefulness of objects and words and a recognition that one is bound to other persons through *solicitude*[81] saves his work from surrendering to a deadly abstraction, but it is nonetheless true that time and again one encounters in narratives of estrangement a sense of withdrawal, and a desire not for novelty as such, but for strangeness as death.

Indeed, Blanchot recounts the story of Orpheus' descent into the Underworld as culminating in an encounter with the night, the heart of all creation: 'All the glory of his work, all the power of his art, and even the desire for a happy life in the lovely, clear light of day are sacrificed to this sole aim: to look in the night at what night hides, the *other* night, the dissimulation that appears.'[82] Euridyce as a shade is the dissimulation that inspires Orpheus' song, her world that of the *negative* into which the poet gazes. Hegel similarly appears to valorise the look into darkness and the turning away from 'mere existence' that produces truth out of 'utter dismemberment': 'Spirit is this power only by looking the negative in the face, and tarrying with it. This tarrying with the negative is the magical power that converts it into being.'[83] But there is probably no clearer illustration of the connection between estrangement and death than Freud's essay on the uncanny. The most uncanny dread of all is the fear of being buried alive, which Freud links to the earlier experience of living in the mother's womb:

> There is a joke saying that 'Love is homesickness'; and whenever a man dreams of a place or a country and says to himself, while he is still dreaming: 'this place is familiar to me, I've been here before', we may intrepret the place as being his mother's genitals or her body. In this case too, then, the unheimlich is what was once heimisch, familiar; the prefix 'un' is the token of repression.[84]

In fact, the mother's body turns out to be the prototypical site of uncanniness which 'represents both home and not home, presence and absence, the promise of plenitude and the certainty of loss'.[85] By this means what psychoanalysis took to be the pre-eminent founding moment brings into association estrangement, death, and the maternal body.

IN SEARCH OF A MOTHER-TONGUE

And it is precisely this disposition of death which Hélène Cixous critiques in 'The Laugh of the Medusa'.[86] Psychoanalysis, she believes, has turned woman into 'the uncanny stranger on display – the ailing or dead figure'[87] at the same time as it has repressed the creative drives in the unconscious. But because women have a privileged relation to the maternal body, Cixous argues they are closer to the drives and hence in a better position than men to affirm alterity, the term she calls 'the wonder of being several'.[88] Woman, she says, makes trouble for phallocentric systems of meaning because she resists death.[89] Cixous appears happy to associate women with the strangeness of difference, but not death, loss, or separation. A feminine economy of representation is therefore apparently unstintingly giving, its writing a gift that does not give in order to give, but because giving is inherent to its nature. By contrast, masculine economics comprehends a 'reductive stinginess' that cuts off libido and life. Since woman has nothing to fear from castration, she cheerfully dislocates the orthopaedic structures of thought by affirming *life*: like Molly Bloom, she says 'yes' to writing.

In contrast to the deadly texts of Blanchot, Mallarmé and Hegel, a writing practice that affirms life assumes it can turn away from what Cixous terms 'the negative'. More importantly, it assumes difference in general can be optimally represented as the *sexual* difference. Estrangement for Cixous lies not in pursuing an elusive Being in order to name it, but in being different names. Woman says 'yes' to her multiple identities, and 'yes' to a writing that defies exile. Undoubtedly, Cixous' quarrel here is not just with psychoanalysis, but with all forms of thought that confine woman to an oppositional signifier within man's discourse. Those conceptualisations that insist on deprivation for their founding moment, she believes, fail to take account of sexual difference as an unstinting process of exchange between and within subjects. And as we have seen, woman according to Cixous, is less afraid of facing up to difference, and more likely to give herself without counting. The (male) philosopher by contrast, fearing to accommodate difference within, but desiring the other sex all the same, takes his stand against the internal challenge of sexual difference in the form of a trembling Perseus or Orpheus, advancing backwards towards what he is most afraid of seeing.

Cixous has been variously claimed by critics for essentialism and anti-essentialism, since in many instances her writing is quite ambiguous on whether *l'écriture féminine* is linked in a special way with the biological female body or with feminine textuality.[90] This particular distinction concerns me less here than the fact that her critique of 'Lack' is a critique of the *Aufhebung* of philosophy that sets man's anxiety and desire as the origin and end of writing.[91] Her essay 'Sorties' accuses Hegel's theory of the dialectic in *Phenomenology of the Mind* as articulating an age-old feature of phallocentrism: the subject acquires knowledge of the other in order to confirm its mastery and its progress towards absolute knowledge. She terms this knowledge a product of the 'Empire of the Selfsame' which appropriates and annuls alterity, producing a single history and reminding man that 'death is his master'.[92] And where the desire for death rules man, woman as alterity will be relegated to a shadowy place outside the time of history. Equally as symptomatic as their preoccupation with negativity and death, Mallarmé's 'tragic dream' and, we could add, Blanchot's fascination for the pre-Oedipal Mother, and even Hegel's celebration of Antigone, reflect a way of thinking that proceeds by excluding sexual difference from history under cover of signifying universality. Woman cannot claim to be living in a home of her own, unlike Nietzsche, remarks Cixous who prefigured his opening to *The Gay Science* with the 'proud' words: 'The house I live in is my own,/I never copied anyone ...'.[93] What if castration, separation and absence were not the be-all of thought, she asks? What if estrangement did not require dead, but living bodies?

Kristeva's response to Cixous' argument that seems to put women outside language and insulate them from loss would be to insist on the foundational nature of separation, which all writing has to take account of. There are no 'back rooms' for women to write in all on their own, nor is there a place of refuge outside language. Regarding responses like those of Cixous as representing a second-stage feminism that privileged woman's experience, she insists that we cannot acquire access to subjectivity unless there has been a radical separation from the mother. She would further add that there can be no writing as such that does not also recognise what she terms 'the murder of soma', the inauguration of the incest taboo, and the repression of the drives in the unconscious. Kristeva is clear that the time of writing for all subjects regardless of gender is the time of exile, and that the language of exile addressed from the edge of the void is often unbearable for humans to contemplate, revealing a landscape of 'broken forms', 'blanks' and darkness. Unlike Cixous, she frequently links the maternal body and the inexpressible pleasure of jouissance with death.[94] Her work often gives the impression of being a fascinated contemplation of the abyss and an intense identification with loss. Her theory of semiotics sternly repudiates the notion of a privileged sexual identity, and even more tough-mindedly insists that a concern for others is an outdated form of anthropomorphism. Over and against Heidegger, in *Revolution in Poetic Language* she criticises his emphasis on 'care' or solicitousness for others as belonging 'to a mere medical ethic that has a kind of patching-up or first-aid function ... anxiety and social work.' (*RPL*: 129)

With the passing of time however, Kristeva has attempted to offer more extensive shelter to the exile. Such a relentless, one could even say militant embrace of negativity, has been softened by an emphasis on the loving ear of the analyst as other, assisting subjects in need of care to have the burden of their suffering lifted, self-love, alleviating the plight of exiles and immigrants in Western countries, and writing the phenomenological discourse of personal narrative into her theoretical texts. Throughout her writing career, then, Kristeva, unlike many contemporary male theorists, has attempted to privilege a modality that is explicitly feminine with and through pursuing an ambitious ('exorbitant') quest to estrange contemporary thought and language. While more recent texts such as *Tales of Love* reflect a rethinking of the nature of exile and the feminine, the notion of the maternal semiotic was first given a history in the early seventies in *Revolution in Poetic Language*, and I will explore this in Chapter 3. It marks one of her earliest attempts to articulate a mother-tongue. But exactly what is the mother-tongue? Lacan had employed the term *lalangue*, 'the-so-called-mother-tongue', in an attempt to distinguish the real from an imaginary or a symbolic knowledge of language.[95] The imaginary and the symbolic are two different registers that represent language as 'work on *lalangue*', and their systematising nature led Lacan to posit an elusive third term, the mother-tongue, as the real reservoir that lies beyond signification. *Lalangue* then is nonsense, inspiring the animation of affects and non-meaning into language. Kristeva tentatively agreed with Lacan, although she accused him of reincorporating the mother-tongue back into a closed structure which ultimately made affect and the drives completely assimilable to the symbolic. By contrast, she wished to show that the mother-tongue could not be so assimilated.[96] When a 'plurality of signifiers aims at and fails at being a signified', she wrote, it produced the 'sentiment of the body'. In one sense the enigmatic body is a testimony to the failure of representation to completely capture the referent, and subsequently to orchestrate a perfect communication between letter and concept or idea. It is not as intimately linked to the signifying female body as Cixous' *l'écriture féminine* (woman according to Cixous writes in 'white ink'). For Kristeva, the opacity of the body makes itself felt through the semiotic mode of discourse, whose over-investments in drive energy return to language in the form of alliteration, rhythm, archaic sounds and enigmatic gaps in sense, what had been lost since castration and the mirror stage. If, as Lacan had said, we have to abandon polymorphous pleasures and leave our mothers, then – and this is Kristeva's original contribution to Lacan's narrative of loss – the semiotic visits language with a compensatory maternal presence, so that instead of incorporating food from my mother, I am sustained by language instead. My hunger is displaced to a psychic level so that I may experience 'the joys of chewing, swallowing, nourishing' myself with words. (*Tales*: 26)

The mother-tongue is precisely, or what really makes language heterogeneous. Kristeva here bypasses the Lacanian interpretation of language as permanent lack to affirm a belief that language, especially literary language, can be nourishing. I have left my motherland behind, but it is brought to life again in signs, in the mother-tongue. As Mallarmé had said, 'the Word presents, in its vowels and diphthongs, a kind of flesh; and its consonants, a kind of bone structure'.[97] The semiotic causes language to thicken and bulge. It gives us something to chew on. Which is why the activity of Communion where the blood and wine become through transubstantiation not just the body and blood of Christ, but also his Word, is such an eloquent symbol of loss and renewal for her. The mother-tongue is what therefore produces the writer's jubilatory fire of tongues, a sublime immersion within a multiplicity of signifiers that redraws the links between the subject and the maternal body.

Despite Kristeva's criticism of Lacan as ignoring the heterogeneous (that is, the maternal) in language, she would equally insist that the semiotic is of necessity apprehended through the Lacanian symbolic.[98] That is, there is no source outside of language, no phallic mother or deity from which the semiotic and the mother-tongue arise. We remain exiles from inside the symbolic. At the same time however, it seems to me that the notion of the mother-tongue or at least the impulse driving it, presupposes a certain degree of *ambiguity* in relation to separation, loss and absence. Such an ambiguity is a state possibly conducive to, but not always claimed for, a privileged kind of female subjectivity. Kristeva's sentiment of the body is intended to renew the relation of subjects to their speech, a renewal which includes tapping archaic drive-laden memories. We are talking here of both a notion of the drives, linguistically represented, and a mysterious transmutation of their affects into language. Furthermore, when a theory of the mother-tongue is articulated by a woman, we discover an interesting complexity. Rather like Poe's Valdemar, the female intellectual, in articulating the loss announced by the symbolic says, 'I am dead.' The point of enunciation for a discourse on the mother-tongue that calls for a separation from the mother before language can be embodied with the semiotic, *when spoken by a woman* is ambiguous, even an impossible contradiction, and cannot be precisely located. When the semiotic's mysterious interchange with language is theorised by a woman we can be sure there is a real and intimate connection being advanced between bodies and speech, a connection that is, after all, an extension of the living practice of psychoanalysis.

The mother-tongue is thus a retention of an uncertain relation between an inside and an outside and represents Kristeva's exorbitant attempt to defy the Lacanian 'trinary hold' of language. It immediately distinguishes her work from her male contemporaries and from feminists like Cixous. As we have seen, she differed from conventional criticism in her understanding of the relation between body and text. Furthermore, her increasingly *personal* investments in the text, her identification with exile, for instance, ran counter to philosophy's insistence on a neutral subject of enunciation, for when writing becomes more embodied, its relationship to narratives of separation and estrangement is a problematic one. By the same token, Kristeva did not usually approve of an overtly privileged female form of representation. This led her to offer only an oblique support for the kind of feminism which tried to closet itself outside the symbolic. So her difference from other women on this question is as intriguing as the rather more subtle distinctions she draws between herself and intellectuals who were men – or at least as she distinguishes herself from the unproblematised discourse of philosophy. But by and large it was not until her work took on a more psychoanalytical cast that the representation of loss, ecstasy, and identity became more complex. Some critics have observed that this difference of emphasis was a gradual progression which culminated in *Powers of Horror* or *Tales of Love* ;[99] I would probably locate the consistent presence of self-inflection from the publication of 'Stabat Mater' in 1976 after the birth of her son. From this point on, a personal enunciation is more apparent in the text, along with a marked interest in the transformation of subjectivity through the interchange effected between analyst and analysand. There is in addition, a more explicit confrontation staged between the (feminine) body, the mother-tongue, and questions of transcendence. There are times, as in earlier texts, when woman becomes the privileged locus for estrangement, but one still equally discovers conceptual structures that allow no single identity to settle in the place of 'the stranger'. The most important difference from earlier writing, though, clearly lies in the thematising of aspects of psychic life, their relation to notions of exteriority, and the self-diagnostic representation of her own case history. I shall explore these questions and the way they produce a different configuration of space more closely in Chapter 4.

In conclusion, the conditions of exile and estrangement as they are diagnosed here by Kristeva share in common with other texts a desire to displace the mundane world of the everyday, a fascination with death and absence, an insistence on the individual as a subject never in complete control of his speech, and finally, a refusal to believe that utopias and epiphanies are ever realisable or recognisable on earth. We apostrophise the fire of tongues, not tongues of fire. What makes the condition somewhat different from a number of other narratives of exile looked at in this chapter is firstly Kristeva's explicit debt to the comforting nourishment of the semiotic; secondly, her persistent fascination for experiences somehow exterior to language; and thirdly, as we shall see in Chapter 2, the oblique relation of her narrative to personal experience. As far as Kristeva is concerned, the strangeness of language makes the phenomenological world uncertain; it renders the 'I' of personal experience problematic, rather than eliminating it altogether. Strangeness is a borderline condition that *complexifies* the representation of identity. In fact, on occasions the 'I' appears to engender the same dazzling obscurity that so attracted Maurice Blanchot. The distinction between an estrangement from language and an exile within language cannot always, therefore, be maintained, and it is in the murky space between the two that Kristeva chooses to locate her own enunciations as a female intellectual. For despite the uncertainty of identity produced by strangeness, Kristeva is determined to claim a place of privilege for her own speech as a woman and an analyst. While rarely extending the same privilege to all women and identifying herself as a feminist, in order to inflect generalised discourses on semiotics and psychoanalysis with a feminine particularity, she plays a nuanced and self-implicating game with language. Taking on the persona of the female voyager, she affirms that the subject-in-process *needs* the wisdom of the former in order to acknowledge that speculative thought and the encounter with transcendence have always been grounded in the world of *seeming*. Calling for an imaginary, empathic inhabiting of language that is both there and not there, inside and outside its space, Kristeva is able to seriously remind us, but with feminine playfulness, not to take our dreams too seriously.

2

The Space of Travel: Reading and the Female Voyager

INTRODUCTION

Reading has always been seen as an itinerant activity. As armchair travellers dedicated to the pursuit of imaginary worlds we become empathically immersed in a universe far removed from our own. Dazzling fantasies eclipse the banality of home and the familiar. The space of reading may of course still be about rediscovering the appeal of the familiar, or viewing a strange new world without ever leaving home, but dominant critical metaphors of reading today, cognisant of human restlessness and mobility, stress its unhomely effects. As Michel de Certeau writes, 'readers are travellers; they move across land belonging to someone else'.[1] Voyagers in transit across lands they do not own, readers live on borrowed time, temporarily inhabiting imaginary places that impose their own forms of seduction and control. When the strange is eventually naturalised, the traveller moves on, perpetually seeking the uprooting effects of what is novel or unfamiliar.

At some stage on the journey of reading, the figure of travel ultimately encounters the representation of gender. In fact, Sidonie Smith has argued that travel in the West has a predominantly masculine subject who achieves his difference from femininity through the culturally symbolic freight acquired by 'journey as narrative'.[2] Whether we ultimately agree with this assessment it has considerable power. Look at Ulysses, for example, who won renown (and manhood) through his travels. As Smith writes, 'Travelling men are men in the midst of becoming "men" through performances of masculinity.'[3] Across the grain of its masculine history then, in this second chapter I introduce the persona of the *female* voyager. What does it mean for a woman to travel beyond the domestic space of home? Does she too become masculinised, or does she find the limits of femininity opened up and expanded? What forms of consciousness are available to the woman who travels? Primarily these questions will be directed at Kristeva herself: the 'female intellectual', but they will also be brought to bear on my own space of reading, which happens to be that of another female intellectual. It is not always easy to tell the extent to which Kristeva as an intellectual has made an identification with femininity, nor the extent to which any woman who becomes an intellectual is able to identify, autobiographically, with being female, and I think in the end that these questions must remain only partially answered. Sexual difference effects subjectivity, but to what degree, and in what direction? Let us see how Kristeva might respond.

I will begin by examining the hyperbolic effects on autobiography when Kristeva begins to narrate her own intellectual journey. Unlike Homer, Kristeva seems to believe that the travelling hero is an outmoded character. What is at issue in the space of reading therefore is not the subject's coming to consciousness, but his dissection by a radical form of writing which travels *him*. The traveller passes briefly across the surface of the text only to fade into the constant play of language. Under these hostile conditions, the self – even more, any privileged female form of self – has a hard time surviving, and depends for its continued presence on the writer's own hyperbolic inventiveness.

KRISTEVA'S HYPERBOLIC MEMORY

When the avant-garde journal *Tel Quel* became *L'Infini* in 1983, Julia Kristeva wrote an autobiographical reflection, 'Mémoire', for the first issue. It was subsequently translated as 'My Memory's Hyperbole' and published in a collection edited by Domna Stanton entitled *The Female Autograph.*[4] Coming back to the essay now, I am struck again by the cumbersome filigree work of the text. Invited to contribute a story about her life, Kristeva sets off through a vast maze of rationalisations about the nature of the social contract, the political process, the psychotic quality of certain forms of personal experience, and the transformation of history into baroque fiction.

The autobiographical persona sketched in 'Mémoire' is hyperbolic, bombastic, although through all the 'verbal oedema' we can still discern elements of a life story. She tells it 'how it was', *tel quel*, a succession of individuals and events beginning with the heady days of Paris in the late sixties when the life of the intellectual seemed the only life worth living. We see the stranger from Bulgaria arriving in the 'city of lights' with novels by Céline and Blanchot in her suitcase; her rapid conquest of the élite Parisian world of thought; her gradual transformation from Marxist to Maoist to a psychoanalyst who affirms Judaeo-Christian values and is afraid of 'the growing Goliath of the Third World.' ('MMH': 276)

We also read her account of the Paris 'revolution' of 1968. During May and June of 1968, there ocurred an upheaval in contemporary French history whose precipitous, volcanic mix of violence and celebration was probably quite unprecedented. In Paris there were scenes of barricades, burning cars, thousands of people massed together, makeshift hospitals. On Monday 13 May students occupied the Sorbonne. Kristeva remembers *le printemps rouge* as symptomatic of the turmoil of modernity, when radical thought seemed capable of shaping the very direction of culture and public life. The foot that she and her friends kept on the barricades was accompanied by a sense that these anarchic events could and should be assimilated by the intellect. Like the intellectual who can maintain a helpful distance from his or her alien status through analysis and reflection, interpreting the experience of revolution, Kristeva believed, enabled the novelty of the contingent event to be turned into a new form of thought. The interpretation of the intellectual, then, is a second order, hyperbolic memory that integrates autobiographical details into an analysis of the explosion 'of bodies, of discourses, of ways of being'. This is the signature that can be read in 'My Memory's Hyperbole'. Kristeva undoubtedly has an autograph, and it is the autograph of the precocious intellectual. But to what extent is it female, and what happens to the female autograph when language turns memory to hyperbole?

The burden of all Kristeva's theoretical work has been to insist that the ego is an illusory construction that denies the existence of the subject's material body. For Kristeva this material comes from the interaction of the drives and affects with psychic representations. The presence of the drives destabilises language and identity because, following Freud, they seek to return the body to death.[5] When they mesh with language however, the semiotic drives can transform it in a productive way. The presence of the drives in language gives rise to a multiplication of meaning as well as to its destruction. In which case the ego, the 'I' of standard autobiography has a shadow of negativity, violence and contradiction to which it turns a blind eye in its insistence on a narrative of personal experience that can always be *read*. The ego is at home in a familiar landscape, travelling only to rediscover the same. Kristeva has been particularly critical of women's writing in this regard, believing that it is preoccupied with producing narcissistic constructions of a biographical or imaginary nature that help shape an ego. Women writers, frightened of the riskier side of travel, reinscribe the social contract of conformity, she says, and to that extent, they refuse to recognise that a *loss* founds human subjectivity.[6] As both Kristeva and Lacan have argued, crucially important for our emergence as speaking beings is an experience of splitting, in effect a series of separations that tear us away from our first maternal support and assist us in becoming individuals. Birth, weaning, the transition from adolescent to adult; these processes of separation shape our subjectivity at the same time as they give us speech. Separation is a universal experience undergone by all subjects in order that they might make the transition from the imaginary, narcissistic world of the child to the symbolic world of language and culture. The doorway to speech lies through leaving the family home and cleaving to another. Thus in bearing the mark of this separation as a scar or hollow in the psychic memory, we speak from the place of what Paul Smith terms the 'enunciatory abyss'.[7]

Hyperbolic language, unlike much writing by women, if we follow Kristeva, thus causes the eclipse of representation. In these terms, it singularly fails to privilege a woman's voice or experience. If the semiotic occurs as a displacement, multiplication, or loss of meaning, then we cannot expect to be the masters of speech. The rational, or conscious aspects of memory fail when language is embodied with the semiotic, and my sense of myself and my speech, my ego, lose their conversational reach. This means that autobiography comes up against a contradictory impulse that works to thicken and distort the narrative of a life. It seems then that writing her hyperbolic memoir has merely given Kristeva the pretext for reflecting on the unreliable nature of any speaking position, and in particular, on the naivety of producing a *female* autograph. Let us look, for instance, at her reading of Nabokov's *The Real Life of Sebastian Knight* (1938) in her text *Strangers to Ourselves*, first published in 1988 as *Etrangers à nous-mêmes*.

In one sense, *Sebastian Knight* seems to be autobiographical, with the intrusion into the narrative of details that closely resemble the life story of Nabokov himself. Kristeva is at pains to demonstrate that the text is definitely not a biography, but a reflection on its own writing.

Sebastian Knight's Russian half-brother tries to write his biography, but all his attempts to compose a life of the famous novelist come to nothing. Knight's life remains as enigmatic as before, in fact as the failed biographer remarks at the close of the book: 'Thus – I am Sebastian Knight. I feel as if I were impersonating him on a lighted stage.'[8] For Kristeva this indeterminacy merely reveals the polymorphous and wandering memory of writing itself which pre-empts the role of the autonomous, self-directed traveller. Our task to construct an identity for Nabokov and Knight is fruitless, for all writing can do is to link and unlink pieces of the puzzle that the subject *is*.

> 'Sebastian's ... image comes to me in a few bright patches, as if he were not a constant member of our family, but some erratic visitor passing across a lighted room and then for a long interval fading into the night.' He is nocturnal, this Knight who has eluded the family of observers and leaves others and himself with only tattered memories. A disseminated 'oneself.' (*Strangers*: 34)

Memory ultimately fails; is banal, even. In the end, it is language and not identity that bears the brunt of recollection, playing with the phonic and semantic textures of the signifier until memory, the origin of autobiography, is nothing but hyperbole. All attempts to make *Sebastian Knight* recognisably biographical would twist it out of recognition. Autobiography may even be a redundant form – *the* redundant form, perhaps.

This is the tough-minded Kristeva, the psychic surgeon who exposes the illusory nature of the ego and delights in the constant play of language. But isn't my reading a shade hyperbolic? Doesn't it read too much into Nabokov's irony? The fact remains that as readers we will probably construct a biography or an autobiography all the same, pushing and shaping the text with 'tender aggression' to fit our projected image of the writer. Besides, the presence of the semiotic doesn't prevent us from following Kristeva's own bright trajectory across the stage of French intellectual life. Nor, for that matter, did it stop Jane Gallop in another context from calling Kristeva the 'vulgar Bulgar' who was always talking about herself.[9] So is the latter's view of self-representation as bleak as Sebastian Knight's? When Kristeva speaks of her experience as a foreigner in France, it is often to stress exile as the state that causes the subject to come to pieces: 'Consequently, as you may have noticed,' she says, 'I have no "I" anymore ...' (*Desire*: 161). The exile cannot claim to have a settled identity, nor can she ever be fully at home with her sex. Everything is disfigured, or escapes in hyperbole. Yet her reflections on exile, foreignness and estrangement are so frequent that one cannot fail to suspect that an autobiography is being written all the same. And over time, this personal inflection has increased, at least in part due to Kristeva's increasing commitment to psychoanalysis, and to providing albeit temporary narratives of recognition for people in psychic distress. Let's return to *Sebastian Knight* for a moment. Only the most intransigent of readers would not concede that her reading of Nabokov is replete with ironic autobiographical echoes.[10] Surely there must be a writerly pleasure in bringing to the reader's attention the story of Knight's encounter with the Cambridge professor when he pretended to be a Bulgarian from Sofia! (His tutor at Cambridge, knowing he was from Russia had addressed him in Russian, but Sebastian pretended to come from Sofia; whereupon the old man, obviously a linguist of some skill, starts using Bulgarian. Unable to speak Bulgarian, Knight makes up a new idiom on the spot and claims it's a special Bulgarian dialect.) And the felicitous pun of *écorcher* Nabokov uses to describe Knight's ambivalent relationship with his adopted language, English, and which means both to mispronounce and to flay the skin, must have considerable resonance for Kristeva herself, the real exile from Bulgaria.

Thus identity and place are present in writing, and although perhaps dependent on the reader's 'tender aggression' to bring them to light, insist on being *read*. Exile may tear us away from our maternal origins, pulverise thought and produce a self-conscious style. But I cannot emphasise enough that writing need not end in permanent exile. As we saw in Chapter 1, Blanchot makes his writer inhabit a dark and lonely space quite unmediated by Nabokovian playfulness. Kristeva's frequently grim preoccupation with exile places her alongside Blanchot rather than Nabokov, but her particular form of self-consciousness and her notion of the semiotic immediately distinguishes her. Indeed, her voyage passes through the night without remaining permanently fixed in its shadow. For a certain degree of playful ambiguity over the act of separation ('did it occur, or didn't it?') imparts a thickened texture to language. Both feminine signature and ironical reflection, Kristevan analysis dramatises the singular voyage of the female intellectual. Style, through the register of irony, and drawing on the semiotic, connects us up once again to the object of displacement (woman, personal affect, and so on).

A final observation: doesn't Kristeva's oxymoron, 'tender aggression', which she uses to describe the activity involved in reading and writing Knight's autobiography, suggest a certain degree of abjection: that is, of incomplete separation? In *Powers of Horror* we are informed that abjection as a borderline state undergone before achieving a sense of separate identity is characterised by 'ambiguous opposition'. (*Powers*: 7) Neither one thing nor the other, it only recognises what elsewhere would be an impossible contradiction. Thus if reading comprehends abjection which in turn borders on the space of exile, then whose is the most authoritative projection on the subject: the reader's or the writer's? Indeed, can we fully separate reader and writer? The reading process, like love perhaps, clouds the issue, obscuring distinctions between inside and outside, me and you, homely and unhomely. I will return to this dilemma towards the close of the chapter, but for the meantime I will suggest that both identity and its dissolution are necessary functions when we read a text, and not least when that text happens to be by a female intellectual so attuned to the metaphorics of travel.

THE FEMALE VOYAGER

In the spring of 1974, Kristeva published a short piece in *Promesse* entitled 'From Ithaca to New York', in which she observes the condition of postmodernity as it is registered in a highly urban society. She offers the figure of the female voyager as the exemplary role to assume in the face of New York's frenetic movement. The time of New York is one of rupture, of perpetual comings and goings which the female voyager can turn into a play that avoids all notions of fixity. In place of Penelope who waits for Ulysses at home, the 'ruse of the female voyager ... lies in not having a "chez-soi," in considering every home a place ... of the Other, and irritated by its fixity, refusing it'.[11] The woman who is able to travel through countries, discourses, and texts occupies a privileged place because she refuses to domesticate the structures that surround her. To her, every potential home becomes an estranging place, offering a site of dissolving identities and structures in motion. If, like Penelope, woman's habitual task has been to transform the places of waiting into comforting homes, Kristeva's ideal woman will turn the waiting game on its head by making the familiar into something strange. Her facility for playful masquerade, we infer, will keep this female voyager from playing the role of the conventional traveller who like Ulysses travels in order to master, because only woman knows that crossing the seas is just a game, and not for real.

And the real is precisely the problem, because American society poised on the brink of aphasia according to Kristeva, has more or less eliminated the power of the imagination from its cultural memory. It even takes its dreams too seriously. Buildings, huge cubes of glass, steel and neon are Mallarmé's 'Un coup de dés' *literalised*, made real.[12] In this place that has conspired to make imagination and dreams a reality, 'everything is free, but nothing is possible.' ('DINY': 498) Such a system fails to allow for any sense of renewal and transformation by the Other, and there can be no epiphanies where consumer capitalism and popular culture guarantee to animate every fantasy and illuminate every dark corner of our dreams with the infinitely marketable commodity. Consequently the superego (the Law, the Other) becomes crushing because the subject identifies with the real, and so exposes himself to the Law's full weight without allowing for a more habitable symbolic mediated by the work of the imaginary. New York, Kristeva claims, *needs* the female voyager's imagination. Gazing up at those towers of black glass that distort one's image, returning it shattered into fragments and blocks, one can only agree that the experience has a disturbing effect resembling the return of the repressed.

Inhabiting this strange world is the American family: 'Come back and bring the family' is the kind of fake homeliness that draws the domestic world of Mom, Dad and kids into the more questionable sensory and erotic pleasures afforded by New York. Contemporary American culture according to Kristeva is deprived of the 'Verb' – only 'the id speaks' – and genuine, imaginative reading or analysis that travels between one and the other is lacking. Other critics have taken up the ethnocentricity and arrogance of such remarks,[13] but what interests me more here is the pretext this assumption provides for speaking about the role of women. The community of women, she argues, is a community of hysterics ('DINY': 510) because the American feminist's rather simplistic opposition of body and drive on the one hand and verbalisation on the other resembles the difficulty of hysteria, a condition whose sufferers deny the final exile in the symbolic. Hysterics find the constraints of the symbolic too confining, and discover ways to return to the comfort of the drive-governed body. Alternatively Kristeva suggests, feminists have adopted (again, like hysterics) an aggressive masculine style and discourse by fighting for political equality or reviving the utopian dream of matriarchy. In either case, the ultimate end is a static situation that allows women to feel too much at home with either the political system or the maternal body. Perhaps, Kristeva adds, the American woman even wishes to abolish the coded discourse of love and romance and replace it with an 'aphasic jouissance', which would turn males into 'dumb troubadors' ready to serve in their own dismemberment. Better still, women in America today may well be in the process of abolishing love altogether. The female voyager by comparison, is in a privileged place to avoid a complicity with the forces of planned obsolescence which prompts feminists to destroy all truth and make men redundant. Her constant moving from place to place that enables her to view everything as strange may actually help her to mediate more productively the relation between body and language. Accordingly, she must keep the subjective unity of the 'I' in a productive tension with the strangeness of what Kristeva calls 'maternal rhythm'.

In practice, it is not clear precisely what would follow from such a generalisation, and its theoretical symmetry leads the reader to wonder if Kristeva's own discourse in relation to feminism does not exercise a too easily-won form of mastery. Just how far she has travelled from what a certain form of feminist criticism would call 'home' is to be seen in the following essay by Minnie Bruce Pratt entitled 'Identity: Skin Blood Heart'.[14] Here Pratt, another female voyager, painstakingly explores the notion of home that she is now seeking to put into place in her own life. Separated from her two children and a privileged white middle-class past through becoming a lesbian, she attempts to understand some of the narratives that have shaped her sense of home and settledness in the context of her new life in a poor black area of Washington DC. Her search is the equivalent of a laboured coming to consciousness of the material advantages with which she had been surrounded, 'stripping away layer after layer of ... false identity, notions of skin, blood, heart based in racism and anti-Semitism ...'.[15] Not that Pratt is insisting that identity be monolithic, but she is making the assumption that underneath the superficial unenlightened self lies a truer one, which if liberated will make the world into a better place. The possibility of challenging the placid assumptions of home is acknowledged, but the Kristevan exuberance in *never* making a home would be quite lost with Pratt. An upheaval in the house for Pratt must result in social and political action, and she would have little patience with Kristeva's call for a renewed aesthetic (imaginary) practice.[16]

More recently, also using the rhetoric of personal history but again at odds with Kristeva, Nancy Miller presented a paper on the question of location and female subjectivity dedicated to 'Mary Ann Caws and Jane Tompkins, who lured me into the dangerous waters of personal criticism.'[17] 'I am working toward a more self-consciously political and personal feminist poetics', writes Miller. In this paper through a variety of voices and positions, she reflects on the implications for feminist theory of problematising its use of the collective 'we' when variables such as class and race are permitted to intersect with the more familiar issue of gender. Miller opens her chapter of dreams with Zora Neale Hurston's *Their Eyes Were Watching God*, and closes with an analysis of the dreams of Jewish and Arab children in Israel and the West Bank.[18] In between and as a postscript, we are given a variety of autobiographical information including a confession of Miller's Jewish middle-classness, and how she has recently turned away from years of academic privilege to take up a job teaching at a college in the Bronx (for which she provides handy directions for the non-streetwise by subway, bus and car). The dream of feminist criticism according to Miller should entail 'textual knowledge of the culture of another country, even if they don't know how to get there',[19] and should grow out of a recognition that 'The Personal is the Positional/The Positional is the Political.'[20]

After long being the doyenne of a feminist-inflected Barthesian criticism, to explore the personal in such intimate terms clearly was a heady but risky enterprise for Miller. For even as exploring the personal affects of reading and writing as a woman led to a new focus, it also threatened with what seemed a dead end: narcissism. Privileging women's subjectivity as Pratt and Miller do risks petrifying it in a specular image, which is precisely the problem Kristeva seeks to avoid in the complex and nuanced representation of her own personal history. In the long run, the confessional or autobiographical mode may be no more productive for female intellectuals than any other genre of writing. Often when women have made use of these self-conscious forms of representation, they have foreshortened the reach of their criticism. Life stories tend to take up *all* the room, and eliminate careful development of intellectual ideas. When criticism becomes frozen in a mode of writing that always reifies the female voice, it loses its savour and tends to become smug and inward looking, grounding the imaginary voyage in a suffocating domestic space. 'Body' overwhelms and devours 'text'.[21] For where the language of criticism and analysis fails to mediate between the text/body dialectic, we find reproduced exactly the same kind of strangely oppressive place Kristeva imagines in New York. Deprived of all sense of perspective, the subject is literally crushed beneath the weight of a hostile textual body, a massive, overpowering landscape that allows no room for difference – and so for the *necessary psychic space* that distinguishes one subject from another. Thus the question of narcissism is a primary structuring one for female intellectuals, who may literally find themselves stranded on the border between a feminine narcissistic focus on the self and the self's objects of love on the one hand, and an effacing of self and identity in writing on the other.

Nancy Miller is one feminist critic among many who confronts the Barthesian injunction that 'the birth of the reader must be at the cost of the death of the Author' and his question, 'What matters who reads?', with caution. Her critical essay 'Changing the Subject' does not warm to Barthes' predilection for death, and I include part of her quotation from the preface of *Sade/Fourier/Layola* (1971):

> For if through a twisted dialectic, the Text, destroyer of all subject [sic], contains a subject to love ... that subject is dispersed, somewhat like the ashes we strew into the wind after death ... Were I a writer, and dead how I would love it if my life, through the pains of some friendly and detached biographer, were to reduce itself to a few details, a few preferences, a few inflections ....[22]

Love for Barthes implies death and dispersion, but does it for the woman, Miller asks, if the female subject has *historically* been dispersed and rendered invisible (dead)? Surely this ought to imply that woman has a different relation to agency, textuality and desire than Barthes' universal man who does not recognise woman's particular discourse. 'What does it mean,' Miller continues, 'to read and write as a woman within the institution that authorizes and regulates most reading and writing?'[23] Miller wishes to preserve a sense of female integrity and intentionality in the text but finally settles for the mode of irony: a 'certain distance to the truth'[24] as a means of securing difference within the constraints of textuality and the semiotics of its 'performance and production'.[25] Language then, will provide the female intellectual with a necessary sense of ambiguity and excess which is less related to a violent disintegration than an ability to manipulate structures, positions, voices. Such a reading celebrates women's liberation without turning the field of language into 'a few preferences'.[26]

Despite their mutual interest in travel, location and irony, Miller would not, I feel, support Kristeva's fascination with the fading of the subject of enunciation. (As early as 1966, Kristeva had read the author as 'an anonymity, an absence', his writing founded on the gap that opens within the subject between the *énoncé* and the *énonciation*.)[27] But for my part, the sense of loss of identity alluded to can on occasions, despite feminist critique, be seductive. A woman can be just as drawn by the prospect of travel as Mallarmé's clearly male protagonist in 'Brise marine', captivated at the prospect of loss of bodily limits as he imagines himself to be a bird 'reeling through unknown spray, drunk with the skies'.[28] In fact, there are times when feminism's emphasis on materiality and the female body becomes a burden for research. If it has given us a more complex understanding of the relationship between the coupling of mind and body in philosophical discourse, and an awareness of the tremendous cost to human experience in repressing the latter term, it has also resulted in a tendency towards a new prescriptivism for those intellectuals who are women: '*real* women theorise gender and the female body'. Kristeva's stubborn distance from this form of judgement is one aspect of her work that I find refreshing. So to return to her writing, precisely what place does the signifier 'woman' occupy? What might its relationship be to questions of exile and epiphany? To the distinction between home and the *unheimlich*? Does it ground and inform these questions, or does it sit awkwardly in the text as an afterthought, an embarassing irrelevance? Further, is it at all helpful to align Kristeva's thought with other explicitly feminist texts? What kind of regard does she have for a category as gendered as the female intellectual which I have represented in this chapter as the female voyager?

Before going any further, I must stress that I have chosen the term 'female intellectual' and not 'feminist' to engage in dialogue with Kristeva's texts, and with the broader question of estrangement and exile. As a working term, it is probably too formal, but at least it avoids the suggestion of prescriptiveness frequently implied by 'feminist'. I have therefore chosen to recognise the difference that gender makes without always choosing to write out of, or towards it. In fact, my reading of gender is sustained by the conviction that sexual difference is to be confronted but equally to be passed through on a voyage to somewhere else. To that extent I offer an oblique exploration of the degree to which women are obliged to be different thinkers here and now, and own a different subjectivity from men. The degree to which sexual difference and its symbolic implications persists poses ultimately an unanswerable question. A direct, phenomenological answer certainly fails to satisfy Kristeva, and cannot be found in a valorised sense in any of her texts. She is undoubtedly a thinker of considerable importance for feminism, but her work is far wider in scope, and must be judged on other terms as well. My own commitments are not always to feminism as an ideology, or as a consistent way of reading, for that matter, but to exploring the question of thinking as a woman. In addition and somewhat contrarily, I suppport the belief that truth may yet be a universal discourse in which both women and men can participate.[29] If there comes a time when 'thinking as a woman' is found to be an anachronism or a hindrance to reading, then I shall set it to one side and attempt to search for a discourse that is more able to privilege shared values across the gender divide, or that internalises sexual difference within each subject. Intellectual inquiry must maintain itself as a country where nothing is forbidden; where no areas are off limits by virtue of one's race, gender, or class. To charge the female intellectual with *always* thinking as a woman seems to me by a strange sleight of hand to return thought and its subjects to an age where access to education was determined according to one's gender, and where women in particular were denied access to participation as equals in the intellectual world. That aspects of feminist theory are currently instrumental in provoking a radical reorientation of much critical inquiry does not lessen my concern, especially where the other (the 'patriarchy') is still represented in paranoid fashion as the enemy on the outside. Here I am in agreement with Kristeva's reading of strangeness which offers an urgent plea that both men and women recognise the strangeness which lives within (as sexual difference, for instance). In that way there can be no other in permanent opposition; simply divided subjects willing to make temporary allegiances, whose only genuine universal is to be found in the mysterious immediacy of language itself, invested with and transformed by affect. The place of the female intellectual therefore, should be one from which gender is both posited and dissolved.

I suspect that Kristeva's thinking about women who make self-reflexive thought their calling is complex and at times contradictory. On occasions the question preoccupies her, on others its insistence is minimal. In the former case she appears to privilege with one hand and take away with the other; in the latter I hear for a moment the ironic autobiographical voice of the female voyager who knows that there are at least some advantages in being a woman and an intellectual. Either way, it is probably inevitable that sexual difference turns aside from the kind of illumination that would discover and name a totality (of identity or theory), and when its elusive nature is imbricated with a 'music in letters' what remains is not exactly a woman but a painting, as Matisse once said.[30]

Admittedly, there are moments when Kristeva's enraptured writing on the jouissance associated with the nameless leads me to suspect that like Beckett's characters in 'First Love' and 'Mouth', she is too preoccupied with obsessional ruminations on loss and death. But clearly as a thinker she ranges more widely than this. In some texts, the reader has a much sharper sense that sexual difference can still be discussed in terms of symbolic identity. Indeed, those who accuse Kristeva of an out and out hostility to women have obviously not read 'From Ithaca to New York'. In the midst of her rather patronising dismissal of American feminism, there suddenly occurs an astonishing outburst against (academic) men. The trouble with these 'senile' male intellectuals (or 'pimps'!) is that they are either full of 'inane gallantry or libidinous paternalism', their avaricious desires fading as soon as the female intellectual begins to speak. They fantasise that the intelligent woman is a phallic mother and, fearful of coming too close, idealise beauty instead. If they do see a woman's body standing there they either can't concentrate on what she's saying or devalue it, and in a 'homosexual purist passion' strive to 'disencumber the theoretical field' of her presence. ('DINY': 513) Surely these observations have considerable affinity with Cixous' objections to the male philosopher whose quest for knowledge permits woman to be mystery, but not to know it. In 1974 when this brief text was written, 'beauty' is obviously regarded by Kristeva as one discourse that expels the maximum of alterity.[31] Beauty might be sublime, but has lost its capacity for revitalising the house of language. It is too *purist* to be able to transpose the language of the body (affect) into the text. Instead, reasons Kristeva, some enigmatic attribute of the feminine body might be able to stand in the same relation to meaning as transcendence and the sublime once did – that is, as both external to the system, but capable of transforming it from within. So she responds by privileging the notion of alterity and equating it with maternal rhythm, which in turn implied that *women*, or at least women who are mothers, might stand in a privileged relation to discourses that included the voices of others. A particular kind of identity or position, then, gave them this hold. What was it?

We need to examine carefully the reasoning that leads Kristeva, among others, to suggest that at times, women occupy a *different* place in relation to language and the body. Ellie Ragland-Sullivan explains feminine identity in the following way: even though the mother is not in reality a source of fullness and presence outside discourse, she does have a 'closer perceptual proximity to the desire that cannot be separated from the corporeal'.[32] And further, 'the mother is the natural signifier for desire, while the father's name offers a measure of distance, the mediation of language, as a phallic third term of flight, escape, or mastery, away from a profound source of affect'. Women, because of their less precipitous flight away from the mother on the way to constructing their identity as gendered, Oedipal subjects, have generally been regarded by Freudian psychoanalysts as preserving a closer relation to the drives, to affect as rhythm, vocalisation, and so on. Luce Irigaray and Hélène Cixous while not Freudian, both affirm this particular quality of feminine subjectivity, as in a more empiricist manner do object relations theorists such as Nancy Chodorow, Dorothy Dinnerstein, Jessica Benjamin and Melanie Klein.[33] The instances where Kristeva herself maintains a belief, even a vested interest in the difficulty of achieving a female subjectivity are legion, and many of these examples will offer themselves in later chapters. In the meantime, an example or two will suffice, the first from 'Women's Time'.[34] Here, Kristeva articulates the unique kind of temporalities that emerge when reproduction of sex, bodies and symbols is considered as a factor common to the experience of Europe and beyond. One of the reasons feminists have for claiming that identification among woman is distinctive rests on what Kristeva has expressed as 'the connivance of the young girl with her mother, [and] her greater difficulty than the boy in detaching herself from the mother in order to accede to the order of signs as invested by the absence and separation constitutive of the paternal function.' ('WT': 204) She notes that because the transition to the symbolic is so fraught, and because woman can never really, unlike the man, restore this maternal relationship to herself except through becoming a mother or through homosexuality, her fantasies about the archaic mother are almost inconsolable. She thus becomes something of a vulnerable subject, never quite recovering from the original loss of her mother, perhaps never fully accepting it even. Despite recognising these handicaps, in case we still persist in imagining that woman's position in the symbolic is identical to man's, we could turn to the following remark:

> I think that for a woman, generally speaking, the loss of identity in jouissance demands of her that she experience the phallus that

> she simply is; but this phallus must immediately be established somewhere; in narcissism, for instance, in children, in a denial and/or hypostasis of the other woman, in a narrow-minded mastery, or in fetishism of one's 'work'... (*Desire*: 164)

The space for the *female* traveller, it appears, is distinctive. Here, woman is in the position of the desired object (she *is* the phallus and so is positioned *in* language, but cannot *have* or symbolise the phallus and thus is exiled to the edge of language). Standing in the place of that first archaic object, she cannot herself be the phallic mother, but is obliged lest she fly too close to her old home, to anchor herself in the symbolic by maintaining a firm attachment to social, intellectual or political projects. Even this anchorage, however, is a good deal less certain than it is for a man, and the reader is left with the impression that woman can *never* feel as at home in the symbolic as can man. As we saw in Chapter 1, she becomes the 'female exile':

> A woman is trapped within the frontiers of her body and even of her species, and consequently always feels *exiled* both by the general clichés that make up a common consensus and by the very powers of generalization intrinsic to language. Woman is a boundary creature who needs to surround herself with *context*, whether domestic or cultural. It is this context in the form of a supporting web of relationships that limits the tendency to fragmentation which Kristeva believes women display.

Lest it be assumed that the above remarks imply that women are permanently exiled from the symbolic and more at home in the unconscious, we must turn again to the universal experience of separation that shapes our subjectivity. Kristeva's work constantly reminds us that indifference to the phallus is simply wishful thinking. Castration and separation we can now see, found society and speech, their painful experiences reflecting a universal condition. Matricide then appears as the crime that will save us all from immobility, asymbolia, psychosis. And if the process of separation is begun but never fully completed we will encounter severe depression, self-contempt, hatred, even violence towards the others in our lives. But strangely enough, Kristeva is immediately led to make the following remark:

> For a woman, whose specular identification with the mother as well as the introjection of the maternal body and self are more immediate,

> such an inversion of matricidal drive into a death-bearing maternal image is more difficult, *if not impossible* [my emphasis]. Indeed, how can She be that bloodthirsty Fury, since I am She (sexually and narcissistically), She is I? (*BS*: 28–9)

Is this Kristeva's personal imaginary delusion, or has she discovered a symbolic difference? The woman in these terms appears closer to melancholia than a man. However, and Kristeva's cavil is discreet here, she is possibly better equipped than men to explore philosophy and literary discourse if she can redirect her narcissism on to a strong ideal. That is, if she is able to find a system of values or ethics strong enough to pull her away from her mirror – or at least strong enough to displace that narcissism in intellectual writing. There is even a hint in this introductory chapter of *Black Sun* that the woman who does survive is indeed one of the fittest, for if she is able to come to terms with her lack in relation to the symbolic order – that is, her secondary position due to her 'castration' (a true Freudian here: for Kristeva, woman's sex is absent, invisible), and if she is equally able to accept the trauma of having to transfer her affections from a mother to a father figure, she will emerge as stronger than man:

> the discovery of her invisible vagina already imposes upon woman a tremendous sensory, speculative, and intellectual effort, [and] shifting to the symbolic order *at the same time* as to a sexual object of a sex other than that of the primary maternal object represents a gigantic elaboration in which a woman cathexes a psychic potential greater than what is demanded of the male sex. (*BS*: 30)

If woman's sex is absent, or invisible, this, Kristeva implies, can be turned to her advantage, since the transition to language also rests on absence and loss. Here, and overturning Freud now (his logic, but hardly his essentialism), she makes women's invisible sex and the universal lack of being that found language and culture not merely analagous, but the first as the privileged condition of the second. It would seem that the creative potential at woman's disposal is indeed prodigious, and if a strong ideal is introjected at the same time as a woman reaches maturity, then the possibility of producing 'sensory, speculative, and intellectual' works is very likely. Surely a self-reflective remark guaranteed to draw attention to her own seemingly endless succession of highly theoretical texts! Such an inference is inescapable. Kristeva's writing is, moreover, speculative work that affirms strangeness as a permanent mode of being which an intellectual woman who maintains her connection to the feminine through a sensitivity to the mother-tongue is in a better position to articulate. For woman's ambivalent relation to specular identification and the body could give her an edge over the male intellectual in theorising a new relation to language. The female intellectual is able, according to Kristeva, to both *reflect* on experience and to stand in its place, her feminine relation to the body functioning as the semiotic's privileged home. In which case the capacity for renewal and transformation of thought lies neither entirely outside language, in raw biology or in the person of a deity (female or male), yet nor is it fully at home within language. There appears to be something quite unique for Kristeva about being the kind of woman who can fully inhabit the material world while simultaneously theorising about the nature of that experience. For that reason the space of uncertainty inhabited by the female voyager both recognises *and* ignores the vicissitudes of separation and exile. It contains the potential to negotiate a complex terrain that moves from an estrangement outside of, or on the edge of language to a place of exile within it. Now Kristeva is not claiming a place of privilege for women over against men. What she is suggesting, I believe, is that the potential space of analysis that opens for the woman who is an intellectual has a distinctiveness about it. At times it may actually afford a richer and more complex reading than that available for male intellectuals. Having a closer contact with the mother's body women are potential advocates of the mother-tongue's pluralising of meaning. But this argument is advanced in a double movement: on the one hand, a turning away from finding a special place for women; on the other a gesture that appears to reinstate the category of the female intellectual.

This movement introduces an unresolved contradiction in her texts, particularly the early work on semiotics where one can read whole stretches of writing that assume a universal voice only occasionally interrupted by a more embodied voice acknowledging its debt to femininity. On the question of consistency, Luce Irigaray appears to have had more success because her critique of the enterprise of philosophy is so radical. Like Cixous, she would argue that philosophy is a house built by and for man; woman's only alternative is to imagine and write entirely new conceptual structures that would affirm the absolute and irreducible nature of sexual difference. Kristeva by contrast works for moments of privilege for women (or for herself as an intellectual woman) within the larger project of estranging being.

Undoubtedly, the biggest challenge to philosophy today is the enigmatic figure of the woman philosopher (the female intellectual). In agreement, Antoinin Artaud once wrote, '... like all women you think with your sex, not with your mind'.[35] How can this exorbitant challenge to the status quo which instinctively would link woman with 'sex' and not 'mind' be dislodged? As I indicated, such a challenge is taken up in all Kristeva's research. If not explicitly, then from across the divide, the enunciatory abyss that separates body from text, her writing is engaged with a supplementary project over and above its explicit aims, namely to work out a justification that would account for both 'the sudden surge of women and children in discourse' ('ANT': 300) and the legitimacy of her own personal wager with language and thought.

But why then is it necessary for this supplementary project to be so oblique? Why have so many critics who have read Kristeva come away feeling she has little to say on the question of woman?[36] I think there are four main factors at work which have produced a discourse that is either surreptitious, or in two minds, about female subjectivity.[37] The first is that she has up to a point accepted the anti-phenomenological terms of reference of much contemporary criticism. The empirical world of experience discovers that the text does not offer a homely reflection. The face that looks back at us from the surface of the text is blank or disfigured. When Kristeva speaks of her experience of exile in the essay 'The Novel as Polylogue', she does so in order to use its estranging effects as the objective correlative for a disintegrated subject: 'Consequently, as you may have noticed, I have no "I" anymore, no imaginary, if you wish; everything escapes or comes together in theory, or politics, or activism.' (*Desire*: 161) The exile cannot claim to have a settled identity, nor can she ever be fully at home with her sex, and when she is deprived of an imaginary, she lacks the ability to put together a coherent narrative in which she could see herself and in which she could be seen. Secondly, as we have already observed, if the Freudian and Lacanian psychoanalytical narrative is accepted with its different *rites de passage* for males and females, woman *does* have a different relation to the social contract and to meaning. Precisely what this difference may mean is difficult to establish, but it certainly exists, both in the relationship that women have to motherhood, and the latter's effects on sublimation and idealisation. Thirdly and as a consequence of woman's position in the social contract, the terms 'mind' and 'body' have conventionally been diametrically opposed, leading to the suggestion that the figure of the woman philosopher or the female intellectual is an impossibility. The first term is incompatible with the second, to the extent that the figure becomes aporetic. Kristeva knows such a conundrum is not evaded as easily as Cixous manages to do in 'The Laugh of the Medusa', where she happily privileges 'unthinking' as a kind of 'spending' that women are most suited to do. Rendering the unthinkable thinkable and the thinkable unthinkable is the dual strategy that Kristeva takes on, which brings us to the final reason for the recessing of female subjectivity: *style*.

When I read Kristeva, I am aware of the very real pleasures that are to be derived from apprehending language as a material texture; from exploring the turns of critical reading, and from observing the transformations in meaning effected from one text to another. Above all, I sense the attraction of distance, of irony, of contradiction and ambiguity: of style, in other words. According to John Lechte, style 'is the transcendence of death and thus of all (banal) realism. Style means that the work of art is inseparable from its production',[38] and implicates the text in an infinitely generative process. In this reading, the death that the subject undergoes before he begins to write is a crucial step in avoiding the banality that arises when a text (and author) fails to reflect on its own productivity as origin. Signs alone can bear the weight of this burden of loss (separation from the mother) that afflicts men and women. The ultimate sign that separation has successfully occurred is when a narrative transcends realism to confront, through language, the founding truth of our being: that that which we most desire is forever departed. The object of our gaze is always viewed by a subject in process – a *voyager* – as if from a wooded ridge. Irony is a form of style that distances itself from realism by the assumption of a mask and in this sense its particular structure fulfils the requirements that a position in language requires a *distance* from that first maternal home. In Nabokov's *Sebastian Knight*, we may not always find a life, but we do get style, and the stylish autobiographer is ironical. But Kristeva also makes it clear that irony as an uncanny kind of *doubling* ('what a coincidence! The theorist also comes from Sofia!') is the indispensable mark of the intellectual. Irony thus involves a kind of turning inside out, of *looping over* our first home that sets up an undecidability at the heart of speech. In the figure of Sebastian Knight, Kristeva is both 'there' and 'not there' in his imaginary place. As she represents him to us, as she accommodates Nabokov's narratives to her own, and her own to Knight's, we have the distinct impression that she is changing the place of things, and using the Nabokovian character as a means of saying something about her own subjectivity. In this way, speaking as a woman must be a highly self-conscious gesture, the product of a style that simultaneously *undoes* style in its double movement of distancing itself from its object (the mother is unattainable except through language) and then doubling back on itself through irony, contradiction and word play to establish a discreet site of privilege for the female intellectual. ('I know I have lost my mother, but all the same.') Separation undoubtedly remains the precondition for thought, yet something else remains alongside: a dazzling narcissistic residue (a new form of 'transcendence' or epiphany perhaps?) which can be read as a speaking against the grain of the text to produce a profound ambivalence or unreadability.

READING STRANGELY

> Life is most fully present when the life of the writer and the writing of the life merge, breaking down the distinction between subject and object; between woman as writer or woman as written, woman as reader or woman as read ...
>
> Mary Jacobus, *Reading Woman*[39]

> Any chain of language is invested with a spending-focus that links the body to its biological and social history.
>
> Julia Kristeva, *Desire in Language*[40]

Listen to the piercing musicality of the Kristevan phrase: perhaps no other theorist writing today has that seductive combination of authority and eloquence. Reflecting on the inevitable intersection in writing of subjective and objective modes of criticism, Mary Jacobus writes with an acuteness and lucidity that makes her work both provoking and immediately accessible, but when Julia Kristeva comes to speak on the same question, I surrender to an altogether different kind of reading experience. Stranded in an unfamiliar zone that is neither metaphysical nor poetic, I witness literally what Mallarmé has called elocutionary disappearance. The void that language opens in the text causes me to experience emptiness, because I recognise that while a 'spending-focus' appears to add a comforting density to discourse, it does so at the cost of identity. 'Subjective' and 'objective' become anaphoric markers constituted on loss, on the gap or space that opens within the subject of writing that adds a dangerous excess to the ego and renders its object unmasterable.

This apocalyptic cast to Kristeva's discourse that draws me in even as it empties 'me' of existence, acts out the upheaval the textual body undergoes when its subject begins to write; when *style* changes the face of things and so opens on to questions of life and death. One of the compelling things about her work is precisely this linkage between writing, the unnamable, and the most fundamental of human processes. The space of travel designated by Kristevan style is enigmatic, its boundaries unfamiliar, elusive. But what gives her the authority to mix discourses and vocabularies traditionally at odds with each other? How much of her persuasion rests on what Roman Jakobson calls a 'contagious voice'? Is there an underlying theoretical strata which energises this rhetoric, and if so, how can it be described?

From the stiff but innovative formalism of the early texts to her latest published reflections on time and nationalism, I am drawn to her voice by the 'need to know'. What does she understand of the search for meaning and desire in language? Of women and philosophy? Or of women and creativity? How does she view the power of institutions, especially that of the State? How does she read suffering? And love? I am led, in accounting for my attraction, to a study of the *reading relationship* that has grown between us over the years, since it is by subjecting this empathic relationship to scrutiny that I will be able to assess the impact of her work more acutely. Kristeva's writing is difficult stylistically and intellectually. For a reader with little knowledge of European philosophy – its tropes and givens, its manner of argument – her thought is formidable, drawing on a huge range of texts and discourses, appropriating, challenging and synthesising. Further, this difficulty is compounded when her work is read in translation, as Margaret Waller acknowledges in her preface to *Revolution in Poetic Language*[41]. In both cases, an easy readability is out of the question, quickly leading the critic (another female voyager) to concede the boundaries of her knowledge. The challenge in encountering Kristeva has in large measure been accompanied by a recognition of the limits of my own intellect as much as it has been a critique of a chosen subject. However, learning to negotiate difficult terrain carries its own rewards – namely a keener awareness of how meaning (as both recognisable product *and* unsettling process) is formulated for a subject.

Let's begin with the way meaning as product works. To read for understanding is in large measure related to finding equivalent terms for those under discussion, to be able to apply them, and to move from one context or place to another. When we talk of product we assume a knowable object and a knowing subject. Initially, the reader as critic accords to the signifying object (the text) a *priority*. That is, criticism assumes its task to be one of respectful explication of an already-there meaning. It invests, writes Kristeva, in '*One Affirmation*'. The author and critic both stand *outside* the system of the text. As Benveniste had observed, 'I'is in a position of transcendence in relation to 'you'.[42] This is even the case when alongside the respect paid to the prior text, the critic is equally involved in a struggle for power, and tries to master the object by reducing it to his or her own terms. To use the word 'understanding' is therefore to imply a sense of arrival or illumination on the part of the voyager, where a light breaks into the mind and transforms the object of its investigation into something homely, comfortable, familiar. Of course, as we have seen in Chapter 1, reading involves a sense of surprise and estrangement. What is oblique often resists illumination; what is at first overlooked may after later associations be reinstated through a second reading, adding to the text's density; the sheer outrageous novelty of an expression or argument may take us by surprise: all of these instances momentarily obstruct the reader, adding to the struggle for lucidity.

Under these conditions where meaning is read as product, the mechanics of thought operates by moving from the unfamiliar to the familiar through naturalising strangeness. Naturalising procedures allow a thesis to be formulated and tested; the imperative to communicate orders the play of signifiers and attempts to fix limits so that the transcendental ego may claim from language a meaning for itself. What happens, however, when meaning is construed as a *process*, and the traveller's map fails? If it is true that understanding works in the way that I have just outlined, it is at the same time an inadequate description. For understanding is as much a constructive process as a reflection of an object that already exists. The mastery of language through the activity of naming and judging is founded on a repression, since formulating an argument turns a blind eye to the dialogic aspect of language. But reading is actually a kind of affective transference or voyage that involves adopting the mutually interchangeable roles of analyst and analysand. Just as the power of the transference derives from the analyst's ability to sweep the analysand off her feet by the unexpectedness of the interpretation, the conviction of analytical discourse rests on a speech that is put together co-operatively. In this way critical reading confesses it is founded on a fundamental lack of absolute knowledge, not an original plenitude. And in confessing its weakness, it allows itself to be transformed by the speech of the other towards which it travels. Knowledge is founded paradoxically on estrangement, on a dazzling that confuses the boundaries between subject and object. In reading no-one knows who achieves mastery, for the reader discovers herself to be both narrator and narratee, the traveller who reads and the traveller who is read. Therefore the space of the voyage of interpretation becomes double, indeterminate, unhomely. For where language is continually oriented to and produced by an Other, it becomes the place where the concept of thesis itself is deconstructed. In these terms, the drive to stabilise a position is more appropriately connected with the egocentric misrecognitions of the imaginary: with Lacan's heliocentrism, in other words. Reading therefore tends to obscure the distinction between the condition of exile from language and exile in language.

When, as Jacobus would have it, the distinction between subject and object breaks down, mastering meaning through knowledge gives place to charting the process of the desiring, enunciating subject through the text. We can see then that knowledge has a fundamental discursive quality whose productivity reflects the intersection in writing between author and addressee (the other) and in a more particular sense, of the writer's work with that of the critic. If reading Kristeva had been a transparent and unresisting activity, there would have been less need to reflect on the *acts and processes* from one to the other, from subject to object, that reading involves. Nor would I have been led to explore what Jacobus calls the 'otherness of the letter', where Kristeva estranges and doubles literal meaning through a 'move that installs strangeness (femininity) within reading itself'.[43] Accordingly, the reader can no longer stand solely in a place of transcendence exterior to the language of the text. Instead, she is drawn into its orbit and experiences its regenerative qualities, as it were, from within.

From the outset, I am attracted to Kristeva's suggestion that language carries a surplus which is material. Its 'spending-focus' is of a materialist and biological nature because according to Kristeva it invokes the drives; and dialectical and historical because these drives operate within and across the subject through the '*linear* order of language'. (*Desire*: 102, my emphasis) However, a material, historical subject for Kristeva is not a subjective, psychological one. Materiality here relates less to experience than to its disintegration through the presence of *affect*, the eruption of the drives into language in the form of 'rhythmic, meaningless, anterior memory'. (*Desire*: 32) When the presence of the enunciation, the act of speaking, is seen to intrude into the utterance, in Kristeva's view it is not registered as the presence of the author, but as the destabilising effects of *signifiance* which work to differentiate the subject from itself and to reconnect it to its primary objects. It is the site of *production*, the unconscious and its effects in language as it pierces the neutral, unified subject that Kristeva insists is the crucible in which subjectivity is produced. In this sense, affect carries the burden of a First Cause without the latter's accessibility to meaning. Where this is the case, elocutionary disappearance causes a personal narrative to fade, or become obscure. Thus from the edge of the void, the voyager who reads confronts both her own nullity, and the prospect of renewal and transformation through the speech of the other.

Naturally, it is impossible for the writer or reader to mechanically separate her own act of criticism into product and production. Our love, our desire for the other is at once irrational and affective as well as open to analysis. Although if it is true that 'it is in the chain of the signifier that the meaning "insists"', then following this chain as I construct it, with all the richly associative bypaths that may be involved is the only course open to me.[44] Kristeva speaks in *Tales of Love* of being 'under the hold of personal predilection as love demands ...'. (*Tales*: 17) Who knows why we choose the love-objects we do? Why we travel to one place and not another? It is just so with reading. We rationalise our predilections after the fact. In the chapters that follow I attempt to account for the idiosyncratic directions of my reading as an intellectual and the extent to which they have determined my analysis of Kristeva. How have her texts moved me? How do they work to transform the domestic into the unhomely? I focus especially on those reading experiences that have had at once a powerfully constituting effect on my own image as woman and intellectual, alongside engendering an acknowledgement that reading (Kristeva) strangely puts all fixed images into question.

When Jacqueline Rose described her attachment to Sylvia Plath, she wrote of her love for the imaginary Plath in terms of a ghost who haunted her with its illusory presence.[45] Could I represent Kristeva in the same light? The publicity photograph gracing the covers of *Desire in Language* and *Powers of Horror* with that enigmatic stare resting on some distant point (rather like one of Bellini's Madonnas, in fact) is a tantalising invitation to construct an imaginary family scene, precisely the kind of construction that Kristeva has frequently criticised.[46] Yet some identification is inevitable, even desirable. Undoubtedly my reconstructions of the Kristeva *I* know are imaginary, but if reading does involve transference, for me it does not exclude whatever transitory identifications that may illuminate this passion of the subject. Therefore, one could ask, what sort of a (textual) model or map was she for me? What was it in her writing, despite its flaws, that I continued to find so attractive? Catherine Clément in speaking of her relationship with Lacan, describes it as love:

> Sure, it was love. When you're always on time for every appointment, when nothing can make you miss one, when you leave disappointed sometimes but always enamoured, what else can it be? I'm well aware that this sort of thing is no longer 'in'. People call it 'dogmatism'. And it's true: love of this sort gives rise to self-betrayal, intransigence, the end of intellectual independence. But it can also give rise to another kind of thought, a kind of thought that is at war with itself and that in the most favourable of circumstances destroys its object. There remains a 'hard core' attached to the love object – the object that originally elicited love. And that hard core of my original love for Lacan is something that I still carry with me, even if I have shed the husks, skins, and shells that used to surround it.[47]

It is inevitable, Clément continues, that we are formed by thinking different 'others'. 'In any body of thought there is an adolescent figure, never entirely effaced.'[48] 'Little by little, hour by hour, week by week, there was woven in us an implacable mesh of language, unconscious but effective, that had the property of rendering all other modes of thought obsolete ... This is how a dogma is born.'[49] In his essay on Leonardo da Vinci, Freud writes that 'biographers are fixated on their heroes in a quite special way. In many cases they have chosen their hero as the subject of their studies because – for reasons of their personal emotional life – they have felt a special affection for him from the first.'[50] He goes on to suggest that he too may have made a narcissistic object-choice in selecting Leonardo in the first place. Discussing the passage, Mary Jacobus observes: 'But at precisely the moment when he implicates his own narcissism, Freud turns away to inquire into the theoretical achievements and limits of psychoanalytic biography ... Freud's account of Leonardo's too great investigative sublimation puts his own theoretical investigation on the line.'[51] Jacobus uses this oversight to return Freud to the maternal body which pushes all forms of theoretical mastery beyond its limits, whereas I could move her speculation in another direction and examine the implications of a particular object-choice: the Kristevan text. For it is clear that the reasons some readers have for preferring Kristeva over Cixous and Irigaray for instance, and the energies subsequently expended in grappling with her work are the product of a chain of relationships complemented by a particular history of reading affects.

But the question of narcissism which, moreover, returns us to Barthes' and Heidegger's anxiety over banality, remains a major stumbling block. Writing of secondary narcissism in the female adolescent, Freud has this to say:

> Women, especially if they grow up with good looks, develop a certain self-contentment which compensates them for the social restrictions that are imposed upon them in their choice of object. Strictly speaking, it is only themselves that such women love with an intensity comparable to that of the man's love for them. Nor does their need lie in the direction of loving, but of being loved; and the man who fulfils this condition is the one who finds favour with them.[52]

Rachel Brownstein in her book *Becoming a Heroine*, responds to Freud's remarks by recognising their perspicacity, and suggests that 'the idea of autoeroticism as compensation for social restriction has real interest for feminists'.[53] Brownstein is interested in women reading novels, and in their desire to be heroines. 'An addiction to fiction, to getting as it were high on heroines,' is quite common: 'All women', she writes, 'with a hungry susceptibility to a comprehensible self-image can be said to suffer from it.'[54] Brownstein additionally recognises that these predilections may be metaphorical: 'I am writing about how the self and self-consciousness are mutually and problematically involved, and involved in literary form and in language.'[55]

Julia Kristeva is more a critic than a novelist. Nevertheless my choosing at this point to emphasise a reading relationship where attention is directed to the problematics of inserting the self into writing, *does* represent a form of narcissism. Brownstein and Freud seem to concur that narcissism is a form of compensation for isolation from the social. To what extent does its inflection here indicate imprisonment in an exchange of images where the other is always reduced to the same, and where estrangement is mastered so that the other neither recedes nor merges enigmatically with us, but comes to reflect our own experience? It seems to me that an answer lies in an emphasis on the transactional, but simultaneously disturbing nature of reading. If we put together a subjectivity, it is provisional; accompanying a 'concentration' of identity is its 'dissolution'.[56] Or, as John Lechte expresses it, 'the history of love will have analytic effects if we read it with love: that is, with the capacity to turn our reading into an "event" of our own subjectivity that is also partly constitutive of this subjectivity'.[57] Autobiography as a mode of analysis that fails to interrogate its own constitution is a dead end for criticism. Producing a thesis through the activity of criticism is principally an act of positing, not auto-eroticism, or confession. The passion of the subject only becomes thetic when desire is displaced in language; in the same way it is not the perception of the apple tree that is of prime concern to the critic, no matter how delightful this may be. As Husserl reminds us when we reflect on its loveliness, it is the perception of a perception that is most important for the intellectual. Yet this does not necessarily imply that our thesis requires a subject blind to its inner differences or exiled from affect. Kristeva's more recent emphasis on the unfinished, co-operative nature of meaning and subjectivity suggests that the mysterious processes of reading and speech draw us out from the enclosures of narcissism into a more generous, transformative space supported by a loving Other.

'Nothing is more common place than the reading experience, and yet nothing is more unknown', remarked Tzvetan Todorov.[58] Kristeva would agree, although her version of the unknown would be very different from that of her compatriot. Speaking on the nature of the interpretive position in 'Psychoanalysis and the Polis', she maintains that the need to engender an object with unequivocal meaning arises because the subject wishes to reassure himself of his own identity when confronted by an enigmatic other.[59] The function of the object, then, may not only be to throw light on the interpretation, but equally to reveal to the analyst what his theory ignores or cannot see: its *unheimlich*, in other words. Because of the constitutive gap on which language is founded, it would therefore be a deception to imagine that interpretation could entirely close it. Meaning, critical analysis, and reading are all inherently limited projects, their formulations of identity at best only tentative. At their most rigid and extreme, they represent a form of foreclosure, a fall into the very first object of plenitude which according to Lacanian psychoanalysis is then embodied in the imaginary figure of the phallic mother.

Kristeva hypothesises that the origin of the desire for mastery lies in an experience she names abjection. Where the object appears as an elusive other just beyond the subject's comprehension, what is aroused in the subject who reads this other is an instinctual memory that recalls a primitive state prior to the formation of subjectivity. In this state that attempts to break away from the all-sufficient mother lies horror, fascination, estrangement: 'This abject awakens in the one who speaks archaic conflicts with his own improper objects, his abjects, at the edge of meaning, at the limits of the interpretable. And it arouses the paranoid rage to dominate these objects, to transform them, to exterminate them.'('PatP': 318) The experience of reading leads us to recognise as abject all that cannot be read, or that resists a determinate meaning. We flee from the enounter with obscurity because its blinding qualities deprive us of a sense of a self at home with itself. The enormity of loss and confusion fills our vision and disturbs our dreams. Thus to be in a state of indeterminacy is to remain a captive of abjection, perhaps the supreme example of estrangement in a world with no God.

This borderline experience where matter appears to exist completely deprived of names and identities is understood by Kristeva as being an indispensable part of the experience of reading. But by remaining permanently dominated by abjection we risk eventually giving the nameless a final identity and final meaning: Man the Enemy; Woman the phallic Master. We can see therefore, that abjection unchecked leads to hatred or destruction of self *and* other. Now up until *Tales of Love* Kristeva appeared to have no mechanism in place to bear the burden of this devastating form of estrangement that abjection gave rise to in the subject. In fact, as I argue in Chapter 3, she was initially preoccupied with effacing all conventional notions of transcendence, a term that might once have been able to subdue abjection. With the notion of the Imaginary Father developed in *Tales of Love* however, one can see the emergence of a figure able to provide relief from pure indeterminate matter. Earlier emphasis on the need for a third party that would intervene between mother and child has now been transformed into the necessary, 'direct and immediate' identification with this Father. I will discuss the complexities of primary identification in Chapter 4, but for the moment my interest lies in the weight accorded to such an experience, for in many respects its representation is remarkably similar to the form of the strange epiphanies read in Chapter 1, epiphanies that Kristeva had apparently rejected as illusory.

If formerly the figure of the sun had been identified by Kristeva as the representative of symbolic law against which the poet struggled in intense Oedipal conflict,[60] by 1983 the Father's agency in *Tales of Love* is redefined as a 'warm dazzling', a 'godsend' that is directly responsible for turning us towards the intimations of an Other. These intimations are from one point of view, traces which the infant *reads*,[61] and so they cannot have the transcendent quality which Beckett concludes lies in the Proustian experience. Nor can we strictly speaking equate them with Hegel's sunflash which bursts across the horizon, illuminating and changing everything in its path. Identification, represented in language as instantaneous and unmediated is in actuality for Kristeva a *performative* act. Furthermore, indeterminacy (and hence abjection) still lies at the heart of reading as performance, since the 'immediate transference toward the imaginary father' gives us 'the impression that it is he who is transferred into you'. (*Tales*: 41) Have we travelled towards the object, or has the object come to us? Yet far from implicating the reader in abject darkness, the very theological cast of Kristeva's discourse leads to the conclusion that indeterminacy and performance have been mysteriously redeemed by an impulse outside language.

Black Sun: Depression and Melancholia, first published in 1987, is more explicit still. Having dispensed with the celestial calm that descends on the writer as an after-effect of epilepsy, nevertheless when she comes to speak on the nature of forgiveness in Dostoevsky, Kristeva describes it as a 'flash' that leads to reconciliation with a Figure or Power that has become distant. Such tones are indeed reminiscent of the apostle Paul's experience on the road to Damascus whose intensity left him blinded but repentant. The time of forgiveness is literally the mercy of the journey that contains a transcendent quality, albeit imaginary, because it momentarily removes the subject from history: 'Forgiveness *renews the unconscious* because it inscribes the right to narcissistic regression within History and Speech.' (*BS*: 205) In addition, the chance for a new loving identification is opened by forgiveness, which re-enacts that first miraculous form of primary identification. Horror and abjection are not so much washed away as passed through and reincorporated in a new speech, in the possibility of new relations with an other. This alternation between pain and redemption is reinscribed in reading ('analytical listening') and writing. Without the miracle of transference to the other however, reading and writing could not occur. Thus it is that the human subject is reminded at one and the same time of his perpetual incompleteness and his capacity for creating works of great beauty.

The brilliant inventiveness of what *Black Sun* names 'aesthetic forgiveness' should not blind the reader to recognising a new emphasis on the foundational nature of meaning which forgiveness presupposes. True, it is not an immutable Meaning, but one arising from 'assertion and inscription', and thus subject to change. Equally, what Kristeva terms meaning is not rationally apprehended, since it is defined as 'an acting out, a doing, a *poiesis* ... without exegesis, without explanation, without understanding.'(*BS*: 206–7) Nevertheless we can recognise that if an indeterminacy still exists at the origins of identification and hence reading, for Kristeva this does not need to lead to a radical scepticism about knowledge or a black despair at the nature of human existence. Instead, it should encourage us to live life in hope of its permanent renewal in creative engagement with the 'speech' of the other. Perhaps this form of enlightenment is one of the few forms of truth today that can remove scales from our eyes.

I do not find in this more recent Kristeva a programme for reaffirming One Identity and Meaning. The figure of the Imaginary Father and the capacity of speech to absorb suffering through forgiveness do not indicate an explicit commitment to phenomenology, although paradoxically they do rest on the associations provided by its discourse. For despite her continued insistence on the ultimate importance of separation for all subjects, I would argue that there are moments when Kristeva appears to perform an about-face and with the assistance of irony, word play, and narcissistic self-reference assert that the position of the female intellectual may indeed be a privileged one. Such a doubling can only add to the forms of estrangement explored in and enacted by her texts. If style is an aestheticising of an original estrangement, then insinuating that separation itself is never a determinate affair (for women; for artists; for melancholics, for instance) gives style a new complexity. It invests it with a new form of 'transcendence', and so reconnects it with the unnamable. Clearly though, this is a hypothesis that cannot be proved. Is the Kristeva I have identified really encoded in the text, or are the signifiers that I have associated to form an argument merely the random effects of language? Have I wished too intently to domesticate the strangeness of reading? What relation exists between inscription as hieroglyph and inscription as readable (phenomenological) sign? These questions persist as a background against my wider text, which examines the relations between estrangement, exile and the female intellectual in a range of

Kristeva's texts. I discover that to a certain degree, she retains metaphysical notions of estrangement that occur as enigmatic moments of 'appearance' in excess of consciousness. She also retains the figure of woman, although she does not permit her a permanently privileged identity. When these forms of 'appearance' and 'identity' are read against Kristeva's anti-phenomenological commitments, they give rise to a paradox or contradiction which cannot be resolved, but which for me makes her work as intriguing as it makes it vulnerable to the charge of inconsistency.

Ultimately I cannot insist on either the indubitability or the exhaustiveness of my argument. It is offered rather as the product of a certain performative reading that has conferred significance on certain aspects of a text and not on others. It has been written out of the recognition that Kristeva's writing contained anomalies on the nature of identity, particularly on female identity which were worth confronting, but it has equally been my desire to explore her preoccupation with estrangement as a radical and often violent revival of otherness, and with language as the only medium through which that elusive notion is at once posited and lived. In her role as female voyager, Kristeva moves adroitly between the shores of a 'chez-soi' and the place of the Other, negotiating the strange terrain that exists where language and subjectivity intersect. In the chapters that follow, we will attempt to chart the process of this voyage, and Chapter 3 begins by introducing us to Kristeva's passion for illuminating the obscure, estranging nature of language itself. If there was one quality that distinguished her from her contemporaries, it was the conviction that the discomfort this obscurity brought to social and sexual identity was most acute in the literary text. Poetic language unsettled the house of being and called its inhabitants to be strangers and exiles to all bounded forms of thought.

Part II
Speaking in Tongues

3

'Language the Unknown'

> More than any other, the criticism of ... [Julia Kristeva] conveys the impression of possessing the complexity and the scope of a genuine work of literature, the intricacy of a city which has its avenues, its dead-ends, its underground labyrinths and panoramic lookouts.
>
> With apologies to Paul de Man.

> The stranger, the foreigner, thinks he is in control, but he has been precipitated into someone else's dream.
>
> Angela Carter

To open language up to 'materiality', to make of it a 'work', is 'immediately to make oneself a stranger to language.' (*Sém*: 7) With these words Kristeva argues that that function as social beings we most take for granted – speech – bears a radical alterity which returns in literature to mock our certitude and give body to our dreams. Language is the Unknown that lies just beyond our line of vision. It is the new sublime, overpowering and mastering us in the same way Africa and the Americas awed the colonial explorers. How can we come to terms with this unhomely place which gives us speech and then changes the rules of the game, dissolving 'us' in the process? For exile alters the shape of subjective space, according to Kristeva. The person who is in exile lacks a sense of her own proper place, a home. Her dislocation is acute, and where language is always represented as the unknowable stranger, the normally comfortable relationship between body and subjectivity breaks down. Reading Kristeva, I recognise my own position to be an unstable one – divided between the space occupied by an ego who judges and a subject-in-process moving from one form of subjectivity and another. Intentional (female) actor one moment; deprived of agency, sex and place in the next, 'my' interactions with the Kristevan text comprise vulnerability as well as a need to master.

In this chapter I will read Kristeva's early writing on language and semiotics, especially the text *Revolution in Poetic Language*, from the point of view of an imaginary landscape of writing.[1] The persona of the female voyager will be the protagonist who negotiates this landscape, although there will be times when Kristeva's injunctions on deconstructing privileged speaking positions will be reflected in the reader's drawing back from the object of identification (the *female* intellectual or voyager) and making a more universal observation. From this shifting perspective I shall examine the estranging characteristics attributed by Kristeva to language, their effects on the reader, and I shall conclude with an assessment of the text's subject of enunciation and its implications for women who are intellectuals. If we discover that the figure of the female intellectual seems very remote from Kristeva's impersonal subject-in-process, we would be both correct and misguided. Clearly, the subject of enunciation here has only the most distant of connections with the ego of experience outside the text. While Kristeva's conceptualising soars skywards towards an indefinite horizon, one rarely if ever hears the unmediated voice of a woman speaking. For all its restoration of affect to language, Kristeva's thought seems driven by an anxiety that femininity and in a broader sense, identity, must submit to a rigorous dissection by the processes of language. Often obscurely illuminating moments of epiphany within the text still leave the impression that they are achieved at the cost of a female voice. On the other hand as I hope to illustrate at various points throughout the chapter, there is ambiguity in even the most impersonal of Kristeva's texts that undoubtedly indicates the subject's passionate relation with her identity. In fact, it is this ambiguity, I will argue, that saves her writing from both extremes of triumphant mastery and theoretical psychosis.

'CE PAYS N'EXISTA PAS'

Mallarmé once said that the realm of language was like a country that didn't exist, in which case the poet must look for metaphors that would disfigure the topography of the conventional landscape. He must seek to pull language away from its deathly ability to refer to objects in the world, and ground it instead in the intersection of his own creative imagination with the blank space of the page. As if in agreement with Mallarmé, Kristeva tells us in *Revolution in Poetic Language* that any discourse which proceeds by enumeration and description addresses a corpse. The moribund nature of contemporary theories of language is for her all too apparent in their determination, unlike the example of Mallarmé, to treat language as an object that has no verticality or history. Linguistics, in claiming a position of transcendence in relation to its object, has denied language its strangeness, its intransigent body, and Kristeva's privileging of a revolutionary poetics reflects an attempt to shift the study of language to an impossible place, to a country that doesn't exist.

A place for everything and everything in its place: such, according to Kristeva, has been the passion and proclivity of a dominant tradition of Western thought:

> Our philosophies of language, embodiments of the Idea, are nothing more than the thoughts of archivists, archaeologists, and necrophiliacs. Fascinated by the remains of a process which is partly discursive, they substitute this fetish for what actually produced it. Egypt, Babylon, Mycenae: we see their pyramids, their carved tablets, and fragmented codes in the discourse of our contemporaries, and think that by codifying them we can possess them. (*RPL*: 13)

In different ways, philosophy has dreamt that the subject could be Master of meaning through exhaustively representing the object. Structuralism, Marxism, phenomenology: all read the text as a recumbent, hermetically sealed body and closed their eyes to that enigmatic remnant, the *opaque* body, that meaning could never address. Linguistics too, Kristeva believes, has tamed and domesticated language in fetishistic structures. More simply, language has acquired a *home*, a comfortable and orderly 'mansion of presence'.[2] Kristeva on the other hand, dedicated to the corrosive effects of negativity, is at pains to demonstrate that while there may be a place for everything, not everything is at home in its place. What she attempts then, is to 'turn the house upside down' ('sens dessus-dessous') (*RLP*: 615) so that what once were familiar modes of habitation become estranged and estranging *spaces.*

'Nous sommes tous *embarqués*,' Kristeva has one of her characters observe in her first novel, *Les Samouraïs*, (*LS*: 22) and so too the reader of *Revolution in Poetic Language* is constantly invited to take part in a journey. Kristeva creates an intrepid subject who is always in motion, eager to depart for an unknown destination 'to the outer *boundaries* of the subject and society.' (*RPL*: 17) Like the ancient heroes who set off on similar epic journeys, we identify with the challenge to venture into the unfamiliar. For Kristeva's text is both epic and travelogue: a guide to an uncharted country – Language – and a celebration of the romance of the epic, where heroes set out on impossible quests and return; disfigured, but triumphant. The legacy of modernity however, has been to place the familiar world of mimesis under erasure. There is no world outside writing, and the subsequent inner exploration of language that takes place is predicated on what we could call the *failure of the mirror*. Accordingly if language has a topography it is an unrecognisable one, if there is voyage of discovery or an adventure of language, as Barthes tells us, 'what happens is language alone'.[3] Where language mimes the path of its own enunciation, style itself becomes the Orient, as Beryl Schlossman recognises,[4] and few capture this fascination for an unnamable region better than Mallarmé. But Mallarmé had been able to refract his preoccupation with language through the prism of a world on the brink of imperial expansion. A different vision inhabits Kristeva's writing, an imperialism that henceforth finds its expression in the unfolding of a textual New World: the terrain of writing and the subject of discourse. Paradise will never be regained on earth, nor is its radiance even momentarily recreated through Art, but perhaps its disfigured traces may be outlined in the unknown country of language.

A New Poetics of Space

Throughout *Revolution in Poetic Language* the notion of place is posited as an outrage to representation. Unwilling to preserve a sacred dwelling for poetic language, Kristeva sites this revolutionary space 'far from the realm of "discourse" and "art"'. (*RPL*: 17) It 'passes beyond' (*RPL*: 101) conventional structures to the 'outer boundaries' of experience, (*RPL*: 17) to an 'other scene', (*RPL*: 27) 'another horizon', (*RPL*: 32) where identity and presence are absent or disfigured. A similar bizarre landscape arises out of *Séméiotiké: Recherches pour une sémanalyse*, one of Kristeva's earliest texts on semiotics.[5] The space of poetic language renders signification impossible: it is an 'empty relation' deprived of entities, (*Sém*: 95) a place beyond the 'bars of rationality' that puts into play an 'impersonal' movement without spectator or actor. (*Sém*: 91) Not content with the surface layers of meaning in language, the text of poetic language 'excavates a vertical in the surface of the word' (*Sém*: 9) and discovers there a 'corridor' (*Sém*: 287) opening on to a 'vast expanse of emptiness.' (*Sém*: 275) Searching for a place to ground herself, the reader finds such a gesture officially declared out of bounds. There is, she discovers, no privileged overview, no panoramic landscape dutifully unfolding in front of her gaze. Like landforms enveloped in fog or seen through the clouded surface of a mirror, the outlines of this new mindscape are frustratingly evanescent.

Kristeva argues that its space is virtually impossible to name or measure because it is 'exactly that which cannot be thought within the whole conceptual system that grounds the contemporary mindset', (*Sém*: 24) but of course this reasoning is true only in a limited sense. To fail to be able to see beyond that mindset implies denying language is able to represent new conceptualisations. Yet clearly our language-bound condition is such that any place which apparently cannot be thought or imagined is still subject to our need to name and describe. The moment a new conceptual vocabulary enters discourse, the subject of language sets about making it a comfortable home through naturalising its strangeness. Even writing that plays over vast spaces of emptiness is vulnerable to the reader's domesticating imagination which attempts to house it in a topography that can be *represented*. Conceptualising such a place is a laborious uncertain task, but not impossible. Indeed like Descartes' subject who drew the certainty of existence from the certainty that he doubted his existence, the reader is aware of a growing psychological response in the form of overwhelming bewilderment and uncertainty. And so there is a sense in which our estrangement is the response to the positing of an object, even if the manner of its positing momentarily confounds us.

In this first uncertain moment of perception when everything other is alien and hostile to us, we find ourselves in an unfamiliar realm that constantly frustrates the search for stable perceptions. The space of poetic language is characterised by a vocabulary of motion and violence. A new textual practice involves 'exploding' and 'shattering' discourse; it 'escapes the ... hold of', 'refuses to identify with', 'exhausts ideological institutions'; (*RPL*: 15) it 'bursts, pierces, deforms, reforms, and transforms', (*RPL*: 103) it tears 'the veil of representation' (*RPL*: 103) and leads to 'decentering ... cutting through ... [and] opening' (*RPL*: 30) discourse to 'plural and heterogeneous universes.' (*RPL*: 14) The subject who attempts to understand and to practise the new textuality is in for a difficult time. Exposed to 'impossible dangers' in leaving the family shelter and in 'dissolving the buffer of reality', he risks the 'violent crucible' of 'mobile discontinuity'. His revolutionary practice produces 'landslides', sets off 'explosions', and gambles with death. Reduced to the puny shadow of an observer watching some primitive landscape in constant upheaval, the (female) voyager is led to believe through the sheer energy of Kristeva's vocabulary that she is witness to the most archaic forces of creation and destruction ever unleashed.[6] Drawn into the strange universe of *Revolution in Poetic Language*, she is left breathless and numbed by its pulverising rhetoric which constantly throws up alienating images.

In actual fact however, the text sets out neither to delineate nor reflect a recognisable landscape where an outside is distinguishable from an inside. As we have seen in Chapter 1, two of the most fundamental concepts in philosophy, outside and inside, assume that a permanent separation structures the relation between subject and object, and between the subject and the world. Philosophy has grounded the subject of inquiry on a distinction between here and there, between this world and another place. The subject could achieve mastery of himself and his objects through reflection, provided this separation between entities be maintained. Since Derrida though, these distinctions have been rhetorically dismantled by such figures as the trace, the hinge, *différance* and writing, which introduce discontinuity within the very structures which had sought to exclude internal difference by expelling it to a second term ('outside', 'there', 'another place'). Derrida's readings were always highly abstract, and his analyses of subjectivity related less to specific problems in linguistics and psychoanalysis than to philosophy. Thus he defines the breakdown of presence as spacing; 'always the unperceived, the nonpresent, and the nonconscious ... *the dead time* within the presence of the living present.'[7] Yet Derrida's conceptualisation of space and its deconstruction were of great value for Kristeva.

genesis of language

Intent on explaining how the subject comes to language, she takes up deconstruction's readings of meaning and subjectivity and addresses them to the subject of discourse and his relation to the Other (the unconscious). Her criticism of grammatology was that it ignored subjectivity, social practice, and jouissance: in short, the dynamic interplay of the drives. It failed to ground the interruptions of space within a theory of the *body*. On the other hand, the deconstruction of presence enabled her to discover that linguistics assumed a phenomenology of presence in the shape of the transcendental ego. Linguistics and the social structure in general she argued, are regulated by laws which assume a subject at home with himself, at home in his speech, who closes the door on dead time. The ability of language to mean rests in the first instance on the clean and proper space of an ego separate from an object, and then in the reduplication of this separation projected in linguistic structures. In turn, language itself is underwritten by the Absolute Ideal, the Logos. But perhaps, Kristeva reasoned, the processes responsible for the separation of subject and object are not as clear cut as we imagine. If what Derrida had named as dead time could be given a provisional identity in the form of biological drives and primary processes, then a space of alterity could be shown to have always already inhabited the subject through the unconscious. Thus the subject never fully separates from his objects and is never fully at home with himself. The real thrust of Kristeva's 'signifying architecture'[8] therefore, is to bring difference as strangeness indoors, so that language is simultaneously undermined and embodied from within.

And so the linear relationship of subject and addressee, or object ('ego' and 'you') presupposed by conventional linguistics is displaced through the addition of a third term: the text as 'stranger', (*Sém*: 181) which we can understand as a metaphor not for a transcendent entity outside the system, but for the space of the unconscious. In this way the fixed opposition between inside and outside is now dissolved, the strangeness of the outside henceforth residing *within* language in the shape of the affect-driven unconscious. Thus if we have previously been accustomed to reading the text as a division between subject and addressee on the one hand and between signifier and signified on the other, the ambivalent logic of poetic language which adds a third term to all binary couples, blurs and multiplies their divisions so that no singular identity can possibly be maintained. Indeed, in *Revolution in Poetic Language* the subject of enunciation turns out to be a construction that has turned a blind eye to its formation through the biological drives, which Kristeva defines as energy flows inhabiting a place driven by 'permanent scission' and destruction. And it is in essence these inexhaustible generating processes that she regards as having transposed themselves on to the linear plane of communicative language and ransacked the house of being. The text's distinctive relationship to *space* thus comes to reflect its revolutionary character. Whereas a metaphysics of presence had assumed that language received the impulse for transformation from without (from divine intervention, the imagination, Art, Truth, or Knowledge), semiotics insisted that the boundaries of language are infinite – and infinitely renewable – from the inside. Classical mimesis with its assumption of a representable world is dethroned by a radically anti-transcendent mimesis which undermines all conventional notions of exteriority and representation. In Kristeva, mimesis becomes an imaginary miming of gesture or spacing that recalls and reproduces the movements of the drives, but in an imaginary linguistic register. *Spacing*, the movement from one system of meaning (or from one body, place, discourse) to another, now must carry the burden of transformation that a form of transcendence or exteriority once did. Spacing as kinesis or gestural energy is the process that will refresh language and thought. Its motion is rooted in the continual movements of the drives, and in this way Kristeva is able to suggest that an ultimately unknowable exterior, biology or unreconstructed matter, when interiorised by the subject in the form of the drives, radicalises the nature of being.

The journey on which the reader is invited then, is a voyage to the interior, 'a descent into the most archaic stage of [the subject's] positing', (*RPL*: 83) which culminates in the 'rhythmical space' of the 'chora'. Representing a key moment in *Revolution in Poetic Language*, the topos of the chora illustrates Kristeva's view of the simultaneous destruction and renewal of language and its subject. From the chora will issue the fire of tongues and the subject-in-process. We could imagine it as a place of blinding flashes of energy, punctuating the surrounding darkness with an abrupt, obscure illumination. Despite all Kristeva's attempts not to give the chora the role of first cause, it is a generative term connoting a primitive form of 'place', 'space' or 'motion' that has been borrowed from Plato's *Timaeus*.[9] Consequently, in order to avoid lending the chora an essential existence which would assume all the paraphernalia of a distinguishable form and content, inside and outside, Kristeva suggests that it lies *before* the separation and object as an abject pre-object which must be 'apprehended without the senses by a sort of bastard reasoning ... This, indeed, is that which we look upon as in a dream and say that anything that is must needs be *in some place and occupy some room*.'[10]

Kristeva's dilemma, of course, is to describe this ephemeral entity without representing it as a conceptual object. It must be an alternative to logocentric modes of thought without either succumbing to their logic or setting up a reverse logic. She hypothesises that the chora is closer to the ruptures and flows of bodily and vocal rhythm than it is to an originating identity. Its space is kinetic or generative, not static. She further suggests that the chora consists of potentially unmediated matter, the most primitive aspect of existence imaginable. As primitive matter it consequently lacks both a thesis or a fixed position, and following Plato who named this space a 'wet nurse of Becoming', she calls it 'nourishing and maternal'.[11] The place that articulates the drives or primary processes, the chora as a *privileged locus of space* supports the continuous passage of flashes of energy across the space that will become the subject, and nurtures the conversion of these flashes into a mobile series of psychical marks. This articulatory function gives its materiality a primitive kind of form or kinesis, and permits the introduction of the term 'semiotic', whose Greek meanings include the sense of 'distinctive mark', 'trace', 'precursory sign', 'imprint'. (*RPL*: 25) The semiotic, together with the topology of the chora, introduce a feminine alterity, an ambiguously mediated materiality, *within* language, in the form of the operation of the drives across a perpetually fragmented body, 'une substance morcelée'. (*RLP*: 19) The chora, therefore, is neither entirely confined by language, nor yet is it wholly outside it. It comprehends Derrida's notions of spacing, but goes far beyond grammatology in its punctuating of primitive space with the continual action of the biological drives.

We might ask in what sense may the chora and the semiotic be associated with the maternal body? Kristeva argues that the semiotic is at its most active firstly in the modern text where it destroys and renews meaning, and secondly in pre-Oedipal relations, where its maternal connotations are clearly more apparent. As Kaja Silverman indicates, the figure of the chora reflects a fantasy of container and contained: the mother englobes and nurtures the child; the child projects its needs on to the mother's body.[12] So we can see that the chora is both material support for the socialisation that takes place between mother and child *and* the locus of negativity, the continual displacement of these supports. Kristeva's version of the mother, however, is not ultimately intended to represent the chora. Rather, this space exhibits aspects of maternity deprived of an identity (that is, the identity of the actual mother who ends up *restricting* the chora's negativity through her socialising role). Maternality as process is privileged, but not the maternity that reminds us of 'milky phonemes' and 'shit and nappy rash'. In the chora we find its life-sustaining energies are supported by a movement that extracts the possibility of human subjects with identities and destinies as effortlessly as colour bleaches from the night sky, or as ink eats into fabric. What remains of the female voyager, therefore, is hardly a subject who owns her own voice, but what Philippe Sollers named 'an infinite perpetuation of the enounced; or ... a generalized *disenunciation* continually demonstrating the absence of any subject whatsoever ...'. (*RPL*: 221)

Clearly in this account Kristeva privileges the elusive kind of articulation supported by the semiotic over and against the sense of structure and restraint as exhibited by the mother. Thus the semiotic is certainly somehow feminine, but equally that place within the subject and within language 'of aberration, incoherence, uprooting' (*Sém*: 99): the place, if we are to hear the echo of Hegel in these words, as most conducive to an overturning of consciousness and a dissolution of all fixed identities. Negativity drives the chora even as it dissolves the identity of the female voyager. And it is this aberrant maternal space that dreams *us*, and that returns within language to cut up the linear orderliness of thought and meaning. Like some inhospitable memory, the semiotic takes refuge within society's signifying architecture only to unsettle its very foundations. That Kristeva chooses to equate disruption and renewal of language with the feminine reflects a determination to restore a certain kind of privilege to the pre-Oedipal mother whom Freud and Lacan had passed over in their rush to link culture and desire with the Phallus. But the feminine is principally charged with the task of revolutionising being. It plays host to a fiery immersion in the mother-tongue, the only form of epiphany she believed possible today, yet its enigmatic qualities could never sustain an autonomous *female* subject. Kristeva's strategy in elaborating a thematics of space, therefore, is to push mimesis and phenomenology to their outer limits. Reading may well naturalise strangeness through the need to make a meaning, and in searching for a ground to support her own identity, the female voyager looks to claim the chora for maternity's privileged support, yet an unsettling surplus remains that actually resists all her attempts to give the notion of space any final identity.

The Thetic

Where the chora meets up with a boundary, the threshold around which the subject will enter the symbolic appears. Borrowing from phenomenology, Kristeva names what she terms the 'thetic' as the threshold of language. Neither fully semiotic nor symbolic but a place of articulation, the thetic is produced by a break or rupture in the signifying process, and so mediates between something exterior to language and its interior. For if the subject is to separate from his surrounding environment (from the mother first, and then from other objects and pre-objects) and exchange meaningful information with an other, a break must come about. Kristeva argues that the thetic is a realm of *positions* or spatialisations, and syntax, which presupposes spacing established by the thetic therefore enables the subject to inhabit a space of *propositions*. The thetic is active at the mirror stage, our first topographic intimations of mortality. It marks the separation between the child and all those things around him, which is later replicated in the separation between, for instance, the noun phrase and the verb phrase of syntax. Positionality or spacing therefore, *precedes* propositionality; or to express it differently, process precedes product. What this elliptical statement amounts to is a dissection of the way language produces meaning. Kristeva wants to assign to space as unpredictable gesture or kinesis the role of preceding order, stability and identity. In fact, going further, it could be concluded that this drive-based kinetic space in some strange way actually *initiates* meaning for Kristeva.

The reader may well find her explanation of the thetic laboured and convoluted, but it is important to understand here that she is directing a critique at phenomenology and in particular at Husserl, phenomenology's founder. Indeed the outcome with Husserl is foundational for her thesis on poetic language, although she does not signpost her reading of phenomenology as clearly as she might. Kristeva begins by stating that the subject of phenomenology is the transcendental ego, the subject of consciousness. This is hardly a revolutionary step, but her privileging of the semiotic on the other hand is an attempt to undermine the consciousness, and so she works hard to develop an elaborate theory of poetics that will reject phenomenology, even while accepting some of its insights. Let us turn to Husserl for clarification, who stated that objects can be experienced intuitively in their essential nature (*eidos*) by the philosopher, so long as thought accepts a certain kind of discipline. The object is always an object for consciousness, but bracketing out the empirical self (*Einklammerung*) avoids the object being contaminated by subjectivity. Thought thus achieves a rigour that enables the essential nature of something to be intuited through the perception of pure consciousness. Provided the intellect can achieve a form of abstraction, the truth of experience can then be connected to the thought of that truth. Now the desire to see the logical working of consciousness clearly represents a mathematician's dream, but in wider terms, that knowledge might transcend itself and know its object recalls the all too familiar dream that longs for purity of vision. Kristeva's response is complex but worth following. She accepts firstly Husserl's suggestion that the thetic is something like a creative fiat where being is engendered by an active positing of name and sign: God's 'Let there be light', and there was light, for instance. In phenomenology, the advent of being as meaning visited language not in the form of an epiphany from on high, but as a result of a constitutive act on the part of a subject whose intentions towards objects *posited* meaning. Nonetheless, unlike Husserl, she views the bracketing out all that consciousness regards as non-verifiable or heterogeneous as a necessary but *imaginary* procedure. Kristeva recognises that a (transcendental) ego must be still be posited for communication to occur, but where Husserl believed intentionality could grasp objectivity and hence meaning, she regards intentionality as having constituted itself *retroactively*, as something that has happened after an event. 'Meaning' is therefore a positing, a projection of the subject's positionality. It is also a dream, a fictional construct. And at this point a subtle redefining of the thetic is occurring, because while insisting that the thetic is somehow related to order and meaning, Kristeva also insists that the separation between subject and object presupposed by the thetic (and thus the syntactic division *NP/VP*) is not really an absolute break, but is occluded by the irruption of the semiotic, which adheres to each of the so-called separate syntactic categories. The division initiated by the thetic, then, is *heterogeneous*. If that is the case, to look back beyond this threshold to the place where meaning has not yet separated from heterogeneity is to direct one's glance to an archaic 'pre-intentionality' and 'pre-objectivity',[13] the dream-world of the unconscious or the semiotic. Upheld by the chora, the semiotic, Kristeva considers, cannot be definitively located either inside or outside language. Through mimesis it has *transposed* its primitive system of difference (represented in language by syntax) upon the normative space of the judging subject so that it may have being:

> A *posited* Ego is articulated in and by *representation* (which we shall call the sign) and *judgement* (which we shall call syntax) so that, on the basis of this position it can endow with meaning a *space* [my emphasis] posited as previous to its advent. Meaning ... is thus nothing other than a projection of signification (*Bedeutung*) as it is presented by judgement.[14] (*RPL*: 35)

To claim a permanent home in language for the *female* voyager would be, according to these terms, a necessary if illusory gesture. The sign posits the ego and articulates the enunciation of the female intellectual, but when heterogeneity enters language that articulation is obscured. We are all, men and women, equally homeless, universally subject to emptiness and loss. Thus when philosophy has done with dreams of epiphanies, it discovers another, perhaps truer myth, if we are to accept Kristeva's reading: that the advent of being is the negativity produced when the archaic semiotic body effects its disruptions in language and negates sexual identity.

Not content with dissolving sexual difference, Kristeva would argue that even syntax is the distant result of semiosis. Semiotic biological processes, moving through the fragmented body that is not yet a subject, operate through division but also to make *connections* between various parts of the body, and between the body and the outside world. It is as if syntax is merely the ghost-writing for a more primitive kind of writing or linkage that takes place between bodily organs. Kristeva argues that this 'psychosomatic modality of the signifying process' (*RPL*: 28) which includes activities of displacement, transposition, and condensation, establishes the preconditions for later socio-linguistic relations: the sign and syntax, and representation and judgement. These relations themselves are in a larger sense transpositions (that is, an alteration through *movement*) of all those primary processes that precede syntax and the sign. Through the disruptive doubling of spacing, the articulation that occurs at the thetic stage permits the divisions inherent to a semiotic modality to be laid down (*projected* or *transposed*) over the linearity of the speech chain. In short, the unconscious returns to language and the subject in the form of a discontinuous succession of epiphanies that constantly redraw psychic and linguistic space. And in this way we can say that the body is renewed and transformed.

More specifically, a unique relationship is established between displacement, transposition, and their kinetic effects in poetic language. Together with condensation, these first two activities form pre-symbolic articulations of the drives which Freud observed functioning in dreams and subsequently named primary processes.[15] When the subject encounters the semiotic, the presence of the drives effects radical changes in the nature of his identity, inviting the unfamiliar to make its home in the familiar: 'The (familiar) abode is for man the open region for the presencing of god (the unfamiliar one),' as Heidegger would say. Kristeva's version of an encounter with God rests, in the early work, on the transformation effected in language and subjectivity by affects: that is, by the drives. The body that linguistics and philosophy have brushed aside, she believed, could thus be restored to speech in such a way as to place it forever beyond the reach of knowledge. Through displacement, an opaque semiotic body is transferred from a realm of biological negativity into a realm of light and forms, bringing to language that music of letters which Mallarmé knew. Mallarméan poetics must be demystified, however, Kristeva argued, by reading his poetry with the help of Freudian drive theory. It was the drives and their representation as primary processes crossing the thetic boundary that were actually responsible for musicating language. Although active entry into the symbolic at the Oedipal stage tends to override their pathways with a system of signs, primary processes can still be seen at work in poetic language.

But how do we understand poetic language which is clearly a crucial term for Kristeva? In his introduction to the English translation of *Revolution in Poetic Language*, Leon Roudiez traces the history of poetic language to Russian formalism. Ossip Brik (sic)[16] founded the Society for the Study of Poetic Language in Moscow in 1917, who posed the term in opposition to communicative language. When Roman Jakobson later wrote that 'poetry protects us from this automatization, from the rust that threatens our formulation of love, hate, revolt and reconciliation, faith and negation',[17] he had in mind less the poem as object than that function of poetic language which unsettles habit, and upon whose murder (or repression) society is founded. The poetic function makes signs palpable by enhancing the material texture of the signifier through multiplying meanings: in short, poetic language firstly opens a radical distinction between itself and language that bears a message, and secondly, between the world of signs and the world of objects. Kristeva incorporates these readings, but revolutionises them so that in becoming the privileged language of the margins poetic language stands for the infinity of the code of language,[18] expressed in its most intense form through the processes of condensation, displacement, and transposition.

Again, Kristeva's interpretation of these activities is intricate, but vitally important to follow, because it lays the foundation for her reading of Mallarmé which forms the practical illustration of her theory of poetic language. We will recall in Freud that condensation related to the tendency a dream-work displayed of combining in one event a number of different experiences.[19] In a broader sense, the activity of condensation produces a plurality of significations and 'non-recoverable syntactic elisions' such as the many instances of interrupted syntax one can find in Mallarmé.[20] Transposition and displacement, on the other hand, operate either by placing signifiers in new contiguous relationships that generate recurring specific associations, (displacement) or by drawing the drives over the signifier/signified divide into the symbolic system so the subject experiences jouissance (transposition). In the case of displacement, the association of disparate signifiers across texts, Kristeva draws on Saussure's remarks on anagrams. Saussure had speculated that Latin poets disguised a variety of proper names in their texts by producing a series of motivated signifiers which could be reconnected.[21] He was unable to prove his thesis, but Kristeva takes up his idea to argue that the kinds of anagrams discoverable in poetic language are numerous, but all are related to the phallus. The anagram is then connected through transposition to the semiotic which is drawn up over the gap separating the signifier from that primary signified now lodged in the unconscious. As we shall discover, she claims that the repressed memory of our incestuous relation with the mother's body is given new life when poetic language taps into its source and draws it up into the text. Such an ingenious reply to Derrida's contention that 'the thing itself always escapes'[22] is, one might argue, the crux of the Kristevan semiotic argument, but while impressive in some respects, its audacity equally leaves it vulnerable to charges of essentialism, even wishful thinking, for I believe there are a number of difficulties implicit in linking transposition and its renovation of thetic space with a motivated arrangement of signifiers. Let us see exactly how this method of argument works with her reading of Mallarmé's 'Prose pour des Esseintes'.

'House-breaking'

The primitive kind of spacing generated in the chora gives place to a new, symbolic representation of space, the mirror stage, illustrated by the way semiotic process is bound as a signifier *in relation to* another signifier. The thetic threshold of language is the agent of this transformation, itself the effect of a positing – or more dramatically, a murder, sacrifice or cut that henceforth acts to orientate the biological body articulated by the drives towards the body of language, articulated by signs. Even so, those first pleasures experienced by the body are not forever out of reach. Instead, the thetic and its positing function is frequently undermined by the modern text and by revolutionary social practice. Kristeva chooses the term *effraction*, with its connotations of breaking and entering a space, breaching a law, and house-breaking, to suggest the multiple strategies implicit in breaking through the thetic, a disruption most clearly marked in poetic language.

Earlier we saw how she viewed the crux of transposition as lying in its ability to draw semiotic material up into language. Fractured and elided syntax, word plays, repetition of sounds and image-associations all bear witness to the presence of poetic language and to the unorthodox work of mimesis. As the text harks back to the place of the most primitive break with the destructive forces of nature, its subject looks for a chance to experience jouissance through drawing into the representational structures of the text the now forbidden pleasure of union with the maternal body. Thus the text re-enacts Freud's Common Crime,[23] but in addition, it *mimes* the constitution of the subject-in-process, unsettling home and hearth by opening language and the subject out to the estranging landscape traversed by the death drives. Perhaps these incestuous recollections are the closest Kristeva comes to representing an epiphany in language. This encounter with the sacred is not in the form of a Pauline conversion or a Proustian illumination, though, but a vehement, almost unmediated return of the repressed experienced directly on the subject's body.

The figure of the house-breaker lies at the very heart of *Revolution in Poetic Language*. His irreverant defiance puts the stamp of Paradise Lost on language, but by the same token, Kristeva's reading of Mallarmé's 'Prose pour des Esseintes' offers an outrageous compensation. If the object forever retreats, its subject founded on emptiness and absence, Kristeva insists that the subject regains its lost hold over the pleasurable body through the radical gestures enacted by poetic language, the fire of tongues. We must not pass over her idiosyncratic reading of 'Prose' too quickly, because it occupies a privileged position in the text. Its interpretation is both the outcome and the motivation for the earlier theoretical section translated into English which had established the interrelation between semiotic and symbolic. It provides the material support, in other words, that will permit Kristeva to connect body with language, but to do so in a most peculiar way. That little critical attention has been given to this aspect of the text seems all the more reason to me why its off-the-wall feel needs to be interrogated.[24]

Let us then follow the stages of her reading of Mallarmé from the beginning. Kristeva hypothesises that in the Romance, Germanic and Slav languages there came to be a conflict between inherited classical metrical patterns and the subject's own rhythmical experience in his national language, which, she argued, gradually resulted in the adoption of the 'word' as the fundamental unit of metre, especially in languages like English, German and Russian which had variable syllabic accents. The word, apparently closer to subjective experience for Kristeva, was able to access the drive-based sound patterns at the base of language. But French, because of its more rigid accent on the last syllable, was not as free to experiment in this way, and so writers turned to 'artifice'. Through experimenting with alliteration and a certain *timbre* or sound texture of the signifier, a number of French poets, and especially Mallarmé, found a different means of accessing the drives. For this reason, Kristeva argues, Mallarmé's verse was a music in letters that opened on to '*another scene*'. (*RLP*: 212) Such an emphasis makes metricality (or rather, metricality as a form of motion or gesture) inhabit language as a privileged if disruptive guest. It also establishes its priority over grammar. But why the need to privilege rhythm? What does it signify in the text of *Revolution in Poetic Language*? Undoubtedly, the answer lies in the central role accorded to transposition and spacing. For if the 'drive-based apparatus' (*dispositif*) can be shown to be explicitly linked to alliterative patterns and chains of signifiers in poetry, then we would have to accept Kristeva's argument that rhythm, its action enhanced through motivated signifiers and ultimately the drives, is simultaneously the condition of syntactic articulation and syntactic displacement. In other words, what Kristeva is offering here is yet another deconstruction of truth and meaning as being exterior to language. The precondition for meaning lies in the semiotic working through language as the mother-tongue, and not in the exterior world of objects, concepts or revelationary truths.

Kristeva believed that meaning and unity in Mallarmé was primarily disrupted through the repetition or association of phonemes that produces 'an effect which is *foreign* to the common usage of the natural language', (*RLP*: 221, my emphasis) and which leads to a 'pre-phonematic' or 'phonetic' state similar to the babble of childhood. Through this estranging procedure, the original phoneme is emptied of its phonematic (or meaningful) character and linked firstly to the 'articulating body' through the apparatus of speech and then, through the drives, to the entire body with its topography of passages and sites of desire. Thus we can see that reading poetic language as a means of providing access to the material body is indeed a revolutionary conception. It literalises the language of exile by connecting the disruptive movements of the biological drives to the subject of the text, and in this sense poetic language becomes a centre for an intense form of estrangement that approaches Dionysiac excess. More specifically, Kristeva follows Ivan Fonagy who linked specific drives with particular forms of consonant and vowel articulation.[25] She reads the 'm' in 'mama', for instance, as 'labial, nasal, liquid'; and the 'p' in 'papa' as 'labial, explosive', and then proceeds to correlate these two sounds with those of 'incorporating' orality and 'destructive' anality in the Freudian 'fort/da' game.[26] Through these and other over-determined sounds, the speaking subject retains a close connection with the 'body proper':[27] 'the phonemes reclaim what the sounds have lost in becoming sounds of a given language: they reclaim the topography of the body which reproduces itself in them'. (*RLP*: 222) These phonemic/phonetic elements that form new semantic associations are the signifying differentials which open language up to an infinite process of generation. Unfortunately, Fonagy's theory is not only dubious, but completely unfounded. In this respect, I would agree with the Lacanian position that insists we cannot possibly access the pre-Oedipal body through language in such a way. Kristeva's ruthless drive for consistency ('the mother is dead, but she comes to life again through language') has led her in this eccentric direction. If the female voyager has thus far managed to stay the course, she now finds herself pitched headlong into a very odd dream indeed. Kristeva's *Bildungsroman* of estrangement falters at this critical spot, whilst the reader's own sense of estrangement approaches the hyperbolic.

Now Mallarmé was clearly sensitive to the sound texture of language, and Jakobson tells us how, despite feeling frustrated with the limitations of words like 'jour' and 'nuit' which in everyday speech in no way reflected the respective qualities of the spheres they named, he had observed that in poetry, through association '*nuit* darkens and *jour* brightens when the former is surrounded by a context of grave and flat vowels, and when the latter dissolves in a series of acute phonemes'.[28] Mallarmé obviously experimented with the sound texture of language and frequently made connections between the sounds of words and their semantic associations. But Kristeva's analysis becomes absurd when she links Mallarmé's observations in his essay 'Mots anglais' with the *corporeal drive-based origin* of the sounds of language. Here is Mallarmé: 'Akin to all of nature and reverting toward the organism which is the depository of life, the Word presents, in its vowels and its diphthongs, a kind of flesh; and in its consonants, a kind of bone structure, the dissection of which is a delicate operation.'[29] Mallarmé had used the *image* of the body to approach the Mystery in Literature. Flesh and bone were metaphors to illustrate the interrelation of sound patterns, yet Kristeva's unwavering commitment to a drive-based theory of language leads her to *literalise* 'Mots anglais' so that its images acquire substantial identity in the form of corporeal, drive-based structures. She demonstrates a similar theoretical psychosis in her reading of *'Prose pour des Esseintes'*. (*RLP*: 239–62)

In this reading the poem's traditional versification[30] is seen to be undercut by what she considers to be the supplementary network of signifying differentials. (Kristeva defines the latter as groups of elements of phonemes that provide a provisional locus for a signified formerly repressed in the unconscious.) In each strophe, the patterns linking sexed body and sounds established by Fonagy are seen to make telling connection with the poet's use of the onomatopoeic qualities of sounds. The semantic quality of the strophe is then examined by turning firstly to Mallarmé's other texts where identical sounds have been used, and secondly, by taking these sounds complete with their semantic properties, and transposing them to the new context of 'Prose'. To illustrate these general remarks, let us look at aspects of the reading Kristeva offers for the first strophe:

Hyperbole! de ma mémoire
Triomphalement ne sais-tu
Te lever, aujourd'hui grimoire
Dans un livre de fer vêtu:

[Hyperbole! can you not
triumphant, today a rune
From my memory stand out
In a book clad in iron][31]

Kristeva claims that the dominant sound pattern here reflects a movement between an 'aggressive phallic drive /tR/, /dR/, /f/, etc. and [an] anal [drive]' and the 'incorporating oral (suction) drive' made of the labial, /m/. (*RLP*: 242) The sound 'm' is represented as the desire for fusion with the mother that Jakobson had first outlined,[32] but Mallarmé's interpretation of what he called the music in letters was somewhat different. On the nature of 'm', he had written that it 'translates the power of making, thus joy, virile and maternal ("*m*âle et *m*aternelle" [my emphasis]); then, according to a meaning that has come from a very long way back in the past, the measure and duty, number, meeting, fusion and the middle term: through a sudden transfer, less brusque than it seems, inferiority, weakness or anger'.[33] Kristeva's startling observation on this admittedly expansive passage is that it too confirms the desire for fusion with the mother observed by Jakobson and others! I find her reading impossible to substantiate. Undoubtedly Mallarmé was happy to offer speculations on the associations conveyed by various sounds in language, but it seems to me that it is at the level of *speculation* at which his remarks must remain. Besides, there seems no compelling reason why maternal joy must be related meaningfully to 'measure' and 'duty', for instance, or 'inferiority' and 'weakness'. There is surely a considerable degree of arbitrary association to these significations, and I can certainly see no justification for amalgamating the multiple associations that apparently cohere around 'm', into the figure of the (phallic) mother.

Having established that the role of the signifying differentials represented by labials connote maternal jouissance, the proliferation of the aggressive /eR/ and its variants in the text are read by Kristeva in the same exorbitant way to signal negativity, death, a destruction of unity and a fading of meaning. The readings of subsequent strophes are similarly structured around drawing equivalences between the semantic and phonic ordering of the poem. At each point we discover how the semiotic enters language and finds, in effect, a home *already prepared for it*, since even the semantic properties of words *literally represent* the pre-phonematic state which the semiotic alone is supposed to engender! If the symbolic anticipates jouissance and the death drive by signifying them, we cannot say as Kristeva had apparently wished to, that language is overtaken by excess, since its structures always already anticipate that excess. This is clearly not a move that occurs 'behind the back of consciousness', uprooting the subject of the text, and confounding mastery. For if memory is hyperbolic and the hyperbolic as such causes memory and its signs to exist, in actual fact the writing subject still remains hyperbole's master. Presumably Kristeva had wanted to equate the quality of hyperbole with drive heterogeneity, but allowing the text to *knowingly* prefigure jouissance makes her wider theory of poetic language a good deal less persuasive, and fails to eliminate a triumphant subject.

Kristeva's interpretative practice is acceptable if it is understood as forming an allegory or commentary on the negativity that may found the signifying process, but when evidence is derived from the repetitive sound patterns generated throughout the text to suggest that these are *motivated*, that is that they correspond with repressed signifieds (jouissance, maternal fusion, and death) formerly resident in the unconscious, is to take the reader too far from home. One critic to my knowledge has alluded to the questionable nature of motivation in language. Mark Adriaens criticised this very tendency when he presented Kristeva's analysis of an extract from Lautréamont in her essay 'Pour une sémiologie des paragrammes'. (*Sém*: 174–207) Kristeva had argued there that the pattern of sounds created by the signifiers in *Les Chants de Maldoror* leapt over subject/predicate groupings to shape the word 'phallus'. Since she considered that Lautréamont was dramatising the moment when the subject realises he is alienated in the Law of the Father, the term 'phallus' analogously effects a unity in *Maldoror* between phonological and semantic components. As Adriaens reminds us however, there is a difference between connotative, poetic language and a semiotic practice that looks critically at its own ideological assumptions:

> Whereas with the Sausserian sign, the relation between *signifiant* and *signifié* is arbitrary, in the poetic sign, the multiplicity of equivalences creates the illusion that the relation between signifier and signified is motivated and hence that there is a 'natural' meaning inherent at the level of expression. In semiotic research, this very naturalization of signifying relations has been exposed as one of the most typical ideological mechanisms.[34]

My purpose here is not to provide a sustained critique of Kristevan ideology, but it is to confess that this section of *Revolution in Poetic Language* is the most indefensible. What began as an ingenious attempt to subvert the fundamental law of language and identity – a law that insists on the separation of the subject from its first object of love – by inviting the object in again through the back door, has failed to convince me. The end result has been a valorisation of a select number of signifiers ('phallus', 'jouissance', and so on) which approaches the condition of psychosis where words and the body are inextricably confused. More importantly, the provocative work on the action of the drives in language, if of purely metaphorical value, is in danger of losing even its suggestiveness. It seems, in fact, that the practical proofs of semiotics have failed. The illustration of a revolutionary form of spacing is not only oppressive but lacks credibility when applied to the microlevel of the text. Perhaps this is one reason why the emphasis of Kristeva's later work becomes more consistently thematic, favouring broader narrative sweeps that do not need to scrutinise the signifier's relation to the body so minutely.

English readers of *Revolution in Poetic Language* are unfortunately deprived of the opportunity to judge the truth of this reading of 'Prose', since the translation by Margaret Waller presents only the first third of Kristeva's thesis. Ironically, we are provided with her hypothesis, but not with the material proof for these general remarks. In the case of a theorist like Kristeva who so pointedly refers to the need to ground the subject in a material practice, it is odd that the reader unacquainted with French and more particularly with the subtleties of Mallarmé's verse is left up in the air, deprived of practical evidence with which to test the mechanisms that engender process within the subject.

For even to the very topography of her style, the preoccupation with revolutionising space examined in *Revolution in Poetic Language*, was clearly influenced by Mallarmé, a point which English readers may well overlook. Her initial debt to the French symbolist poet had arisen from his search for an allusive but visually seductive writing that would 'Peindre non la chose, mais l'effet qu'elle produit.' It was 'the horror of the forest or the mute thunder strewn in the foliage' rather than any realistic account of trees that Mallarmé wished to produce.[35] Since Kristeva places his poem 'Un coup de dés' at the very *centre* of her thesis on a revolution in poetic language, we can conclude that as in 'Prose', she has appropriated his reading of space for her own ends. Notwithstanding the value placed on the generative qualities of space though, the performative nature of rhetoric in *Revolution in Poetic Language* actually contests this value. Considerably at odds with the experience of Mallarmé's 'mute thunder', reading a Kristevan text for the first time is to become lost in an impenetrable thicket. Its pages are crammed with specialised terms, lengthy complicated sentences, and compressed allusions to other intellectual discourse. The typography of Kristeva's page is frequently interrupted with graphs and equations from logic and mathematics. Thickly branching syntactic trees add their flourish (*RLP*: 276–9) and the whole daunting effect is underlined by an impressive array of italicised print, which as Bachelard so nicely puts it is 'but engraving while we write'. Kristeva's style is emphatic and triumphant, and these typographical markers convey an implicit message: 'master builder at work!'. Thus although Kristeva needs Mallarmé's rhetoric to energise her own, in the process it undergoes a profound alteration which in important respects is unable to be sustained.

Mallarmé had sought to provide a bouquet where the flower was absent; his poetry was built on a 'lacuna' ('a lucid contour … which separated it from the garden'). In his country that did not exist, 'Each flower more flagrantly bloomed/Without our discussing it'. He lifted an exploration of absence to an art-form and despite his fetishism and aestheticism, we can admire this refusal to fix meaning and identity in texts that would so easily yield up their repressed truth to the observer. In her eagerness to claim him for her own country, Kristeva has quite driven off the sense of mystery that pulverises the 'Idea' by its evasion, its sheer slipperiness. For under cover of supporting the 'imprecision' of rhythm and the 'effect and not the thing', her theorising actually crushes the delicate flesh and bone structure of poetic verticality. Mallarmé's 'dazzling music' quite loses its power to illuminate once Kristeva gives it eyes. I am reminded in fact of his comment in 'Mystery in Literature':

> For whenever She sniffs out the idea that obscurity may be a *reality*; that it may exist, for example, on a piece of paper, in a piece of writing (heaven forbid, of course that it should exist within itself!) She rises up with a hurricane fury and, with thunders and lightenings, blames the darkness on anything but Herself.[36]

As Bachelard had written, the imagination calls us out of ourselves and submerges us in an ineffable place. His dreamer is a voyager charmed or disturbed by literature's 'function of unreality'. When an attempt is made to *deprive* the subject of this unknowable territory, those evanescent, beckoning horizons are closed down, their obscure brilliance extinguished. We will recall that Kristeva's project was to name the unnamable. In announcing her intention to press behind reason using reason's tools, she has successfully managed to turn the obscurity of Being into a prosaic (banal?) reality. Behind poetry lies biology; behind the reticence of the image lies Freudian drive theory. To a large extent Mallarmé ranged himself against interpretation, and although criticism today has scant respect for intentionality, I consider that Kristeva's exercise in transposition has taken us too far from home and common sense into a hallucinatory realm that has a good deal less life and interest than the impossible country to which Mallarmé always alluded, but never reached.

A MAP OF THE BODY

Kristeva's intention to embody Mallarmé with the violence of the biological drives illustrates her preoccupation with a destructive kind of negativity. The subject of Kristeva's modern text is obsessed with a *fin de siècle* mix of madness, death, and pleasure. From Podolski and

Artaud, from the narratives of Judge Schreber and the Papin sisters popularised by Lacan, from the more sedate accounts of madness by Charlotte Perkins Gilman, Doris Lessing, and Janet Frame to the delirium of Lautréamont and Hélène Cixous, and to the melancholic or aggressive suffering that ravishes Marguérite Duras or Sylvia Plath, modern writing drapes itself with a deathly blanket of permanent mourning. Or if not madness, then disgust and despair steep its discourse. Mutilated bodies, decaying cadavers, streets pasted with excrement and human blood, roses that mutate into corpses, and the lacerating experiences of incest are all mixed with a jubilant defiance: 'only the criminal is truly free'. That language can have a *body*, even if it exposes its subject to psychosis, opens literature to a different kind of reality: a place of negativity and jouissance, where everything is put into play.

The dust-jacket of Kathy Acker's *Empire of the Senseless* draws a map of a new New World: the waves are dotted with tattooed sailors and floating ships filled with blood-drenched pirates.[37] Violence and sexuality dance together in this strange commonwealth that eventually defeats the forces of law and order in a horrific urban civil war. Acker blatantly celebrates the dangerous, anarchic side of ourselves that most of us would rather not acknowledge. Her characters are voyagers learning to negotiate the sublime, terrifying world of the unconscious. Bodies get out of control, run amok, and burst apart or fragment. This kind of destructive carnivalesque spirit is similarly reminiscent of Kristeva's fascination with the links between pleasure and death. She produces a map of the body, a (female) voyager's guide to a place where all is permitted and where the ultimate erotic pleasure derives not merely from a loss of bearings, but from the threat of complete annihilation. It is interesting that Acker chose to represent the ultimate sign of criminality in *Empire of the Senseless* by the figure of the tattoo which tore the body up and turned it into writing: the conceptual become flesh, the flesh, conceptual. Like the intellectual – and the exile – the tattooed person is a sailor with no home, a voyager forever passing between ports.

On a similar theme, Tzvetan Todorov gives a fascinating account in *The Conquest of America* of the Mayan rulers who were chosen for their capacity to interpret signs.[38] The successful candidate was marked on various parts of his body by the tattooing of pictograms, and addressed as 'the possessor of red ink and of black ink'. Like the Mayan ruler, the intellectual is faced with the same challenge: 'Interpret or die', and like the Mayan too, the intellectual who listens for poetic language approaches the place of the subject of the text, who bears within himself the inscriptions of red and black, of language *embodied* with the mother-tongue. In this sense then, whether undertaken by a man or woman, intellectual activity is the turning of an inward eye towards a writing that ruins representation, including the representation of sexual identity. Unlike much theorising that ignores the body or social practice, Kristeva's intellectual is preoccupied with the way the semiotic inscribes a new map of the body on language. Through the work of negativity and the drives, the maternal fabric of language itself envelops the subject in an ineluctable process towards jouissance, death, and renewal.

Negativity and the Drives; Jouissance

The quintessential moment of negativity that Kristeva identifies as occurring in 'Prose pour des Esseintes' is the moment that rhythm overwhelms the symbolic constraints of metre and threatens to sweep away signifying structures. Rhythm without metre is a radical dislocation of space which dismembers the subject and opens social and artistic practice to the devastating work of the drives. The instinctual drives were originary psychic structures or energy flows that Freud named 'Triebe'.[39] We can only treat the drives hypothetically, formulating their existence after the fact, but from their operation through the unconscious and through observing the psychic and linguistic development of young children, psychoanalysis suggests that these archaic structures are the product of the very first attempts of the subject to map over the body a number of spatial limits against the flux of the real, an impossible place of fullness outside language.[40] In other words, the threatening and completely unrepresentable nature of the real is opposed to the orderly symbolic (in itself a contentious point which I shall discuss further in Chapter 5 of this book).

In linguistic terms, the coming of the real into the symbolic reflects the eruption of what cannot be fully symbolised (drives, energy cathexes and so on) into language. In reinterpreting the drives, Kristeva distinguishes her reading from Lacan's. For Lacan, lack, which emerges at the mirror stage when the child perceives the loss of its mother and/or the breast, is the essential precondition for the formation of the drives. He opposes instincts (the order of the animal world) to drives (the order of the symbolic and imaginary worlds), and distinguishes the sex-based drive from need.[41] Whereas Freud in many instances gave us to understand the drives were biologically determined, Lacan insisted that they were dependent on the effect of the Other: it is the signifier that directs the attachment of the drive to an object.[42] Kristeva wished to attach the signifier more emphatically to the body than did Lacan so she compromises between the two positions. Yet rather than relegate the drives (and 'objectivity') to a realm of pure biology outside human experience remaining therefore permanently exiled from a space subject to dialectics, as we have seen with the chora, she maintains that the drives simultaneously articulate a pattern of psychical marks across the body, thus investing it in a dialectical signifying practice: the 'red' and the 'black'. The full force of their activity cannot be grasped or measured by consciousness, but instead their constant division and multiplication reflects the repeated division of matter that engenders *signifiance*, the production of meaning in excess of consciousness. (*RPL*: 167) In confronting the inescapably violent and implacable character of instinctual forces, we are brought, like Hegel, face to face with the 'negative' or 'negativity', which when recontextualised by Kristeva, internalises and multiplies sexual difference within the subject.[43]

Kristeva borrows the term negativity from Hegel. Somewhat similar to the destructive activity of the drives, negativity for Hegel comprehended a continual deferral of consciousness from itself, a recognition that the moment of truth is only apprehended in the movement between the fixity of the object and its difference from itself. Like the subject-in-process, Hegel's 'Subject' is 'pure, *simple* negativity', a reflection on the otherness within itself which leads to 'the moment of the "I"... in the process of becoming'.[44] Negativity is what mediates between self and other and for Hegel what enables the same to distinguish itself from the other. It puts thought and its subject in process, being the privileged figure of heterogeneity and excess. The subject of negativity does not recognise a permanent opposition between inside and outside, but understands whatever transitory self-identity it may acquire as having emerged out of a struggle. Seeking enlightenment, but recognising the intransigence of the alien object as a challenge to consciousness, it accommodates the other within itself in order to master it.[45] True subjectivity then lies in *departure*. The self is like a traveller who in a state of unrest, continually flees the fixity of being to make new conquests and discoveries, but the self is also a being 'which has returned into itself', transformed and revivified by its unrest.

Hegel anchored excess and alterity finally in the circle that returns the other to Absolute Mind, but along the way he established a path that would permit Kristevan semiotics to use these privileged instances when consciousness is uprooted as *founding moments* for all subjectivity. In *Revolution in Poetic Language*, Kristeva removes all connotations of transcendence – as it has been conventionally understood – from Hegelian negativity by lifting it out of its former conceptual system, calling it 'rejection',[46] and grafting it on to her own theory of signifying matter. Negativity now becomes a *foundational semiotic moment*, and one of the preconditions for language. (Kristeva also claims that those so-called unmediated moments of creation or recognition when the object first appears such as in Proust, or in Dostoevsky's visions, are merely variations of uprooting, and can also be attributed to the 'jolts' of matter in constant process.) *Rejection* is the mapping on to the body of negativity, and refers to the destruction and renewal of drive charges which are *transferred* from the space of the semiotic to the space of the symbolic through *signifiance* as articulation. Its introduction provides the tangible means to link poetic language with an embodied theory of negativity and *jouissance*.

The path of ex-istence[47] which Lacan had linked with the unquantifiable economy of jouissance experienced by 'Woman' in Kristeva comes to represent an '*infinitisation* of meaning'. (*RLP*: 613) No-one, she remarks, 'not a single person, nor any linguistic, discursive or rhetorical unity can contain ["embrasser"] the infinity of the process.' (*RLP*: 615) A remark surely intended to be as pungent as Lacan's observation that 'there is no sexual relation'.[48] And so through the eruption of the drives into the literary text and in the subject-in-process, signification is exposed to the infinite. Kristeva derives this expression from the mathematician Cantor. Conventional set theory expels the infinite to the *outside*, just as the nineteenth-century French state had an exterior notion of the infinite which resided in the respect it accorded religion, mystery and poetry. In Cantor's infinite set, however, no absolute distinction or separation exists between inside and outside. There is no single highest power, for each part may be equal to the whole. Poetic language is the ideal representative of the infinite, she considers, because it is never static or localisable and thus cannot be contained by an outside. It is both equivalent to the whole *and* one of its parts, or subsets. Similarly, jouissance is a metaphor for the infinite because it informs and, as negativity, destabilises the whole.[49] Thus Kristeva shares neither Lacan's nor Irigaray's fascination with the female mystic, whose supplementary sexuality (their orgasmic capacity) links them with God. Her use of jouissance as a notion is therefore less voyeuristic than Lacan's,[50] but equally encyclopaedic. In *Revolution in Poetic Language* the term is indicated in and associated with a whole gamut of occasions from *signifiance* and rejection to the destruction engendered by erotic and textual excess. The most critical locus of jouissance that throws the subject into crisis is held to be Freud's notion of expulsion (rejection), an infinite form of repetition.

In Freud's article on 'Verneinung', expulsion (*Ausstossung*) constitutes the real object, establishing an outside that is never fixed, but which must always be posited.[51] Its symbolic representation is the sign of negation.[52] Freud like Lacan reads the symbolic as the site of repression of all pleasure, a site dominated by the superego, but Kristeva asserts that underlying the symbolic's 'black ink' is the specific pleasure of expulsion which in turn derives from the anal stage. In the anal stage the openings on the surface of the body are eroticised through drive charges, which makes expelling substances from these sites pleasurable. Anality, she argues, may be mimetically reactivated in literature, where non-symbolised form as negativity tears up the domestic space of the body and inserts paragrams and glossolalia into the signifying chain.[53] Destructive urges in poetic language underlie both oralisation (music, rhythm, prosody, paragrams), and the more phallic, positing aspects of language, represented by the aggressive image of what Kristeva terms the 'homosexual phratry', presumably to identify it with the first Crime of incest. Rejection by this means announces in the literary text the return of the repressed and ensures that jouissance is always *outside* the household scene, a sacrificial inscription of erotically embodied writing.

Although I will read Kristeva from a more critically female perspective later in the chapter, it is important to comment in passing that these pleasures that are so glibly held up here as the most desirable kind of *jouissance* – incest, anality, a fetishistic orality – are by and large sheer fantasy on Kristeva's part. Deprived of its imaginary allure, incest remains a real and painful experience, and it is interesting to see that in her later work where she maintains a more active role as theorist and analyst, and has probably encountered many incest victims, its aestheticisation fades in importance. I am also intrigued to see the repeated connection made between sexuality and violence and it disturbs me to watch a capitulation to some of the more unpleasant practices worked on the figure of the female body in the name of bliss. Earlier, we had seen how both male and female as privileged positions of enunciation were equally at risk from the force of the semiotic. But when it comes to illustrating how poetic language works, Kristeva frequently turns to what could be termed male forms of pleasure and fantasy. Indeed, these fantasies approach the grotesque kinds of violence inflicted on the protagonists in William Burroughs' 'The Naked Lunch', and would surely not accord with the inclinations of most men either. There is absolutely no room for tenderness in the early Kristeva, and little obvious accommodation to the female subject of desire. Such vehemence gives her writing an apocalyptic resonance, but herein lies its weakness too. Because the semiotic is associated with firstly the death drives (negativity) and secondly the biological body, its destructive effects become difficult to contain. While insisting on the mediating role of the symbolic, it is clear that Kristeva is infatuated with forces that wipe out all forms of consolation and security. Her disavowal of joy, beauty and delight, not to mention female subjectivity, evidence a refusal to relate the body and matter to a more compassionate and differently embodied form of sublime that I believe a different reading of language, subjectivity and the psyche could provide. Both women and men suffer when loss is aggrandised in this way. Poetic language as inscription tears the maternal body to pieces at the cost of producing a mother-tongue, a 'divine' form of speech. Yet the pleasures of jouissance and rejection she describes and privileges which are supposed to engender her notion of the maternal sublime are more often than not destructive and misogynistic. It is interesting to note that this kind of aggressive dream is rejected in the later *Tales of Love*, which celebrates not eros but agape, whose subject loves without mastery or annihilation of its object.

However, credit must be given where it is due. The complexity of Kristeva's argument means that we must give space for its large claims to unfold, even if as readers there are aspects of her theory we find questionable. And in summary we can say that jouissance borders on the unrepresentable, the inexplicable. Through the destructive pleasure that results from the explosion of the unconscious into psychic life and discourse, being is divested of its comforting supports and brought face to face with the negative, or negativity. Whether it arises from plunging meaning into the infinite or multiplying subject positions, Kristevan jouissance diverts the female voyager from her intended path to a place of non-being: ex-istence. It shows her a new map of the body, and commands her to interpret or die.

Fetishism

Interpretation assumes a distance from the object, a space in which observation and reflection may occur. With Kristeva, this space is frequently under threat. As we have seen, the conceptual edifice of

Revolution in Poetic Language is a *filled-in* space, a landscape dense with vocabulary and figures synthesised from other disciplines. In fact, Kristeva's prodigious denominative power gives the impression that she is a true obsessional, her preoccupation with naming creating an armature for the text that makes it impervious to critique. It can be suggested with some legitimacy, I think, that just as the obsessional feels led to fill a space with words, the fetishist invests it with highly-charged objects. Kristeva's thought tends to manifest both of these extremes and so it is intriguing to follow her discussion of the place of the fetish in French society, since we could argue that her own reading of Mallarmé's 'Prose' replicates this condition.

France at the close of the nineteenth century was a bourgeois society driven by a spirit of rationalism. Into this claustrophobic space, Kristeva argues, the writing of Mallarmé and Lautréamont released dramatically new forms of representation that were to have powerful effects on language, aesthetics, and social practice. Social transgression, jouissance, and the radical dereliction of being are at their most developed, in Kristeva's view, in the experimental writing of modernity, but she believed that as early as the late nineteenth century, Mallarmé and Lautréamont had taken the first steps toward modernity, each viewing their writing as fundamentally shaking the foundations of literary and social convention.[54] A whole host of social identifications associated with a conservative French society, she notes, were challenged in their texts: questions of sexual difference, the figure of the father representing the Law or God, the images of a fascinating mother or a castrating woman, the power of the State, religion; all the above, *when opened to the full force of language*, touched the most painful and intimate sites of culture: 'les lieux névralgiques'. (*RLP*: 612) Kristeva's explanation for this preoccupation with aberrant sexuality and unconventional literary style lies in fetishism: a state like the French bourgeois republic of the late nineteenth century experienced power as fragile, and so fetishised it in the forms of religion, feminine mystery, and poetry. In an attempt to ground her hypothesis in social reality, in the final section of *Revolution in Poetic Language* Kristeva studies the phenomenon of the salon. The salon existed as a micro-society both in contradistinction to social and family life, yet also as a representation of the State. Frequently presided over by a woman, its feminine power, argued Kristeva, functioned as a fetish, a substitute for the 'feminised', eroded forms of power at work outside the salon. She assumes then that women's leadership role in the salons reflected a *structural weakness* in the power relations of wider society. So far from applauding feminine initiative, she actually seems to believe that their visible presence was an indicator of the decadent underside of the French State.

From a psychoanalytical point of view, the nature of fetishism is to deny that the phallic mother is castrated, and to pretend that separation from her has never really occurred. That is, the subject ignores his difference from objects. (Kristeva suggests that the problem is one of spacing, and could actually originate in a difficulty in separating the ego's image of itself in the mirror from the pre-symbolic, semiotised body. [*RPL*: 63]) At the same time, the process of fetishism sets up a substitute object strong enough to stand in front of the phallic mother's imagined reality and screen its threat. This object then absorbs the full force of the thetic function of language, which has now been displaced from the symbolic on to the drives, various parts of the body, or a host of objects associated with the body. Despite the fact that the text at the end of the nineteenth century allegedly challenged the fetish of representation in its hostility to naturalism and realism, its denial of or anxiety towards sexual difference limited the radical scope of its discourse. The aesthetic in Mallarmé for instance tended to take the form of a fetishistic regression or a holding back of signification, according to Kristeva. Through the different figures of absolute woman, fascinating mother, dancing animal, and absent father, Mallarmé's artistic practice attempted through fantasy to close the gap opened by castration. Lautréamont's writing was of a different order. In *Maldoror* and *The Poems*, Kristeva tells us, there is a continual struggle between 'I' and 'you' which she links with Orestes' murder of his mother. (*RLP*: 470) This murder seems to be the condition for a radical upheaval in the text's language – nothing is forbidden any more once a man has murdered his mother. Here, the mother is seen as both phallic (aggressive) *and* castrated (waiting to be punished). An abiding fear of her 'étreinte génitale' ('genital grasp') seems to have led Lautréamont to a conception of genitality completely unlike the inaccessible and fascinating mystery it became through literature for Mallarmé. In Lautréamont genitality is rendered as something so terrifying that it must be dominated by a sadistic and phallic possession: 'Maldoror courageously excavates the vagina of the unhappy child with an American knife.' (*RLP*: 471)

Now in some respects Kristeva is critical of these two writers for their problematic representations of femininity, but in other ways she admires their innovative rhetoric. Their refusal of the conventional norms governing sexual and familial obligations and above all, their struggle to defeat bourgeois convention and put language on trial, she argues, lead to jouissance and to a dizzying multiplication of subject positions. (*RLP*: 470–2) Every subject may now participate in feminine jouissance (the coming of the semiotic into language), thus bringing into the light the mother's forbidden sexual pleasure and appropriating it. Her forbidden place, rendered so acutely by Lautréamont and Mallarmé, is then no longer voiceless, or inhabited by a faceless Someone, but lives on as a 'chant' in the subject of writing. Yet this does not mean giving real woman a real voice, since the language and the subject here are not normative or communicative, but semiotic; and since the latter's presence in discourse still depends on the suppression (as sublimation) of *actual* (or sexual) jouissance: '*That is to say that the text exists to give a language and thus a subject to jouissance.*' (*RLP*: 491) Kristeva's privileged subjects are men fascinated by the *gestures* of femininity but frightened by real women.

Yet if we were to extend the range of our investigation, we would have to agree with Kristeva that in some respects every text is a fetish, halting the signifying process by investing it in semiosis or the mother-tongue. Its music in letters appears almost tangible, and recalls the power of the text to evoke imaginary and hallucinatory resonances in the reader, as we saw in Chapter 1. The text as an eroticised object now becomes the fetishistic sign of the phenotext, that visible aspect of discourse which registers meaning and structure. As a boundary between subject and object, the symbolic and the real, the text as (imaginary) fetish maintains the difficulty, perhaps the ultimate impossibility of ever clearly separating these two orders. For Kristeva, then, there is a sense in which subject and object, symbolic and real, are never clearly distinguished, ('jamais nettement distingués') (*RLP*: 362) because negativity has established that a *doubt* underlies all activities of positing and erasing being. Now this particular form of fetishism does not necessarily need to lead to a devaluation of women. In fact, as I have argued in earlier chapters, as a female intellectual Kristeva on occasions makes use of this kind of doubt herself to suggest that women's incomplete separation from an original object provides them with a different narrative on identity, representation, and negativity. Just as the presence of poetic language gives rise to a difficulty in distinguishing the class of elements spoken about from the class doing the speaking (the notion of the infinite having broken down this distinction), we can also see that the *énoncé* cannot be clearly be separated from the *énonciation*. The woman who writes therefore always retains something of the maternal in her speech, even when that 'something' is *gestured* towards, but never explicitly formulated. And in the following section we will explore some of the convoluted, reticent strategies that are necessary when a woman turns the feminine into the locus and support of poetic language.

Yet there are other instances in Kristeva when incomplete separation becomes a dangerous pathology. At times, the conflation of symbolic and real in the text leads to a state of abjection. Spacing, that necessary separating gesture performed by the thetic, is minimised to the point where the reader feels crushed by the massive weight of theoretical apparatus towering over the horizon, obscuring the sky with its ambitious spires and turrets. In this environment where the urge to master the unknown leads to the writer's enclosing herself in an impregnable stronghold, we could suggest that the text itself becomes the ultimate form of Law, psychic space collapses, and the subject experiences abjection. Thus there are times when the vastness of scale abruptly contracts in a mass of detail, threatening to crush the reader in the relentless refusal to allow room for the *imagination* to mediate between the Other and the real. Such a lack or failure of space points to the recurring difficulty I maintain Kristeva has in developing a structure that would mediate between semiotic and symbolic so that neither entropy nor a deadly abstraction prevails. Her map of the body is produced by an interpretation that makes no apologies for celebrating violent rivalry, hatred and destruction: the failure of the space of transcendence, in short. These marginalised forms of social experience have here been recast by Kristeva to assume a position of dominance in the construction and deconstruction of speech and identity. Indeed, they are primarily responsible for the distinctive landscape of writing produced by *Revolution in Poetic Language*, and add astringent emphasis to Blanchot's understanding of the country of writing as a disfigured space that leaves 'the lovely, clear light of day' far behind.

While it may now be impossible to reintroduce an unproblematised form of metaphysics into a reading of the text, I feel that Kristeva's early alternative posed in *Revolution* – to make semiotic processes and the drives carry the burden of a first cause – has not been altogether successful. On the one hand, the affective landscape is profoundly alienating. More importantly, I consider that the foundational notion of spacing as negativity or kinetic gesture is not conceptually robust enough to do the work Kristeva's poetics requires. Firstly, the homologous relation set up between bodily space and linguistic space is unable to be sustained at the microlevel, as we saw with the reading of Mallarmé. That both forms of space may be sustained by tenuous divisions between outside and inside, and that psychic anomalies are often connected to linguistic anomalies (as, for example, in abjection) does not necessarily lead me to conclude that there is a *consistent* causative relation between them. Nor does it necessarily follow that both spaces can invariably be collapsed into the same primal container (the unconscious, the semiotic, biology). I am aware that in relation to Freudian psychoanalytic theory this is an unorthodox response, and am further aware that new readings of the body/text problematic would need to be unfolded within the context of a very different book from this one. As I have chosen by and large to work within a psychoanalytic framework, particularly a framework that assumes the primary importance of the drives, my criticism can only be presented as questions asked in passing. But the second observation concerning spacing and the work of the semiotic is, I feel, vindicated by my readings throughout the chapter. Although Kristeva insists that the semiotic is in a sense articulatory and thus always already in language, the sense of thetic restraint she allows is actually too fragile in the face of the dominant aspect of the semiotic, which is its hostility to all forms of meaning and identity. I cannot help but associate the notion of the semiotic with a vengeful, unregenerate Nature which allows the imagination *no room* to negotiate the path between drives and signs. The very locus of Kristeva's theoretical argument exists as a potentially Manichaean opposition between anarchy and order, conscious and the unconscious. Kristeva ignores the possibility that a subject whose identity is grounded in a non-dualistic or, better still, non-antagonistic psychic structure may be more productively revolutionary than a subject grounded in negativity. Consequently the (female) voyager's body has a tendency to become indistinguishable from raw matter, an 'unbearable monstrosity'. Neither at home in the house of being nor finding shelter outside, she discovers the red and black inscriptions of language have been elevated to the status of a murderous law which *always* reads the semiotic as a place of destruction in which *she* somehow belongs. I shall develop this point in the following chapter, where the standoff between semiotic and symbolic becomes more apparent. But whereas by *Powers of Horror* the spacing mechanism is so jammed that body and sign are locked in constant opposition, *Revolution in Poetic Language* still attempts to forestall this failure of genuine and renewing transformation by insisting that the place of the subject is empty – a *blank space.*

'WOMAN WHO IS NEVER THERE'

> What, therefore, is important in the *study* of *Science*, is that one should take on oneself the strenuous effort of the Notion.
>
> Hegel, *Phenomenology of Spirit*
> Julia Kristeva, *Revolution in Poetic Language* [55]

'The Woman-effect'

Bataille had suggested that the most revolutionary poetic practice should be sustained 'outside the family shelter'.[56] Kristeva's response is to insist that the house is ready to be turned upside down from within, in order that it might stand on the very edge of human society. The topography of estrangement that has gradually been revealed in a reading of Kristeva's texts illuminates the disfigured landscape that results when the topos of the house is turned inside out. This strange place is without an inhabitant, or at least entertains one in the process of being perpetually dissolved. Phenomenology's judging subject has been led to an elsewhere, to a place of negativity that threatens to push him over the edge or reduce him to an impossible unity, struggling, as Mallarmé says, like Hamlet 'against the curse of having to appear'.[57] In which case the female voyager can hardly insist, in any direct way at least, on her own feminine specificity. She too must allow herself to be dissolved by the semiotic. Barely resisting the semiotic's negativity, Kristeva's masculine and feminine are merely notions or marks of enunciation rather than gendered behaviour codes capable of signification. The early chapters of *Revolution in Poetic Language* therefore set out to amass a more comprehensive form of representation for the subject absent from the surface of speech, and pluralised by its deepest structures. In essence Kristeva's desire is to grind down the surface topography of phenomenology and dismember the transcendental ego assumed in different ways by modern linguistics, in order to make visible a radically new signifying architecture. On the site that she maps out, no-one is at home except Language. The semiotic is logically anterior to yet also synchronous with the subject posited by the symbolic, and because of its pre-eminence, especially in poetic language, its presence introduces *death* for the subject. Yet when I follow Kristeva through interminable landscapes silent as the grave, I sense an enunciating subject, a female voyager, who is *alienated* by the architecture of her own text, overawed by its monumentality, and dazzled by the self-generating energy of signifiers that on one level, certainly do not require a *subject* to direct them. Reading *Séméiotiké* and parts of *Revolution in Poetic Language* is to lose one's identity and one's face, finding in their place the troubling inscription of the 'woman-effect'.

The condition denoted by Alice Jardine as 'modernity' demands as its indispensible aid a new space that has been designated 'the woman-effect' or 'the feminine'. Modernity announces the death of Man and the end of History, and looks for solace to the figure of the woman, unrepresentable and monstrous, but feminine nonetheless. More than any other contemporary writing, Jardine goes on to say, in French (male) writing 'one finds an erotic merging and withdrawal across and through those spaces internal to signification, spaces that have been gendered as feminine'.[58] Roland Barthes had visualised the writer as someone who played with his mother's body; Maurice Blanchot in his turn linked the experience of childhood fascination with a powerful maternal figure who exerted a fascinating attraction 'because, appearing when the child lives altogether in fascination's gaze, she concentrates in herself all the powers of enchantment'.[59] Whenever the experience of fascination recurred in later life, for these writers it was always accompanied by an intense moment of perception that seemed to cohere around some faceless, impersonal presence, immensely powerful, invisible, unknowable.

The reader does not have to work hard to realise that this indeterminate Someone is not God but in psychoanalytical discourse the 'phallic mother', that figure who represents plenitude and infinite jouissance, but also absolute power. To return to the mother through the imagination, or rather, through the writing practices of the modern text is to engage in a writerly kind of incest as well as to turn her body into a text. The (male) writer experiences jouissance because he is playing with something forbidden. Clearly this something does not exist as a literal act but in the form of an imaginative transposition or a *mimicry*. In fact, rewriting Nietzsche, we could suggest that even when he 'gives himself' – he '"gives himself"'. The male is so artistic. Or as Kathy Acker ironically expresses it: 'The realm of the outlaw has become redefined: today, the wild places which excite the most profound thinkers are conceptual. Flesh unto flesh.'[60] To restate, mimicry or mimesis explores language and the enunciation rather than an object in the world. And since modernity, philosophy's privileged tropes have been lifted from the language of sexuality and morality, which in turn cannot avoid implicating the *desire* of the philosopher in his own philosophy. If Kristeva is correct, performance is an embodied gesture, not just an abstract intellectual concept. The intellectual's body therefore, subject to the marks of the 'red' and the 'black', is implicated in his or her speech. Jardine implies that these new incestuous explorations of inner female spaces are part of modernity's challenge to the incest law, and so to the patriarchy. It is just as likely of course that one of modernity's indisputable effects is to sustain a 'penetration' of 'woman' under the Law, a penetration that even when read in the figural sense inevitably contributes to the confrontation between the sexes instead of easing it. Needless to say, any thoughts of returning to some blissful, incestuous time before the Law existed are not just naive romanticism, but also ignore both the pain of incest for the *real* female subject, and the fact that the reverse fantasy – mothers taking sons – is not one that frequently appeals to women. Spivak's reading of Derrida's *Glas* concludes that the end result of these images that are invariably expressed in the language of male (heterosexual) desire indicates that 'man can problematise but not fully disown his status as subject'.[61] The image then, is never uncomplicated, nor is it pure sitelessness, without an inherited set of meanings. So how does Kristeva fare in all of this? What use does she make of these inherited meanings invested in the woman-effect? She certainly doesn't invite us to witness the spectacle of the woman's sex organs in the unabashed way that Derrida does, for example, nor does she imitate Lacan's arrogant imperialism when he looks at Saint Teresa. Neither does she play directly with the woman's body in an exhibitionist, self-pleasuring way as does Irigaray. Rather she insinuates, re-reading Hegel, that the 'negation of the object in its alterity as an "independent life"; [and] the introduction of this amputated object into the knowing subject ...' (*RPL*: 133) must be *refused*. To what extent the object in its alterity may be equated with woman remains to be explored in the final sections of this chapter.

Let's begin with Lautréamont. Reading his *Les Chants de Maldoror*, Kristeva finds that the entry of the drives into language eclipses the subject at the level of enunciation: 'je' becomes internally divided between a 'tu' and an 'il', she writes. (*RLP*: 316–7) The ground between I and an other therefore becomes the place of a struggle. Crucially, Kristeva acknowledges that the difference between the two pronouns can be correlated with sexual difference, and every time the pronominal polarity is disturbed, it results in a change in the sexual conflict. Conversely, a change in the balance of power may initiate an alteration of the pronouns. Because the pronominal struggle corresponds to the sexual battle, the other is the other sex, and the most primal other is the mother, illustrated in Lautréamont's symbol of the ocean. As the other sex, the mother never was the direct subject for Lautréamont, but rather a force of negativity who decentred the one who said 'I'. Woman is little more here than an 'amputated object' marooned outside language, and it appears then that Irigaray is correct when she reminds us in her reading of Plato that the house of being whether constructed by humanism *or* by semiotics, requires that the female body be estranged and silenced in order to let the body of language speak. In bringing woman from the opaque shadows where she had been left by philosophy and narrative, Kristeva seems no more capable of giving her a voice of her own than do her male contemporaries. And yet there is within *Revolution in Poetic Language* some excess that does not quite accord with the appropriative gestures of modernity. Kristeva's enunciative position is, like that of Lautréamont's protagonists, an ambivalent one. Although ultimately poetic language is the privileged limit, there are times when the text clearly gestures towards a lived form of femininity. Here she is in the concluding chapter:

> On the one hand, an enjoyment which does not verbalise itself but lodges in the frayages and stases of the drives; on the other hand a language which is always that of others: between these two borders of 'not yet' and 'not that', in the throws of a heterogeneity, informulable or else lost as such as soon as formulated, passing immediately from one into the other, the woman is the utopic but privileged addressee of the text. As much as she wonders how to speak that which the social-filial code does not represent of her joy, she listens to poetic rhythm. As much as she wants to make herself subject of her enjoyment and not only a reproducer or repeater of already made languages, she asks herself what sets symbolism in motion. As much as her enjoyment does not have an object but, trans-symbolically produces itself from its rupturing, the woman is fascinated ['se fascine devant'] by the process of objectivity in all that is *practical*, and thus also in ['devant'] the text. (*RLP*: 614)

This quite lengthy passage is the closest Kristeva takes us to a sense of where 'her' position might be. It requires the reader to visualise a representation of woman as always inhabiting a borderline position, exiled like all subjects *in* language, but additionally experiencing estrangement *from* language. Lodged in the drives, speaking the language of 'others', neither one nor the other, she is the privileged but silent Other that compels language to go beyond itself. So far then, woman's evanescence is valorised and textualised. Woman is *the* stranger. But reading further, what interests me are the discreet markers that indicate there is, simultaneously, a consideration of real identity occurring. 'As much as she wonders how to speak'; 'As much as she wants to make herself [a] subject': these are signs that witness a subject of enunciation not effaced by poetic language, but engaged in an effort to establish a critical distance for (feminine) analysis to occur. The customary image of woman gazing into the mirror is here transmuted into the woman who stands, 'fascinated' in front of the *text*. Intellectual analysis, it seems, when faced with the threat of eliminating a female subject, gathers up the feminine energies of narcissism, and through a distinctively nuanced and self-implicating style, transfers them to the imaginary realm of poetic language, where its subjects are free to fly uninhibited, so long as they don't forget their practical streak which keeps them objective analysts of textuality.

The (Female) Theorist as Hysteric

Even in that telling passage, however, there is a refusal to people her text with a domestic scene where familiar characters reflect back our imagined sense of ourselves to us. Woman forgoes her mirror and loses herself in the spectacle of the text, a gesture, I suggest, that is consonant with *hysteria*:

> The glance by which I identify an object, a face, my own, another's, delivers my identity from *frayages*, nameless dread, noises preceding the name, the image-pulsations, somatic waves, color frequencies, rhythms, tones. Intellectual speculation derives from this identifying, labelling glance: the hysteric knows something of the process when, endlessly unable to find a sufficiently satisfying mirror, she finds herself at last in the theory itself – target of all sensible and senseless intentions, shelter where one can *know without seeing oneself*, for one has relegated to another (philosophical contemplation) the problem of representing an … identity.[62]

'One can *know without seeing oneself*': is this reticent desire the sign of an enunciative position? That is, the desire to find a place from which to speak where we are already spoken? Perhaps it indicates the desire to wake up in someone else's dream? If so, whose dream might that be, and what does 'intellectual speculation' deliver us from?

Hysterics frequently failed to achieve sexual maturity, according to Freud, refusing passive feminine sexuality in favour of a 'masculine' orientation. Unable to identify satisfactorily with either parent, every mirror-image encountered provided only a strange and estranging double, mimicking the hysteric's bisexuality. The patient was cured when the transference achieved through therapy enabled her (or him) to name the initial symptoms as psychic or textual manifestations of a resistance to normal sexuality. More particularly, hysterics were those who were feminine, but denied their femininity (as sexual difference), imagining a perfect and uninterrupted fusion with the mother. ('I know, but just the same.') Such a refusal, according to Freud, led to the emergence of the somatic symptom that stood in for the original trauma, and which in Lacanian terms amounted to an imperfect transition from imaginary to symbolic. The relevance of hysteria for us here is that just as the 'body of the hysteric becomes her text',[63] the text of the hysteric becomes her body. Inasmuch as the (female) writer is a hysteric, unable to represent her femininity, or find a place for a sex-marked enunciation within the language of theory, analogously, her writing must be 'masculine': doubled and estranged from its originating feminine body. Naming the theorist as hysteric thus illuminates one of the fundamental dilemmas for a female intellectual like Kristeva, who finds her female body so estranged from itself that home must finally be sought within the text of theoretical discourse itself. Intellectual speculation then becomes Perseus' shield used to deflect Medusa's terrifying image, a deflection that often removes a space for an imaginary dialogue between reader and writer. Yet the shelter afforded by theoretical discourse is a transitory and ephemeral identity for the subject, especially when confronted by modern literature which redraws the whole problematic of hysteria as a doubling or split identity that the mirror cannot contain.

The failure of the mirror is referred to in Kristeva's essay, 'L'engendrement de la formule', (*Sém*: esp. 286–8) and although this is an early text, its comments on the estranging effects of poetic language on identity are germane to the larger questions of identity under discussion in *Revolution in Poetic Language*. We know already that for Lacanian psychoanalysis a recognisable form of doubling first occurs with the intuition of the symbolic at the mirror stage when the subject is formed out of a primary alienation. The subject becomes both 'I' and 'another' simultaneously. It could be suggested that when this phenomenon of doubling occurs within the text under the influence of the semiotic so that it becomes both product and process, or alternatively, *énoncé* and *énonciation*, it gives birth to the phenomenon of the hysterical body. Figure for the text's estranging excess, the hysterical body is a lure ('un leurre') that pathologically mimics the hysteric's 'bisexuality'. And the reason the text's monstrosity 'affronts the mirror' is because it transgresses the laws of the *seen* ('le vu'/'la vue'). Its 'eyes' see neither itself, nor the *signifiance* that produces it, since its true image is to be found in the unconscious. What we have before us then, is the spectacle of the inconceivable. Like the hysteric endlessly dissatisfied in front of the mirror, the text is permanently estranged from itself, never settling into a final reflection. Now we know that if the correct sense of spacing is not established during the mirror phase of human experience, and if the explosive motility of the subject is not provided with a stable imago, psychosis will eventuate, hence the necessity for the thetic. Kristeva tells us that the mirror stage 'produces the "spatial intuition" which is found at the heart of the functioning of signification – in signs and sentences.' (*RPL*: 46) But when the text doubles under the generative energies of *signifiance*, the thetic is breached, and the Other returns within the subject, causing massive dislocation and estrangement. By and large it is true then that Kristeva believes the only way to represent the object or the other in its alterity is through negativity. But as I have suggested, she also places a number of small restraints on negativity to prevent the complete loss of subjectivity, and these are most noticeable in her style that doubles back on itself to suggest that somewhere, buried in the text, is the desiring body of the writer herself. These markers or restraints set up a resonance in Kristeva's work that rescues it from absolute facelessness, while still allowing her to remain critical of a femininity tied to a visible material world.

'A Material Girl'

To what extent does Kristeva surrender the problem of femininity to theoretical discourse? In discussion with Louise Burchill conducted in Paris in June 1984, she comments on the way her writing had become more personally marked over time:

> A transformation is, I think, entailed, firstly, in the greater importance assumed by a personal implication in my theoretical work. In my earlier work I sought, despite all, a kind of neutrality of enunciation. This was never pure – implied in the interweaving of genres and theory there was always an extremely large personal element;

> but from a stylistic point of view, from the point of view of a more immediate implication on the lexical, the syntactical, the stylistic level, this was less evident. The idea of, the desire and the ambition for a certain neutrality were maintained, whereas this neutrality is now more and more effaced and the personal implication very large. ('TLW': 23)

We can only speculate on the extent of 'an extremely large personal element', but it clearly involves an ironic re-reading of conventional feminine gestures that doesn't so much eliminate as supplement their validity. 'Practical', 'material', and 'experience' are all words that have been traditionally applied to women. It is intriguing to find them played on and transposed into contexts where they acquire new associations. The word 'dédoublement' for instance can be read as a doubling introduced by the semiotic apparatus through signifying differentials so that the sense plays on splitting in two, dividing, and the unfolding of cloth. (*RLP*: 220) Leon Roudiez refers to the image of the text as fabric in his introduction. According to Webster it is a texture, 'a disposition or connection of threads, filaments, or other slender bodies, interwoven'. (*RPL*: 5) At different points Kristeva defines the text as interwoven and intersecting threads ('fils'); (*RLP*: 148) a 'linguistic texture' ('tissu'); (*RLP*: 154) a splintered 'linguistic fabric' ('sa trame linguistique'). (*RLP*: 228) Her theory is a 'materialist' one, but lest the reader imagine that the text was identifying too closely with women's experience, then a practice was always social: 'Experience is not Practice', we are reminded. (*RPL*: 195)

Concluding the theoretical section of *Revolution in Poetic Language*, Kristeva makes the following remark: 'The ethical cannot be stated, instead it is practiced to the point of loss, and the text is one of the most accomplished examples of such a practice. Mallarmé writes: "I revere Poe's opinion, no trace of a philosophy, ethics or metaphysics will show through, but let me add that it must be *included and latent*"' (*RPL*: 234, my emphasis) Traces of personal enunciation then, are 'included and latent', projected on to the screen of the text as it were, *from a distance.* But why insist that 'the ethical cannot be stated'? What is Kristeva's objection to making a position statement? I cannot insist enough that to do so, to present a final product in language (for example, ethics), is for her to deny the negativising qualities of poetic language which destroy all fixed positions. Whenever we traverse a discourse (philosophy, another language, a genre, another subject's speech), we have an erotic relation with the other that can only be mastered as an 'amputated object' by the consciousness at a cost. The ambivalence engendered by the drives that stream into poetic language projects one of the most intense forms of strangeness and alterity imaginable, because it is the other we have repressed that returns: the mother-tongue. But this kind of strangeness that the text discovers and displays only consists in a moment of textual negativity: 'when the stranger (discursive or national) wishes to fix himself as identity, value, continent ... the process which drives the text refuses him this fixity and indicates that strangeness *does not exist*, except as a cause of process (as negativity).' (*RLP*: 542–3)

The text is hostile to the stranger who searches it to find and hypostasise an identity, and if his search is frustrated, accuses it of 'racism'. Its drive-based violence can be seized by reactionary ideology, but in actuality the text dissolves all identities. Which brings us, briefly, to the question of feminism. 'Racism' here could quite profitably be exchanged for 'feminism'. When the feminist comes looking for an identity and a vindication, what does she find? That strangeness privileges no unitary identity, champions no oppressed class or sex, stands up for no-one. It accuses feminism of being reactionary in response to the feminist label of sexist and accepts no political programme other than analysis of itself as the hidden (semiotic) potentiality of speech. Perhaps the only sort of identity it sustains is that of 'woman who is never there':

> A feminist practice can only be negative, at odds with what already exists so that we may say 'that's not it' and 'that's still not it'. In 'woman' I see something that cannot be represented, something that is not said, something above and beyond nomenclatures and ideologies.[64]

Elizabeth Grosz in commenting on this passage suggested that Kristeva viewed feminism as 'a negative and reactive counterstruggle against sexism. It does not provide the materials needed for developing alternatives. Its function is to say "no" to this or that view, opposing what exists, without actively contributing something new.'[65] But this is a misreading which ignores the effect Kristeva was aiming for throughout the whole article that she entitled 'la femme, ce n'est jamais ça'. What characterises the above passage is the obvious indebtedness to negativity, which could be seen as a constant denial of fixed positionality and identity 'above and beyond nomenclatures and ideologies'.[66] Written at the height of Kristeva's dialogue with feminism, it adds that there are certain men who understand what this negative procedure means, which is at its most lucid in the modern text. At the same time, she argues against a naive kind of feminism that expects a belief in identity (which she names as the reverse of 'phallocratism'). Women have to be able to link negativity and ethics. In this sense, saying no in the form of 'not yet' or 'not that' is an exemplary activity on all levels of social intercourse that invest themselves in a practice, and probably the *only* practice that Kristeva could conceivably support as feminist.

It could be suggested that as the semiotic is to the feminine, the feminine is to Kristeva's performative reading of the semiotic in *Revolution in Poetic Language*. In the same offhand way that the pre-Oedipal phase is labelled 'feminine': 'ou si on veut', (*RLP*: 604) and in the same way that this phase as the semiotic is an 'already structured' one; speaking from the place of a woman appears in a similar apparently offhand gesture: 'ou si on veut': that is, if one wishes. Surreptitious, established after the fact, always already structured through the symbolic activity of separation and differentiation, but present as a potentially challenging alterity and strangeness, the presence of the feminine in the enunciation of the female intellectual mimes, *in the fullest sense of the word*, the semiotic's functioning. Bolstered by the feminine strategy of mime, Kristeva can then take on herself what Hegel calls the 'strenuous effort of the Notion'. What astonishing arrogance. And what a playing with fire if theoretical rhetoric (as mastery) fails! This appropriation of Hegel is symptomatic of a more aggressive kind of vision, traditionally relegated to the 'stronger sex'. I acknowledge the solitary and indeed vulnerable position being articulated here, and the enormous intellectual energy that needs to be expended simply to live up to that exorbitant challenge. And yet, doesn't Kristeva displace Hegel as soon as she quotes him? Doesn't she change his place? There may well be a radical difference between Hegel's use of these words and Kristeva's. If we accept her reading of woman as being indispensable to the social contract but simultaneously marginalised by it, a marginalisation all too evident in the male intellectual world Kristeva belonged to, then for a woman to take on 'the Notion' has additional resonance far beyond what Hegel had in mind. If we are willing to agree that women may sublimate differently than men, are less interested in the purely theoretical, and are generally sustained by a more intimate sense of their own bodily existence, then the Notion becomes differently strenuous.

It inhabits us other-wise, and Kristeva is keenly aware of this difference which manifests itself in a flash of recognition: just when everything seems the same we are suddenly aware of another voice speaking quietly from a distance, changing the place of things. With woman, the Notion comes to stand on the boundary between the world of the body and the world of signs: an impossible, risky place 'raging with intelligence'. (*RLP*: 616) But this head-on challenge to Hegel and the humanism he represents requires that any exploration of the feminine be conducted as the discreet underside of a larger inquiry, lest the totality be too harshly dismissed as 'racist'. Unsatisfied as I am by the equally hasty dismissal of woman and her experience, and estranged as I travel through Kristeva's highly textualised landscape grounded in negativity, I nevertheless admire the enormous conceptual edifice that has been constructed: 'a monumental challenge to all of us', as Alice Jardine remarks.

In conclusion, Kristeva's writing of herself into the text is deliberately 'asymptotic'. When her discourse takes a recognisably feminine turn, it steps cautiously back from its usual breathtakingly ambitious, stylish, and self-conscious voice to become in her own words, 'modest' and 'chaste'. Any form of personal enunciation is always in the form of a trace: an ironic reference, a displacement, or a form of ventriloquism. A ventriloquist *throws* his voice, transferring it from the register of one body to that of another. So too with the enunciative strategy of *Revolution in Poetic Language*. Speaking through the register of the text's formal structures is another voice, another position. Ironic, dislocated, ambivalent, yet passionate, unannounced it transposes the text into the estranging site of one subject's (feminine) desire. In so doing, it inscribes through the speech of a female intellectual the subject's exile in language. This speech functions as a temporary dwelling within a primary discourse on poetic language and the pleasures of homelessness. That such strange pleasures were unable to be wholly sustained by Kristeva became increasingly apparent however, leading to a deeper, more troubling sense of estrangement from language. Her turn to a more marked form of personal enunciation and the reintroduction of the notion of transcendence as a safeguard against unlimited negativity will constitute the major themes of the next chapter.

4

'Into the Cellar of the Native House': Kristeva and Psychoanalysis

INTRODUCTION

Around the same time that *Revolution in Poetic Language* was published in France by Seuil, *des femmes*, a feminist publishing enterprise, released Kristeva's diaristic account of her travels in China in 1974: *Des Chinoises*. Its intensely personal response to the Chinese cultural revolution represents the underside to the dispassionate accounts of subjectivity presented in her doctoral thesis. Kristeva had travelled to China with Roland Barthes, Philippe Sollers, Marcelin Pleynet, and François Wahl, and represented herself on the first evening the party arrived in Peking as 'an eternal stranger ... Ill at ease in a group of men. Neither Asian nor European, unrecognized by the women and detached from the men.' (*ACW*: 1578) Even while later wishing to distance herself from some of the naive and ethnocentric shortcomings of her Chinese travelogue, Kristeva nevertheless here offers the reader a more *familial* subject of enunciation.

In *Revolution in Poetic Language* Kristeva had read the language of the text as indifferent to the stranger's needs to construct an identity and find a domesticated shelter. Instead, she argued that the topography of the text estranges comforting architectural structures and refuses sexual identity, transposing its elements into the very processes of signification. Under this scrupulous regime, providing an ego for the author is prohibited: the place of the subject is a mobile positionality, and if it were to be filled with an authorial presence would result in a turning away from the renewing effects of negativity and jouissance. Experience, she reminds us, is not *practice*. Ventriloquism then becomes a vital device, for in the form of transposition, it allows the writer a provisional strategy for throwing her voice across the veil of language. However, in reading *About Chinese Women* we hear a distinctly personal voice; we note the markers of the subject of enunciation, the structurings around 'I', 'we', and 'them' that signify real identities and real places. Homely anaphoras 'here' and 'my' designate the writer's cultural estrangement that is paradoxically represented in her sitting '*here* in front of the typewriter, trying to write about *my* experience in China'. (*ACW*: 11, my emphasis)

It is my belief that this turn to the personal equally marks the beginnings of a confessional history of estrangement and abjection, a history that finds its fullest expression in Kristeva's text *Powers of Horror*, first published in 1980. Kristeva's argument in *Revolution in Poetic Language* had been that if the mother remained mysterious and unattainable, her unexamined power would return as fetishism or psychosis. The tentative solution had been to insist that drawing the forbidden signified up over the bar and into language in the form of semiotic disturbances would defuse maternal phallic power, all the while adding to language a destabilising, feminine lining, the only permissible gesture acknowledged towards transcendence. In this fourth chapter I will suggest that when Kristeva begins to speak more insistently about the place of this lost object, that is, when her discourse attempts to give the maternal (and women) an emphatic history and a home within language, it encounters horror and abjection; when she reflects on women's writing it is to be repelled by its bodily viscosity; and when she begins to speak of her own life history a terrifying image of the phallic mother shadows every page. Overwhelmed and burdened by a female materiality it had sought to introduce, Kristeva's discourse then finds itself in the uncomfortable position of having to appeal to more and more textually sophisticated means to keep the maternal at bay. What needs to be redrawn in the later work, one discovers, is the relation between transcendence and the body – whereas *Revolution in Poetic Language* announced the death of transcendence and the triumph of the semiotic body, a decade later that body is rearticulated in relation to a new metaphysical vocabulary. The subduction of the body in Kristeva's oeuvre does not take place, however, until the reader has encountered a series of narratives apparently predicated on intense hostility towards women that represents them as derelict.

Dereliction is a state of utter abandonment where human identity is maintained in a state of loss. Dereliction is also, according to Luce Irigaray, a homelessness peculiar to women.[1] In Western culture, she argues, women's identity is not as clearly symbolised as men's because it is too closely fused with the identity of the mother. Without the means to represent what has been lost in culture (the mother's subjectivity), women remain to an extent outside the symbolic as residual or waste objects. *Déréliction* is then a hopelessness in the face of an exclusive order which has abandoned the feminine to a place of permanent exile. In Irigaray's account the female body is the abject ground that supports culture's investments in a disembodied sublime. Kristeva's increasingly psychoanalytical reading of the body is in some respects similar.

While *Revolution in Poetic Language* regarded the site of estrangement as language itself, in later writing the focus on semiotics becomes less prominent. It seems in fact, as if the deconstruction of transcendence and the failure of an associated sense of space or perspective has given rise to a return of a *more intense* version of what that metaphysical discourse had repressed – that is, the body, and the female body most especially. What we increasingly discover is a thematic, psychoanalytical discourse on those disturbing borderline experiences undergone by the psyche during times of change or crisis. Now Mallarmé's figure of the black gaping cellar in Igitur's native house comes to stand for an abject *somatic symptom*. The reader equally finds that this new discourse explicitly plays on her affective, as well as intellectual responses – with estranging consequences. *Revolution in Poetic Language* is marked by a problematising of the distinction between exterior and interior space, but all the same, procedures of reading were still able by and large to establish a *distance* between the critical subject and the object of investigation. Despite its impulse to efface identity, the site of language seemed too conceptually remote to pose a real threat. Its estranging landscape remained somehow exterior to the subject's embodied existence. In contrast, the journey that is offered the reader in a number of subsequent texts is a voyage to the psychic interior of the subject, where cartographic instruments measure and map bodily architecture and its imperfect mediation through culture and discourse. Moreover, the deliberate destruction of transcendent space now poses an insuperable dilemma, for it seems that space is the necessary prerequisite for psychic formation, not to mention a creative renewal of language. The disturbing world of the borderline that I alluded to in Chapter 1 intrudes once more, but unless the perceptions it gives rise to can be stabilised, extremely intense forms of psychic disintegration will result. We cannot become subjects unless we separate from our mothers, but separation presupposes the very kind of distance that the semiotic eventually manages to eliminate. Sharing some points in common with Holbein's *The Corpse of Christ in the Tomb* which Kristeva discusses in *Black Sun*, the failure of transcendent space here comes to be identified with the subject's helpless anguish to see beyond a horizon that lowers to annihilate him. When Derrida deconstructs metaphysics, everything becomes a text. But when Kristeva deconstructs metaphysics, everything becomes a body; a body in the process of breaking up, a murderous body that must be put to death before it destroys *us*.

Can we say that Kristeva invents maternal abjection through rhetorical performance, or discovers its existence? And if the latter, is there an end to her journey through the night? The publication of *Tales of Love* in 1983 suggests an answer in the affirmative. Here the figure of the 'Imaginary Father' appears as the necessary support for love; an imaginary identity whose configuration as Kristeva tells it alleviates estrangement and suffering by opening out the paranoid enclosures of narcissistic subjects to the loving embrace of the Other. It is in *Tales of Love*, read from the exemplary position of the female analyst, that an enunciative position is finally constructed capable of bearing the weight of estrangement without permitting its homeless subjects to be devoured; and it is this text that finally enables the personal voice of the female voyager to parcel out suffering and renewal over a social body no longer regarded as the ultimate threat to subjectivity.

To my knowledge, drawing connections between a discourse that displays a greater personal content, a corresponding sense of abjection and antipathy towards the mother, and an increasingly inventive series of (anti)phenomenological strategies developed to console this antipathy, has not yet been fully acknowledged by critics. Victor Burgin, Cynthia Chase, Barbara Creed, Elizabeth Grosz, John Lechte, Juliet Flower MacCannell, Kelly Oliver, Jacqueline Rose, Jennifer Stone and others have in various ways outlined the Kristevan thematics of horror and abjection.[2] Grosz notes that the emphasis on psychoanalysis, especially the pre-Oedipal mother/child relation is a crucial factor in linking abjection with the maternal.[3] In conversations with Louise Burchill and Rosalind Coward in 1984, Kristeva herself acknowledges a gradual effacing of neutrality in her work, and its more personally inflected style and scope. The autobiographical turn has equally been recognised by Madelon Sprengnether and Marianne Hirsch,[4] although it is Jacqueline Rose who has made some of the sharpest observations on the connection between desire and thematics, thus: 'Kristeva is also a self-diagnostician, and the psychic drive or investment of much of her writing can often be lifted straight out of her texts.'[5] My argument takes the element of self-diagnosis further than Rose by suggesting that the inscription of personal desire in the Kristevan text colludes with a horror and paradoxically a *celebration*, of maternality.[6]

Need it follow however that a fear of intimate space invariably returns to the mother's body as its primary site of anxiety? And if the above anxiety is introjected as a cultural paradigm, how does it bear on the way we understand (and read) women? Clearly, Kristeva has not escaped those very antipathies she seeks to overturn. She is still a victim to a primordial vision of animosity towards the (female) body and an anxiety that this body will transgress the limits culture has prescribed for it. When she emphasises more explicitly the personal and the subjective, her negative critique of the mother apparently increases *exactly in proportion to* that emphasis. The essay 'The Novel as Polylogue'[7] is, outside of *Powers of Horror*, one of the clearest examples of the relation between explicitly acknowledging the female subject of enunciation and a corresponding need to strike at maternal identity, depriving it of consciousness.[8]

Intellectuals who read Phillipe Soller's novel *H*, claims Kristeva in the essay, are drawn to identify with it through a form of narcissistic fascination:

> you talk about it, because *H* sends you into analysis; you assume its writer as an object of transference, as a character on your Oedipal stage ... You tend to see *H* as a person, to fashion its negativity into a psychological or sociological case, and to search for an identity that is a threat to itself – and a threat to you. (*Desire*: 160)

These phenomenological reflections provide the pretext for Kristeva to talk about herself and her own identity; about why it is that she is now compelled to speak in French, and how Soller's polylogical writing that plays with multiple signifying practices is able to have a disintegrative, yet renewing effect on her subjective identity. Her use of the metaphor 'Yalta' represents both the historical reasons that led her to leave Bulgaria and take up a scholarship in Paris, and initiates a sequence of reflections on the nature of identity and its relation to history: 'to the extent that I am allowed to use the pronoun "I," is to speak about my right to speak, in French ... To put it bluntly, I speak in French and about literature because of Yalta. I mean that because of Yalta, I was obliged to marry in order to have a French passport and to work in France ...'. (*Desire*: 161) The privileged figure of the female voyager that she takes on under Yalta is marginal precisely because the experience of exile can exist only on the edge of the imaginary.[9] Subject to 'death and violence', this estranged 'not I', reminiscent of Freud's frontier or boundary creature,[10] inevitably cannot have the same placid relation to subjectivity entertained by those who are at home in their culture. Nor can it place the same optimistic faith in history as its socialist and capitalist signatories.[11] For if Yalta also represents obversely the triumph of the ego, it allows its subjects to bypass the estranging effects brought by a revolution in language.

But whatever Kristeva's biographical explanation, the desire to deconstruct identity alongside an inclusion of the personal constitutes a major aspect of 'The Novel as Polylogue'. And the 'personal' includes addressing the question of identity as a woman: 'I was obliged to marry in order to have a French passport and to work in France ...'. Woman's ambivalent relationship to culture is nowhere so tellingly expressed as in this autobiographical confession. But the crucial question for this woman now a stranger in a foreign country concerns the issue of whether a relationship may be established between personal affect (as confession, for instance) and the music in letters (that is, the presence of semiotic affect in language). Undoubtedly, including the expression of subjective feelings in speech *is* a kind of affect. It humanises what could otherwise remain a remote, impersonal narrative. To describe oneself as 'obliged to marry' and live in a foreign country is to admit to a sense of home-sickness and alienation. Yet Kristeva is unable to let this form of confession stand on its own unmediated by *style*. She believes that style must problematise the enunciations of a sexually marked subject, transforming her sense of exile into an affair with language, the universal mother-tongue. And so confession merely provides the pretext for a discussion of a crisis in enunciation and its destabilising effects on identity. Not wishing to turn away from sexuality altogether, though, Kristeva views the path to this problematised identity as lying through an appeal to maternal sexual pleasure, an experience that culture has generally wished to ignore.

If there is a sense in which criticism has refused the expression of subjectivity in analysis, it is also true that language and culture generally turn a blind eye to maternal jouissance.[12] Thus to read the figure of the mother as the source of a disintegrative kind of jouissance working its way into language by defying the boundaries of reason and propriety could be the perfect opportunity to reinscribe woman in society while simultaneously preserving her alien status. Moreover, to speak of woman's desire might also allow for a new dialectics of intimate space to be elaborated. But what would this signify for Kristeva's representation of herself as the exile, the female voyager? Working in concert with the maternal as privileged representation of the semiotic is a substantial personal implication for as Jane Gallop observes, Kristeva deliberately emphasises narcissistically her self, body, and her history in outlining a theory.[13] Gallop terms these 'self-pleasuring reference[s] to her own body'.[14] On the one hand then, narcissistic reference defies the conventions of criticism, since traditional practice has not usually encouraged an autobiographical commentary on theoretical writing. On the other, attributing the site of upheaval in language to maternal sexual pleasure is equally challenging to the symbolic. But can we regard Kristevan textual strategy in 'The Novel as Polylogue' as privileging women and their quest to find a home of their own in language? I think not. In fact, the performative intent that puts woman into play here is not ultimately to affirm feminine subjectivity in its familiar sociological or psychological aspects, even if the effects of reading 'Polylogue' *are* experienced somatically. In reality, the presence of narcissism evoked through the text's biographical confession sparks off a train of analysis that leads to an attempt to *empty out* or *cordon off* female sexual identity. These rhetorical procedures are always incomplete, leaving islands of self-implicating discourse; nevertheless 'woman' and the 'mother' in Kristeva become ambivalent figures that function as both locus and metaphor for all that phallocentric language excludes, creating the threatening phantasm of the phallic mother, whose destructive energies, moreover, must be restrained by an increasingly theoretical narrative.

Similar in some respects to the earlier strategies adopted in *Revolution in Poetic Language*, unveiling the phallic mother in 'The Novel as Polylogue' is seen as analogous to unveiling language, revealing the myth of transcendence that it inhabits, and celebrating the passion of the letter through the advent of the semiotic. Kristeva's reading goes beyond those offered in *Revolution in Poetic Language* though, when in seeking to challenge the transcendence and identity that she believes the mother supports, she vividly embroiders on Freud's myth of social origins. Freud attributed the origin of the incest taboo to the sons' murder of the Father of the Primitive Horde, whose rulings against incest were subsequently internalised through the first Communal Meal. In her essay on Sollers, Kristeva stages a bizarre reversal of Freud's myth and asserts that the mother must be 'eaten' in order for language to destroy the boundaries of sense and sensibility within the self, and to give rise to a heterogeneity of voices speaking at once: a polylogue. Here we see the ludicrous lengths Kristeva's text has gone to concoct a series of manoeuvres that will first aggrandise maternal identity in paranoid fashion and then permanently bar it from entering the scene of representation. The son-artist is invited to ravish his mother and devour her in a cannibalistic meal, overlooked by an approving daughter-critic.

Kristeva had insisted that subjects blind to their own debt to the semiotic were inevitably preoccupied with avoiding negativity by producing banal ego-centred narratives. Unanalysed, representation of the personal, she believed, became one more mystifying effect of paternal law. Its equally misguided corollary lay in assigning the semiotic as the privileged representative of femininity a room of its own. Kristeva claims that she supports neither a valorisation of female essence nor making a comfortable home for women in the semiotic. This is because, she argues, the unchecked presence of the semiotic tacitly supports the paternal function of language. But if the dangerous negativity of the drives can be fed through language, then there will be no chance for the 'Mother as Master' syndrome to develop, or for some kind of essential identity to fill negativity with the form of an object or phantasm. As Mallarmé reminds us, 'ce pays n'existe pas'. Accordingly, to allow the mother to speak *in and for herself*[15] is to risk psychosis or fascism. An explicit female subject, we infer, would merely underwrite metaphysics and its repression of the body, or would invite the body's violent return.

Ironically though, Kristeva's own form of analysis leads to representing power attributed to the mother through metaphors of violence and aggressive incorporation. Now I do not think that one can simply dismiss her as someone who at this point fails to give a sufficiently correct feminist reading. To mete out this sort of judgement in the context of writing so rich and complicated would be to radically underread. Although as time has passed I have come to find Kristeva increasingly unsatisfying in many respects, I have appreciated that alongside exploring the feminine question, her enunciation does not permit idealisation on the part of the (female) reader. When we come to her texts looking for the subject presumed to know, looking for someone to believe in, we find a discourse that refuses such narcissistic identification: 'I am not the one you love', it says. The subject 'Kristeva' remains a familiar character on the Oedipal stage at our peril.

Yet it would be another kind of blindness not to concede that the term 'woman' in her discourse from 1974 onwards introduces a personally inflected enunciation spoken by a female voyager whose effects, readable as well as equivocal, produce a maternal figure at once horrifying and valorised.

In her haste to judge women's narratives as maintaining too close a relationship to the body, she has in the same breath created a lonely position for her own speech as a woman. By insinuating that such narratives are the primary supporters of a repressive, symbolic mode of representation (even if the symbolic as such has not always recognised women's claims to speak publicly about a personal history!) she is reaffirming the solitary position of the female intellectual who visited China in 1974, 'unrecognized by the women and detached from the men'. And by accompanying the turn to autobiography with the figure of a hostile mother against whom we all must strive, I suspect that she has descended into an interior purgatorial world of grotesque forms from which there will be no Virgin to deliver us.

JULIA KRISTEVA AND THE VIRGIN MARY: ALONE OF ALL THEIR SEX?

It is probably too simplistic to attribute the introduction of a loving mother figure solely to Kristeva's own experience of motherhood, although 'Stabat Mater' shows we cannot discount that involvement either. I find a crucial difference in tone in this essay: less stern and uncompromising than those pieces collected in *Desire in Language*, it marks a noticeable softening of an earlier intellectual austerity. Here there is a more consistent emphasis on locating a subversive feminine voice that will interrogate language and philosophy. Several years later, the essay 'Women's Time' suggests why such a voice is required: 'women ... seem to feel that they are the casualties, that they have been left out of the sociosymbolic contract, of language as the fundamental social bond. They find no affect there, no more than they find the fluid and infinitesimal significations of their relationships with the nature of their own bodies, that of the child, ...'. ('WT': 199)

The staged interplay of pregnancy, its representation in language, and the place of the female intellectual in 'Stabat Mater', suggest that the figure of the mother may yet provide support for a *woman's* speech. Written in 1976 following the birth of her son, the text reads language and childbirth as originating from the site of a primary wound. In conflating the experience of pregnancy and the experience of reading, Kristeva opens up our very first primal shelter to the scrutiny of critical practice and disfigures its homely connotations through the addition of an unreadable surplus. By no means, though, is motherhood represented as being all tears: here too are its pleasures, mixed with the pleasures of the text and celebrating in their interplay a succession of epiphanies in language: 'As if a geometry ghost could suffer when collapsing in a noiseless tumult'. (*Tales*: 242) In an attempt to encourage two different discourses to engage in mutual interaction the typography of the page is divided in two: a bold typescript denotes a biographical, lyrical intrusion alongside a formal analytical commentary. Signifying the topographical and material differences between symbolic and semiotic, the text's divisions literalise the animosities in idealism between matter and form, flesh and spirit, phenomenon and inscription, while simultaneously attempting to deny this division through performing what could be termed an 'enigmatic sublimation'. For where the hysteric denies the separation of body *from* words and produces somatic symptoms, 'Stabat Mater' similarly denies the purity of the signifier, but it does so through displacing the effects of the body *into* words.

The experience of motherhood, argues Kristeva, threatens conventional discourse with collapse. Its agents are 'grinders of volumes, expanses, spaces, lines, points'; a geometry of the maternal body that confronts the discourse of idealism with a subversive feminine resonance. Its most privileged representation is of course the Virgin Mary, whose enigmatic, sublime kind of identity both prefigures our own experience of maternity and overwhelms it with an excess in language – the unnamable. Reading, like motherhood, summons epiphany in language, and when this mysterious kind of sublimation is mediated to us through the embodied discourse of the female analyst 'alone of all her sex', language and philosophy become accessible to radical subversion. Can such an eccentric discourse on motherhood then, creatively subvert the notions of transcendence and the divisions between outside and inside that have conventionally supported philosophy? A discourse that sublates the notion of the good into a transcendent ideal accepts the accompanying devaluation of the body, the material. Is there a new relationship between matter and form that could provide an alternative to their otherwise hostile opposition? Can its linking of personal narrative and divine love provide a way out of the phallic mother syndrome? And finally, can there be a personally inflected subject of enunciation who is female without her superior kind of knowledge exiling her from the wider community (of women), and meaning?

It is almost impossible to separate a discourse on the mother from our own experiences of mothering and/or being mothered.[16] When we speak of motherhood, we end up affirming primary narcissism: 'this motherhood is the *fantasy* that is nurtured by the adult, man or woman, of a lost territory; what is more, it involves less an idealized archaic mother that the idealization of the *relationship* that binds us to her, one that cannot be localized – an idealization of primary narcissism.' (*Tales*: 234) What exactly comes to mind when we think of 'mother'? Our own experiences of being mothered? The ideals of being a good (and bad) mother that we have internalised? The discourses of religion and psychoanalysis and their varying degrees of idealisation of motherhood? Why is it so difficult in fact, to see the mother as a subject in her own right? Why is motherhood surrounded by a fantasy produced by the richest resources that the imaginary has to offer – the fantasy of a 'lost territory'; and why should we find it easier to speak of our relation to her? And why is it that when I want to speak of 'mother' I end up by speaking of myself? Kristeva has correctly located a gap in discourse about the mother. This gap is experienced by all subjects, but for *women* to talk about the mother becomes even more difficult because of the trouble they have in separating from their own mothers, in being different from them, and then in separating from their daughters.[17]

Another way to express this is to state that there is a confusion of the relation between subject and object. We blur the boundaries between subject and object because when we attempt to speak of the existence of an other, we are led to speak of our own subjectivities. And with women, such a transference of personal affect to the site of what we desire to know, is, according to Kristeva, more exaggerated. In that case, is Kristeva indicating that her own discourse may be no more than a repetition of this site of transference; that she too will speak of *her* own mother when attempting to speak of *the* mother;[18] that she too will be drawn to elaborate a discourse of her own emerging subjectivity? The risks of writing entail constructing a narrative of the mother that will not solely reproduce our eternal struggle with her or sentimentalise our memories of her love, but will present the maternal relation as something that is ultimately separate from our infantile fantasies and desires. The language of analysis *displaces* our fantasies even as it re-enacts them. It creates a necessary distance between body and word. Kristeva's performative strategies insist on the dangers of recalling a nourishing maternal fusion because it is inseparable from a hatred directed toward the mother that represents a terror of coming too close, of failing to separate. But her (borderline) analysis equally produces the knowledge that these risks can never be entirely eliminated from speech because the work of separation from the mother is never complete.

'The paradox: mother, or primary narcissism.' You, or me? Implicated in the rhetorical structures of the text I encounter a further dilemma: the problematics of reading. For when I read Kristeva, I look for a reassuring shelter, a 'mother'. This part of reading meets the needs of my *ideal ego*,[19] my need for narcissistic gratification through incorporation. A second aspect of the reading relationship insists on the ability to be able to idealise this mother, to admire her life or speech, and to wish in some way to emulate it through introjection. This satisfies my *ego ideal*, the part of me that needs someone outside of myself to idealise and love. Reading 'Stabat Mater' endorses these expectations: it nourishes and exhorts, but its conceptual strangeness forbids any permanent identification. The discourse of maternity as I read it according to Kristeva swallows the necessity for a paranoid reader ('alone of all her sex') and sustains us instead through a vibrant play with the textures and tongues of language.

What could possibly be the strategic virtue in choosing the Virgin to speak of motherhood to a contemporary audience? Kristeva argues that Mary exemplifies primary narcissism, but in a unique way. Men and women could identify with the Virgin, Kristeva believes, because her freedom from sexuality and death puts her on a par with God and thus gives them leave to love her in a whole host of ways that can range from sublimation to masochism. As Lechte comments, Mary is also the perfect mother because she gave up her son,[20] and her experience of loss is able to sustain us in the variety of losses that might be ours. While I agree that Mary may well symbolically be Other for us, she is not without humanity. Mary's standing at the foot of the cross; her tears, her suffering, is like the hysteric's 'I know but all the same' and signifies her fleshly implication in maternity. Yet with one important difference: when our sense of identity and our grasp on language is overwhelmed, if we have any feeling for Catholic iconography at all, Mary's privileged position allows her to stand as a representative of the first primal mother: 'Archaic maternal love would be an incorporation of my suffering that is unfailing, unlike what often happens with the lacunary network of signs.' (*Desire*: 252) Unlike the gaps and lacks that language opens within us, maternal love absorbs our sorrow. Kristeva suggests that maternal love is founded, like all our loves, on loss, but that it retains something distinctive – the capacity to remind us of and compensate us for our fleshly identity. Thus any discourse on motherhood that refuses this identity and insists purely on the Virgin's spirituality and perfection will come to grief and will, moreover, reinforce the dualisms of idealist philosophy that Kristeva is attempting to subvert.

Kristeva therefore seems to be offering herself as someone who will clear away conventional discourse (on motherhood) by dismantling fantasies about the mother, but she also narcissistically positions herself in the mother's place. To repeat, 'Stabat Mater' is prompted by the birth of her son. It deals in part with her own experience of pregnancy. Identification, through a mimetic displacement in language involves both narcissism and its critique, which in turn assumes a complex relationship between the semiotic and the symbolic. Kristeva here implies that when the experience of motherhood is analysed as knowingly as she herself has done by transposing its estranging effects into language, the result can only be 'an identification with love itself'. (*Tales*: 253) Such a mysterious, sublime form of identification challenges all localised identities and may be the only way to effectively displace idealism. Her strategy also provides an opportunity for a covert 'feminine' enunciation: 'I know language is "lacunary", but all the same ….' Undoubtedly her earlier rejection of conventional iconography had made this kind of reconciling identification impossible.

For 'Stabat Mater' gives us the impression that there is more to an analysis of motherhood than its enigmatic representation in language. There is the implicit suggestion in the text that an analysis of the critic's own experience is the most lucid way to proceed. In an act of renunciation and passion, a narcissism not unlike Mary's in fact, Kristeva herself stands in the strange place where the woman as mother dwells, implicated in its 'underground swarming of seconds … folding in unimaginable spaces', (*Tales*: 235) yet mediating its strangeness to us through the 'surge of anguish' that writing is. Elsewhere this literal psychotic identification with the object of thought is acknowledged as reflecting the necessity of being 'a *woman* [who will] attempt to take up that exorbitant wager of carrying the rational project to the outer borders of the signifying venture of men …'. (*Desire*: *x*) Kristeva's own body has now become the privileged site of sacrifice. Giving birth to a text *and* giving birth to a son defies the philosopher (Hegel) who once remarked that women could be universal or particular, but never the singular subjects of consciousness. It never occurred to Hegel that women who were *mothers* could also become intellectuals. But the woman who writes adds new meaning to the figure of the mother who loves in her impossible fusion of flesh and words. This is because writing about motherhood enforces a separation from the body whereby the writer must confront *through language* the alterity of pregnancy. But when that writer is a mother as well, the degree of displacement effected is more subtle still, as at the same time she returns us over and over again through the potentially self-implicating layers in discourse to our earliest embodied memories of primary narcissism.

Separation from the mother and thus from the bodies we inhabit is only ever partial and never complete, as language and its materiality – 'weavings of abstractions to be torn' – remind us. I think we can understand Kristeva's identification with the mother as being a celebration in its own right, but more importantly, as a strategic riposte to the kind of theorising that would sweep feminine experience, along with the material lining of thought ('negativity') into a void. She is consistently taken up with forcing this conceptual blindspot of idealist discourse to declare itself and in the figure of the Virgin as represented to us by the analyst-as-mother, she has found the perfect relation for ravishing speech.

At this point we are returned to the original intention set out in *Revolution in Poetic Language* which was to estrange thought and language, but now in 'Stabat Mater' the project passes throught the mystery of the 'Incarnation' that language *is*. On this side of the incarnation lies home and all that is familiar, where predictable egos inhabit predictable bodies. On the far side of Mary is the *unheimlich* to which Mallarmé attributed 'the primitive lightning bolts of logic'. We inhabit our bodies and minds so thoroughly that there is no space for innovation that will take us by surprise and jolt our habitual procedures and organisation of thought. 'Stabat Mater' offers, in the words of Hegel, 'a sunburst which, in one flash, illuminates the features of the new world'.[21] Its epiphanies point the way not to a revelation of transcendent being, however, but to a moment of striking perception on the *far* side of consciousness: 'FLASH – instant of time or of dream without time; inordinately swollen atoms of a bond, a vision, a shiver, a yet formless, unnameable embryo.' (*Tales*: 234) In this coming face to face with an unrecognisable identity our sense of continuity breaks apart, and we are unsettled, beside ourselves, because the Other has returned to confront us with a sense of our finitude.

When alterity is mediated through a discourse that so self-consciously mimes (reproduces) motherhood in relation to an imaginary transcendence, the Other appears at its most intense, yet restrained from its radical destructiveness. There may be no more effective place from which to estrange language than through an unthinkable dialogue effected between Virgin, sexually active mother and female intellectual. Beginning with Hegel, Kristeva informs us, Mary has been thought of as universal and particular but never singular. (*Tales*: 261) Kristeva is fascinated by Hegel because he too sought to grasp at what lay beyond recognition; but his reasoning eventually led to the other being naturalised and subdued by the consciousness. This is why she reads 'because of and in spite of Hegel', attempting to construct a space for women and language that being neither inside nor outside, neither subject of a specular masterful gaze or its mute object, will resist naturalisation. If this attempt succeeds, it will establish subjectivity not as phallic or paranoid, but embodied and differentiated, and thus acknowledging the symbolic without being enclosed by it.

'A woman will only have the chance to live her life either *hyper-abstractly* ("immediately universal," Hegel said) in order thus to earn divine grace and homologation within the symbolic order; or merely *different*, other, fallen ("immediately particular," Hegel said). But she will not be able to accede to the complexity of being divided, of heterogeneity, of the catastrophic fold-of-"being" ("never singular," Hegel said).' (*Tales*: 248–9) In these terms, Mary can be seen as universal because her conception was immaculate, and singular because she was, all the same, a mother who grieved at the loss of her son. Generally speaking though, because women usually invest all of themselves in the family, according to Hegel their existence is particular. Particularity means that its form (reproduction for instance) can't be negated through critical self-consciousness, hence transcended. A particular identity cannot engage in making history, for instance, or transforming culture. Because women by and large refuse to risk their lives in struggles for power and since they lack the necessary means to be actively engaged in a reflective life, they are cut off from the recognition of their own finitude, which for Hegel circled back to produce the subject of consciousness. The fundamental energy of the self-conscious (intellectual) life concerns loss, differentiation and doubling, and this is what women's preoccupation with ensuing the continuity of family life is unable to accept. Death's significance for women only lies in the particularity of its loss (that is, loved ones die) but never in its significance as a graspable, reproducible concept, nor as the precondition for the re-creation of the world through reason. Hegel therefore deprived human reproduction of a consciousness and women of an active, enunciative role in discourse.[22]

While Kristeva attempts to show against Hegel that in pregnancy the mother actually experiences the heterogeneity of folded being that he claimed only for men, she still considers that the maternal body is a being *in extremis*; it does not properly belong to the order of signs and so lies outside of women's active knowledge. But only a truncated reading would then conclude that this must leave women permanently exiled from the world of thought and creative life. We can see therefore that subjectivity for women, however different from men's and however difficult to achieve, is not only a reality, but may exist as a permanent challenge to the notion of autonomous identity. A challenge, moreover, which receives its most intense expression in the figure of the female intellectual.

Hegel had assumed a certain unity of the self when self-consciousness and the assimilated object were united. 'Desire is the agent of this unity;' Kristeva remarks, 'it acts as the agent of unification by negativizing the object.' (*RPL*: 134) This is the paranoid moment, when the ego splits, projecting the bad object out to the exterior and erasing difference (Hegel's 'independent life') within. However the subject still finds this unity threatening because it is potentially heterogeneous, always vulnerable to the semiotic's challenge. To ward off the threat of disintegration from what Kristeva reads as the semiotic and to come to terms with internal difference, desire in Hegel subordinates difference to a self-consciousness ultimately submissive to the One, the Spirit. She comments: 'The "I" is divided and doubled only to become reunified within the unity of Self-Consciousness. This is the ambiguousness of the idealist dialectic; it posits division, movement, and process, but in the same move dismisses them in the name of a higher metaphysical and repressive truth ...'. (*RPL*: 135)

And what of the object outside consciousness? Kristeva reads 'Force' ('Kraft') in Hegel as negativity in its most alien, material form, which she associates with the semiotic. Hegel reclaims force for the symbolic under the category of the Notion (force 'driven back into itself', *RPL*: 114), but not before the disturbing recognition that it is actually heterogeneous and other to thought and knowledge. 'In conceiving radical negativity as an *expression*, the idealist dialectic deprives itself of negativity's powerful moment: the scission that exceeds and precedes the advent of thetic understanding.' (*RPL*: 115)

Interestingly, the privileged metaphor that Kristeva uses to illustrate her re-reading of 'Kraft' is that of *childbirth*. Here she quotes Artaud: 'In it we feel a grinding of sluices, a kind of horrible volcanic shock from which the light of day has been *dissociated*. And from this clash, from the tearing of two principles, all potential images are born in a thrust stronger than a ground swell.'[23] Idealism amputates Force by erasing its painful conception and birth; similarly the reality of motherhood and its mediation of the semiotic is amputated by procedures which continually ignore its powerful moment of negativity. Like the Notion, the place of motherhood before being naturalised by thought is 'that of a non-being which contains the system, which conditions the becoming-system of the process, at the same time that it threatens the subject ...'. (*RLP*: 539)

I am aware that other critical readings of Kristeva on maternity have not seen in 'Stabat Mater' what I have. For instance, her ambivalent borderline position between separation and fusion, body and text seems to have passed almost unnoticed.[24] Elizabeth Grosz criticises the fact that women in this essay and elsewhere have 'no special link to the maternal body ...',[25] which Kristeva evacuates of all lived content. She cites the figure of the 'maternal container' as reflecting Kristeva's hostility to the lived quality of women's experience. Grosz's reading certainly highlights the weaknesses of a non-essential reading of maternity, and Kristeva's apparent reluctance to credit the activities of nurturing and socialisation with an agent. Yet if we read Kristeva's surreptitious readings of Hegel correctly? differently? we can see that when representation presents an aggressive, incorporating face to alterity, neither sex emerges unscathed. If consciousness amputates motherhood's strangeness, the mother in turn 'gnaws' at the symbolic's 'almightiness'. But we can also see the limited nature of a reading that repeatedly reiterates the fact that Kristeva is not a good enough feminist (by extension, not a good enough woman, and clearly 'not I'!). Do we, like Simone de Beauvoir, too hastily see here a feminine defeat?[26] If 'Stabat Mater' is measured against a programmatic notion of motherhood that can assist women in their struggle to acquire a better status for themselves in the world, obviously it is lacking. But although Kristeva's intention is not to endorse feminism, nor is it solely to show that the maternal body is a depersonalised biological filter. The privileged link that a woman has with maternity is maintained in 'Stabat Mater', despite the obscure way it is conceived and represented. Through the enunciative markers that inscribe a woman's desire, and through a narrative that operates on several levels at once by means of allusion, word plays, interposition of other discourses, irony, and ambivalence, Kristeva has foregrounded the crisis in meaning anticipated by motherhood and has extended the horizon of her discourse to a meditation on identity and primary narcissism that implicates us all.

Indeed, 'Stabat Mater' is hardly indifferent to the question of identity. Women and their relationships are quaintly represented as 'a community of dolphins', (*Tales*: 257) but in case we find this metaphor too fanciful, we should not forget that it then allows Kristeva to ask what happens when the other woman wants to be considered a singular voyager? What happens if some women wish to be intellectuals? The experience often has negative connotations: alone of all her sex, the female intellectual is rejected by this underwater community, either through indifference or through hatred of her unnatural, inconceivable ambition. These confessions persuade the reader that the personal stakes are indeed very large, and that personal affects are not as erased as Grosz has suggested. The hostility levelled at Kristeva's reading of maternity arises, I believe, from two sources. Firstly, her preference for conducting a discourse at a high level of abstraction – executed with obvious panache – is regarded as hostile to a deeply feminine need to insist that practice and experience are domesticated, that they are ultimately comforting and not estranging gestures. Intellectual activity must for feminists be accompanied with a corresponding degree of 'objective' application. It must be 'practical' and it must correspond to '*my*' experience. Thus Madelon Sprengnether writes: 'Whereas Lacan believes that he can speak in the place of "woman" without being one, women themselves seem to have greater difficulty in discriminating between the position of cultural disruption signified by the Imaginary and the fact of being female.'[27] Figural reading strategies by women themselves sooner or later are intimately connected to the fact of being female. Our questions are our bodies. In these terms, 'Stabat Mater' is only partially acquiescent, since it finally privileges modern art and not women as the most knowing source of maternal love. It insists that the semiotic fire of tongues is the most sustaining expression of a divine encounter for subjects. As I have argued however, the enunciation of the text *is* personally inflected. The analyst who advocates a subversive mother-tongue is a woman and a *real* mother. Which leads us, paradoxically, to the second resistance feminism might well have to 'Stabat Mater' that lies precisely on the wound of primary narcissism, for in reading Kristeva we are led to ask whose mother is she talking about anyway: ours or hers? When we read Kristeva on the female intellectual do we let her discourse stand alone, or do we turn a blind eye to its alterity, its singularity, by expecting to find reproduced there solely our own memories of maternal care? It occurs to me that our responses to motherhood reflect a conceptual outpost we have constructed for ourselves in the face of what is perceived as Kristeva's relentless negativity: an outpost which is often represented as a last ditch stand against the forces of rationality, perhaps even intellectualising. Childbirth as both ultimate sacrifice and supreme reward is something we can't be deprived of, and an instinctive response on the part of women has been to put out a franchise on its discourse that will hedge it from life's losses. But this discourse sometimes binds itself in a sentimental wrapping – 'I' to 'my mother' – that 'Stabat Mater' recognises and interrogates. We need a discourse such as the one offered in this essay as the necessary corrective to sentimentality that will accompany other narratives of motherhood, estranging through a profusion of metaphors its domestic mansion.

Of course, Kristeva doesn't really acknowledge that turning to Mary today is an antiquated gesture; probably limited to those among whom I count myself who feel the need to explore the founding myths of their own faith. In subsequent texts however, we read how Mary's unoccupied space has today collapsed back into widespread abjection. In *Tales of Love* the Virgin is seen as a 'safety lock for feminine abjection' that has failed, and whose loss we have been unable to compensate for. Our secular society can admit no transcendent salvific identity, and in completely removing the maternal body from a renunciation of the flesh, Kristeva argues, social experience is marked by a growing hatred towards women, a kind of suffocating self-hatred on the part of women themselves, and a lonely narcissism for men. This culmination of negativity also appears in Kristeva's own writing. Thus one could argue that the earlier attempts to speak of maternal love or jouissance, admittedly always shadowed by ambivalence, eventually succumbed to a wholesale fear of female sexual excess. 'Stabat Mater' was only a temporary respite since there are Virgins no longer, only abject 'females who can wreck the infinite', as Louis-Ferdinand Céline was to write in 1936.

ABJECTION

> Her lips opened up as she howled so that she offered him, without her own intention or volition, a view of a set of Chinese boxes of whorled flesh that seemed to open one upon another into herself,

> drawing him into an inner, secret place in which destination perpetually receded before him, his first, devastating, vertiginous intimation of infinity.
>
> Angela Carter[28]

Today infinity explodes perspective, and the vertigo that terrified Peter in Angela Carter's version of *Peter and the Wolf* into taking up religion is no longer enclosed by a woman's body but offers itself everywhere. The sky has left off holding up the heavens or as Angela Carter puts it, the thing 'which they feared most, outside, was now indoors with them'.[29] That the outcome of a fully secular logic should lead to a collapse of the space of intellectual reflection may come as no surprise to Kristeva's readers who are familiar with *Tales of Love*, but when in *Powers of Horror* the boundaries of the psyche collapse, we witness a similar logic at work, yet with considerably less alleviation of its symptoms.

Kristeva believes that those individuals who suffer from abjection are either estranged from language, or live a precarious existence on its margins. Neither language nor social relationships are sufficiently sustaining to permit an identity to be articulated that can withstand the existence of an other without paranoia. However, according to Kristeva abjection also appears to be a founding moment for *all* subjects. As a revolt of and against the being that gives us existence, Kristeva argues that before we have yet been formed as speaking beings and before our world has acquired the coherence of objects for us, there exists an abject borderline state we inhabit. Our identity runs all over the place, and in this phase of psychic development, whenever it meets up with boundaries and barriers, we experience a traumatic sense of upheaval. This moment therefore marks the beginnings of separation from the undifferentiated relationship previously experienced with the mother (thus 'I expel *myself*, I spit *myself* out' [*Powers*: 3]. The maternal relation is the most primitive representation of intimate space, yet this relation opens on to a landscape of estrangement. For the peculiar organisation of abjection actually *founds* the signifying economy of our culture and its characteristics of 'rejecting, separating, repeating/abjecting' (*Powers*: 15) are present in the symbolic in any cultural and intellectual activities relating to denial and negation, differentiation, repetition, moving from inside to outside, setting up boundaries. Abjection enables us to differentiate between clean and unclean, proper and improper, inside and outside. What the symbolic system expels as waste or defilement becomes abject, but its very persistence indicates the ongoing difficulties of any final exclusion. The threat of abjection comes from a maternal entity that is neither 'us' nor 'not us', but somewhere in between that summons up an archaic state in the development of the subject prior to the desire precipitated by the mirror stage. As the emerging subject attempts to free himself from this entity, the mother's body becomes the 'horror vacui', the Absolute beginning and end of space into which one can avoid falling only by endlessly repeating the gestures of separation.

Kristeva derives the rationale for abjection from Freud, who argued that the superego appeared at the same time as the castration complex when the child internalised the paternal prohibition on incestuous desires for the mother.[30] According to Kristeva's reading of Freud, what the superego represses are those aspects of my/my mother's body still caught up in instinctual drives, not yet differentiated from each other and thus not yet able to be articulated as signs. Expressed another way, this fallen object's presentation to consciousness as a 'discharge' or 'convulsion' is a return of the repressed. Abjection unchecked recalls a state *prior* to signification, where there are destructive, self-seeking drives, but no symbolic system in firm enough position to repress or displace these drives into speech, thus the corpse 'does not *signify* death'. It *shows* it. (*Powers:* 3) When the superego's function is radically weakened, sufficient structure or spacing has still been given to the drives to organise them into a rudimentary pattern of pathways or articulations, but insufficient to definitively separate inside from outside, and subject from object. The abject is a realm where drives and signifiers are all mixed up; where there are some kinds of sublimating (symbolic) attachments, but only imperfect ones. As Kristeva notes, abjection is 'a composite of judgement and affect, of condemnation and yearning, of signs and drives.' (*Powers*: 10) That is why the abject person is the supreme example of the voyager, always straying, torn by these 'somewhat Manichean' aspects and lacking a strong third term (the paternal function) that will attach him securely to language and the symbolic (the Other).

Accordingly, a borderline patient who suffers from abjection will be unable to differentiate between his own subjective space and another's. He will view himself as an ideal for an Other (originally his mother), and thus as having a *false* self or selves. The subject of abjection is an exile preoccupied not with his name but about his place, which Kristeva tells us he endlessly builds and rebuilds. If abjection is a disorder associated with the mirror stage, its subject demonstrates quite serious problems with living and conceptualising space. When our first attempts at marking off a boundary that will eventually distinguish us from the mother are stifled, then the necessary linkage between psychic interior and a material exterior never develops, or it does so only in the most rudimentary of forms. Under the shadow of a maternal relation that is too sexual, too (auto)erotic, the abject person constructs his own shaky dwelling. Never able to fully depart from the first 'natural mansion', his work is always in progress; estranged from notions of fixity and rest, ceaselessly on the run, he can never get far enough from a devouring interior that threatens his fragile sense of identity.

In a paper on narcissism, Freud had suggested a possible causal relation between the organisation of the body and the organisation of the ego: 'For every such change of erotogenicity of the organs, there might then be a parallel change of libidinal cathexis in the ego.'[31] The ego and consciousness rely for their initial organisation and coherence on a sense of corporeality: 'The ego is first and foremost a bodily ego; it is not merely a surface entity, but is itself the projection of a surface.'[32] When the body fails to acquire a coherent psychic and conceptual spatial organisation, there has been a corresponding failure to perceive the physical space occupied by the body. Obviously these two modes of perception (interior and exterior) are interrelated, and abjection occurs when their mutual differentiation is frustrated. In fact, when differentiation does not occur successfully, the materiality of the drives (which are the most primitive form of interior psychic space) returns to add a dangerous overlay of negativity to the subject's problematic identity: 'The body's inside, in that case, shows up in order to compensate for the collapse of the border between inside and outside. It is as if the skin, a fragile container, no longer guaranteed the integrity of one's "own and clean self" but, scraped or transparent, invisible or taut, gave way before the dejection of its contents.' (*Powers*: 53) Hollowed out yet crushed beneath the weight of an intimate infinity, the abject person is caught in a place of shattered forms, remainders and residues. The sublime is powerfully present in abjection, but unable to be supported or sustained by language, its epiphanies have the tendency to collapse on to the subject's own body, causing it to fragment or become dejected. Kristeva believes that the profound ambiguity of abjection is at its most relentless in literature, which manages at the same time to provide some form of cathartic relief through sublimation.

Catharsis is possible because the abject's 'symptom is the rejection and reconstruction of languages', (*Powers*: 45) and the writer is a subject who transfers primary phobic fears of a too-present mother through metaphor on to the literary text. The 'signifier that terrified, flees its signified' (*Powers*: 49) is the transposition into language of this life or death struggle and is at its most extreme when the literary text appears to split the signifier from the signified and reinvest fragments of words with affect. Is the reader mistaken then, to connect the topology of abjection with the body of the mother or more drastically, with women? Does abjection produce dereliction? If Victor Burgin is correct, ultimately, it is 'not woman *as such* who is abjected, but rather woman as privileged signifier of that which man both fears and desires: the extinction of identity itself'.[33] So how can we read *Powers of Horror* without being overwhelmed with loathing for the female body? How can we recognise abjection without gouging out our eyes? Here is Kristeva's response: restraining abjection is possible if, and only if, 'we hear in language – and not in the other nor in the other sex – the gouged-out eye, the wound, the basic incompleteness that conditions the indefinite quest of signifying concatenations.' (*Powers*: 88–9) She reiterates that language, and not unmediated experience, is our daily reality. If we wish to avoid falling into perpetual conflict with the other (sex), we must let language, particularly literature that is potentially more invested with the mother-tongue, absorb our terror, our aggression, and our disappointment, not to mention our identity. Clearly, Kristeva is striving here to restrain the potentially life-threatening energies of unchecked abjection by insisting on the spacing gestures of language alive to the semiotic. Nonetheless, it is impossible to keep the pure borders of theorising about abjection ('woman as privileged signifier') from drawing on a reservoir of personal affect (woman *as such*) and implicating both in a horror of the derelict female body. In *Powers of Horror*, Kristeva aligns abjection, the grotesque and the maternal. One of its most objectionable aspects is the attitude to birth, and in the following passage, Kristeva makes little attempt to distinguish herself from the position she is describing, thus:

> When Céline locates the ultimate of abjection – and thus the supreme and sole interest of literature – in the birthgiving scene, he makes amply clear which fantasy is involved: something horrible to see at the impossible doors of the invisible – the mother's body. The

> scene of scenes is here not the so-called primal scene but the one of giving birth, incest turned inside out, flayed identity. (*Powers*: 155)

This distaste is merely the other side of the artist's fascination with the woman as 'Ideal, artistically inclined, dedicated to beauty ... the focus of ... [his] gaze.' (p. 157) Céline's attraction to good bone structure in women is something that Kristeva can't take her eyes off, and I suspect that in a subliminal sense, it is homologous to her own preference for the good lines of form. The asexual, the child and the homosexual woman are categories that appeal to Céline because they do not offer a female bodily lining to the male gaze, thereby transmuting all the more easily into form. Comments Kristeva, not without narcissism: 'A ballerina is the most perfect example of it, preferably a foreigner – the opposite of the mother language, without language if need be, all sensitivity and acrobatics.' (*Powers:* 166) One can tolerate the eccentricity of Céline's personal tastes however, without turning them into a dissertation on the conjunction of abjection and the sublime. Kristeva's fascination for Céline's discourse is such that she has elevated his narrative of hatred and fear into a universal condition.

Apparently, the experience of what Kristeva has named abjection is also the prerogative of psychotics who are bound to fantasies of the phallic mother through refusing to introject as verbalisations what they incorporate of her. As a result, they believe that castration literally occurs (that is, they refuse, in a certain way, to accept the incest prohibition).[34] Jennifer Stone tellingly criticises Kristeva for her literal and therefore borderline psychotic reading of Freud.[35] In the same way that psychotics believe the mother to have the power of castration, and in the same way that they acquiesce to the negativity of the drives over symbolisation, we could say that Kristeva mimics their dissociated condition, and *mimics Céline* in the horrific place she accords to the maternal function. Psychological and linguistic aberrations, made homologous through the intervening figure of the abhorrent mother, are seen firstly as the precondition of language, and secondly as its indispensible inner lining which reveals itself most particularly in the literary text. *Spaltung*, first used as a term to describe schizophrenia and developed by Lacan in his explanation of how the subject enters and remains a split being in language, here takes on a new dimension as we see its presence manifested as acute condition in the theoretical discourse of Kristeva.[36] The phallic mother appears to have considerably more than descriptive and metaphorical status in her work. Presenting itself as symptom in the troubled writings of

Céline, its phantasmatic presence is no less apparent in the case of the analyst, where its description invokes Kristeva's fascinated acquiescence (incorporation) instead of critique (introjection).[37]

It seems abundantly clear that Kristeva's quest for estrangement has led her to forget her own space and leap to a jubilant identification with the body of Céline's texts. The female voyager *identifies* herself with Céline's voyage through the night. As she writes of Bataille in another context: 'Experience, its authority and method cannot be distinguished from its contestation.'[38] Just as abjection fails to distinguish between subject and object, the experience of horror and its intimate connection with maternal space cannot easily be distinguished here from its critique. When we read Céline and Kristeva on Céline, the language of the text fails to offer us consolation for the rottenness, the horrible sticky violence that streams from the representation of a maternal relation now utterly deprived of love. Reading Kristeva on abjection therefore has real effects, even if these must be registered as fantasies arising from the imaginary.[39]

To what extent is this impression sustained? Can critique be cleanly railed off from empathic listening in the text? Is there a catharsis of suffering which emerges through reading, despite everything? How is Kristeva's own enunciative position a response to the effects of abjection on the discourse that produces her as woman and as analyst (intellectual)? For despite its estranging effects however, Kristevan discourse is complex, often maintaining a carefully orchestrated dialogism between valorising and denigrating the feminine. The pleasures and challenges of reading become more nuanced, until the text that most appears to lay waste to the maternal simultaneously offers a unique relation to the object, which the woman who is an intellectual may be in the most strategic place to articulate. Since *Powers of Horror* was intended as 'something other than an intellectual exercise', (*Powers*: 209) we can assume that the writer, far from establishing herself as a disengaged observer contemplating the object, instead identifies herself with it. Yet throughout that fascinating and repellant journey, Kristeva labours to construct a speaking voice that will move between identification *and* analysis, between abject proximity *and* interpretation: 'You have to have been *removed* from the spot' writes Céline in *Entretriens avec le professeur Y*.[40] Elaborating a new kind of space, neither entirely outside or within abjection, her study is the practice of a phenomenology of reading characterised by a considerable degree of reflexivity, where the text represents and scrutinises the affects produced from the speaker's intimate engagement with the space of abjection, and the bearing of this abjection on the practice of reading. As she remarks, 'When reading Céline we are seized at that fragile spot of subjectivity …' (*Powers*: 135), and abjection seizes us similarly because it occurs 'within our personal archaeology'. At times then, the text's discourse is produced at a distance from the writing/reading subject, whose utterance reflects on the nature of subjectivity; at other times the enunciation seems to overwhelm the subject to produce abjection.

What redeems *Powers of Horror* in my judgement however, is the fact that Kristeva's reflexivity leads her eventually beyond an identification with Céline to an elaboration of a different relation to the theoretical object (and hence to the notion of space) that a *woman's* discourse may, under certain circumstances, produce. One of the distinguishing characteristics of the borderline experience of abjection is that its weak relation to the Other as a third term results in two warring factions, each reducing the other to abjection: 'Nature, the body, the inside. Facing the spirit, others, appearances.' (*Powers*: 143) Kristeva suggests that the closed-in nature of the binary relation – the real pitting itself against the symbolic – could be opened up by an influx of the imaginary, an investment in seeming and appearances. Elsewhere she indicates that women do not experience the abject in the same way that men do; usually they '*imagine* rather than experience abjection.' (*Powers*: 144, my emphasis) Thus in reading Céline, we are informed that the writer is '*seemingly*' going to deal with a number of themes. Playing on the potential investment women have in the imaginary and recalling the figure of the female voyager in 'From Ithaca to New York', she takes up this potentiality and uses it as the site from which, coyly, to confront truth bereft of seeming, an abject truth 'without makeup'. (*Powers*: 143)[41] The woman and the analyst at this point coalesce as a privileged kind of home from which to view abjection and through its interpretation, to restore a cathartic discourse/distance of seeming ('makeup') to the standoff that has developed between the real (that is, the woman's body, or unmediated matter) and the symbolic (theorising about interiority). Which in the light of her remarks on the privileged position of women intellectuals, acquires considerable resonance.

In 'Stabat Mater' Kristeva argued that maternal love was a necessary comfort to the speaking being at times of suffering, 'a refuge when his/her symbolic shell cracks and a crest emerges where speech causes biology to show through'. (*Tales*: 263) If the figure of Mary has now become obsolete, there is the implication that her sublime body which absorbs suffering will henceforth be transferred to the body of the (maternal) analyst who suffers with her analysands that she might assist them in becoming resurrected beings. The role of the analyst is thus both sacrificial and fully maternal. As a form of catharsis, analysis offers a shelter to the suffering subject and effects not purification but a 'rebirth with and against abjection.' (*Powers*: 31) For unless analysts and critics permit their discourse to be affected by the estranging qualities of abjection, then speech will not be transformative, renewing or sublime, but will block the productive forces that have assisted in its birth.

But can literature deflect social animosity by providing structures that allow for an interchange of inside and outside without promoting abjection? In *Powers of Horror* the cathartic experience receives the following definition: 'A discourse of sex that is not the discourse of knowledge – it is the only possible catharsis. That discourse is audible, and through the speech that it mimics it repeats on another register what the latter (knowledge) does not say.' (*Powers*: 289) The 'discourse of sex' circumvents knowledge because its informing energies do not arise from the consciousness, but from the unconscious which can never be known in conventional terms. Speech which comes from the unconscious is like ventriloquism, a voice thrown from a distance, which as we have seen in Chapter 3, is an obliquely inflected enunciative position that works by saying what it does not seem to say. It is this distance of another register (literature as mediating abjection, analytical speech as mediating a woman's voice) that effects catharsis. Mimetic identification, an act that I have suggested is the prerogative of the feminine in Kristeva, is the enabling mechanism of transposition as spacing, but its energies do not simply repeat information or reinscribe with exactitude a phenomenological object (woman, for instance). On the contrary, they creatively transform it. Through 'the "poetic" unsettlement of analytic utterance [the text] ... testifies to its closeness to, cohabitation with, and "knowledge" of abjection.' (*Powers*: 30) Kristeva's enunciative 'I' that mediates the disintegrative effects of abjection on identity follows its 'skewed topology', giving us the impression that the boundaries of the subject of enunciation are under threat of collapse, a collapse whose proximity is elaborated by *style* as much as theme. But if style is intimately related to the relief of an intolerable closeness, how does style as catharsis bear on the place of the female analyst?

Powers of Horror does not disguise its ambivalent investment in phenomenology and personal narrative, which is probably why it is so vulnerable, ironically, to feminist critique. The effect of reading Céline and reading Kristeva on Céline is 'quite other ... It calls upon what within us, eludes defenses, trainings, and words, or else struggles against them. A nakedness, a forlornness, a sense of having had it; discomfort, a downfall, a wound ...'. (*Powers*: 134) It causes Kristeva to recall the discomforts of her own childhood experiences; to emulate abjection's hold by continuously naming, designating, repeating, in her own use of style; to play, like Céline, with the homely, colloquial turn of phrase ('How come?'); to ask question after question; to re-create lyrically the ecstatic experience that she believes occurs where abjection comes close to the sublime: 'When the starry sky, a vista of open seas or a stained glass window shedding purple beams fascinate me, there is a cluster of meaning, of colours, of words, of caresses, there are light touches, scents, sighs, cadences that arise, shroud me, carry me away, and sweep me beyond the things that I see, hear, or think ...'. (*Powers*: 12)

In the above meticulous elaboration of Célinian style, we are additionally offered a commentary on the nature of the reading (analytical) relationship. Quoting Leo Spitzer's analysis of Céline, Kristeva explains the 'mutual combat and fascination' between subject and addressee, a paradigm for abjection, as a tearing in subjectivity between a preposing subject who is too self-confident and a subject who constantly supplements information offered, indicating a lack of confidence in both the self and the other. Somewhat like the struggle within manic eros that Kristeva has observed at work in Plato's *Phaedrus*,[42] the fascination the subject feels when he approaches the other and then draws away from its threat is to construct the abject person as someone who finds himself simultaneously in more than one place. Kristeva uses this analysis to demonstrate how enunciation subverts grammar and logic in Céline, but the resonances can be interpreted more liberally still, I feel. Surely we have in the following comment an elaboration of the problematics of reading (and analysis): 'The binary message thus effects a shift from the *I* of pleasure to the *you* of the addressee and to the impersonal *one* that is necessary for the establishment of a truly universal syntax.' (*Powers*: 196) On its most fundamental level, this is an explanation of how the doubling or spacing within enunciation between narcissism and objectification paves the way for a subjectivity that can begin to distinguish between outside and inside. Secondly, it suggests how abjection may be mediated through the third term of writing and analytical speech (that is, the Other as language renewed by the semiotic) in a way that

Revolution in Poetic Language had been unable to. Thirdly, it contains a more nuanced observation that to be in at least two places at once is symptomatic of the transactions and uncertainties that occur within reading, and that occur when *female* intellectuals take up the question of style. Style transformatively redraws the woman's relationship to her own voice by opening up a distance between the speaker and the object spoken about without eliminating the connection between both. Such a confession is what Kristeva's discourse skirts but if it is to be consistent, cannot say directly. With Kristeva, like Céline, we forget that '[s]he can show it to us only because [s]he stands elsewhere ... within writing.' (*Powers*: 134)

From an uncertain distance then, we follow this journey through maternal space, certainly horrified, but probably also even fascinated by a reading experience which may, if we submit to its style, lead us to the very edge of our identity as speaking beings. That Kristeva uses the indeterminacy of identity as a metaphor for the indeterminacy of reading is illustrated in *Powers of Horror* by an account of phobia. Fear and object are linked, she argues, because the passage of the drives is checked in the process of separation and this frustration produces a phobic distress which nevertheless is unable to find its place in speech. The phobic is frightened not only by the all-powerful mother, but also at the prospect of separation or castration. Because such a position is 'non-representable', reflecting *'a drive economy in want of an object'*, (*Powers*: 35) he displaces his anxieties on to some improbable object: for little Hans, it is horses. Kristeva takes the impossible entity of the maternal phallus as the ultimate origin of all fantasy, and while it is clear that phobia is concerned with the anguish surrounding separation from this object, it is not quite so obvious from the exposition in *Powers of Horror* that want is predicated equally on separation's antithesis: that is, fusion. Yet I think such an emphasis is clearly intended. Phobia is a condition where its subject dreads maternal fusion, but equally fears separation from the mother. Agreeing with Freud that little Hans is afraid of castration, Kristeva proceeds to turn his passive subject position: 'I am afraid of being bitten', inside out by remarking that underlying paranoia where the bad object threatens from the outside is an anxiety over one's own devouring mouth: 'I am afraid of biting.' What is termed 'syntactic passivation' (*Powers*: 39) is a necessary procedure in the subject's uncanny ability to simultaneously maintain and separate from the maternal *within* by putting himself in ambivalent relation to the object, hence: 'the ab/object is me; I am afraid of the ab/object'.

Kristeva uses this recognition to move the phobic person (and the origins of subjectivity) away from incorporation to the support that can be provided by language and the speech of the other. Unlike hysteria, abjection (which includes phobia, as well as perversion and obsession) turns from constructing an index of somatic symptoms to indicating want through signs. Its subject makes a metaphorical leap from phantasmatic pre-objects to signs, whereas the specular ego, according to Kristeva, is taken up with pursuing phenomenal objects. In a sense we could see this distinction as alluding to the appropriate way to read abjection, which must be understood in its most vital sense not as a discourse on the horror that pertains to a phenomenal object – woman – but rather an attempt to privilege literature through elaborating the figure of the mother as the dread of an unnamable void. *Powers of Horror* argues that this dread is an inseparable aspect of the separating activity that constructs us as speaking beings and is both brought to light and mitigated through signification and most especially through the literary text's access to the sublime – that is, to alterity. But could we not also agree that just as the relation to the phobic object represents what Kristeva calls 'an avoidance of choice' (that is, 'I am the object'/'I am afraid of the object'), in the same way the processes of separation and abjecting may reflect a similar avoidance? That an indeterminacy of identity underpins all subsequent states of separateness, and that the pleasures of maternal fusion cause us to relinquish a clean and proper castration in favour of a relation that is thoroughly ambivalent and that by the same token, cannot entirely forsake filling the void with an embodied entity, 'more or less' phenomenal? And by extension, couldn't castration be understood as a gap and/or a knot, with the difference being indistinguishable? In which case to understand separation as the dominant narrative of love and abjection, as does John Lechte, is perhaps underreading. For if the fear that links itself to the emerging object is both a fear of separation and a fear that separation will not take place, we would then need to read Kristeva as profoundly more ambivalent on the question of woman than a first glance would imply. We would see again how for Kristeva women are in some measure foreigners on the edge of language and culture, yet as exiles they also recall the difficulty *all* subjects have in coming to terms with the space of the body.

At one point in the text, there is the suggestion that contemporary feminism's privileging everything prior to symbolisation as feminine aligns itself with Céline's anti-Semitism. (*Powers*: 180) Later Kristeva adds that the Jew (read feminism in its struggle for power) makes the

Aryan feel unnaturally feminine and masochistic. Where does the woman stand here? On the side of the anti-Semite? The Jew? Or both? And how can we be saved from gouging out our eyes in this standoff where both parties are implicated in abjection? If woman may claim identification with Céline *or* his protagonist, and if Kristeva by implication casts woman as both envied 'subject' and hateful 'object', then woman's position in signification must be the chosen sign of signification's uncertainty.

Woman's place, the product of a spacing gesture that is never entirely complete, is therefore neither quite empty (a signifier), nor a replete home (the ego, which Kristeva considers to be the 'reflection of the maternal phallus'). Moving between and confusing the distinction between the two sites of representation (imaginary and symbolic), the real is both elaborated and displaced. The space of abjection that crosses the boundaries of language and pre-language, paternal and maternal, castration as painful wound and castration as denial, offers us a commentary on the complexity of a woman's relationship with that space – neither within abjection, nor outside of it; neither its object, nor fully removed from its borders either. I would argue that Kristeva's reading of abjection knowingly mimes the indeterminacy that abjection *is* and in so doing, pays a considerable debt to hysteria, despite evidence to the contrary. The woman who approaches abjection through writing inhabits it differently, improperly perhaps. Never fully at home in the body nor fully at ease within signs, the writer's body, both *heimisch* and *unheimlich*, is (seemingly) her text. I suspect that the estrangement produced by inhabiting improperly is what the writer of *Powers of Horror* desires above all else.

Why is it though that when I read this text I am immediately struck by the force of hatred and aggression that is directed at the maternal body? And why do I along with other critics instinctively rush to connect such hatred with 'woman' and then with 'me'? As in 'Stabat Mater' is the point the abject mother, or primary narcissism? The signifier, or my experience as a woman and mother? Can women simultaneously name the exile of Being and be different names? And is my reading reaction misguided, straying across places (the ego, phenomenology) where it has no business? Or in imaginatively feeling myself closer to this archaic object, am I not beginning to elaborate a kind of reading that is not so much wrong as different? A difference that may lie, if we work within the psychoanalytical narrative, in a different relation to the phallus, and one that Lacan has expressed as the difference between being and having (the phallus). Yet once more, even a reading that begins with specular identifications is caught within the displacing logic of signification. Nor can it neglect the complex effects of separation, through which we all must pass to take up the order of signs. Kristeva's exchange with abjection incorporates a phenomenological approach and thus gratifies even as she wounds the reader's narcissism, but while not relinquishing phenomenology, voyages beyond its limits to find and name, like the phobic, an impossible lost object – Heidegger's 'Nothing' – whose recovery eludes every speaking being regardless of their sex. Thus the unique kind of perspective offered by a female analyst unquestionably provides some relief from the abject collapse of spatial boundaries, yet its ironic, double emphasis on separation and identification is ultimately too self-reflexive to stand in the place of the support formerly offered by an Ideal from *outside* the body / text's system. What is required then is a new third term, preferably with a paternal inflection if it is to be consistent with Kristeva's loyalties to Freud, that will convincingly redraw the connection between the subject's body and his speech.

SPEAKING OF LOVE

> The speaking being is a wounded being, his speech wells up out of an aching for love, and the 'death drive' (Freud) or the 'unbeing' (Lacan) that are coextensive with human nature determine, if they do not justify them, the discontents of civilisations.
>
> Julia Kristeva, *Tales of Love*

Love and love's losses are universal experiences but they are also, as Julia Kristeva reminds us, universal topics of conversation. In speaking of love we lose our sense of ourselves and the securities of dwelling; thus, she argues, is the speaking being and the nature of being itself transformed. But if we are to be loving subjects, the modalities of enunciation available must contain structures able to shelter loving speech. *Powers of Horror* had unveiled a speaking subject locked within abjection, unable to transcend an opposition between matter and words which left the female body derelict and the subject broken in pieces, no longer capable of finding the idealisations necessary for life and love to exist.

Tales of Love is the working out of this dilemma; the attempt to accomodate the speaking subject in relation to a loving, mediative Other.[43] Given that the collapse of Christianity has, according to Kristeva, deprived our speech of mystery and left us with no transcendent space to absorb abjection, this text aims to designate a subject of enunciation whose reflections on love are supported and maintained by a new third term – the Imaginary Father. Once, the ideals of romance – and religion – consisted in bringing together the figures of a loving father and a nurturing mother, whose happy duality would be further cemented through the bonds of parenthood. In *Tales of Love*, Kristeva argues that changes in Western society have so eroded these boundaries that we have become fragmented individuals, estranged, shipwrecked beings who can find no self-image with which to feel at home. Nor can we reach out to others – our love objects are irretrievably lost, indifferent, or punitive. If idealisation is lacking, so too is catharsis: conventional social structures, habitual patterns of speech and ideal images fail to absorb pain and violence and so alleviate the burden of human suffering. But the solution, Kristeva maintains, is not to return us to couple love, narcissistic self-love, and Oedipal love which may be dead ends in themselves. Nor is it to return to an unproblematic notion of metaphysics. Rather she advocates an opening out of these enclosures to the mediating influence of a loving but imaginary figure: a point, place or structure able to absorb the shocks and disappointments of human love simply because it draws its subjects in a loving gaze directed away from an enclosure towards an elsewhere. It is thus a new kind of perspective that is offered in *Tales of Love*: not the vanishing point of a perspective that supports absolute transcendence; nor the abject collapse of contemplative thought in upon itself; instead Kristeva puts forward the argument that the aporias of love and intellectual reflection call for a new form of dwelling altogether; a space that will be lovingly transformative without endorsing metaphysics on the one hand or a destructive negativity on the other.

The history of love subsequently developed by Kristeva assumes two levels of estrangement at work. Firstly as we have seen, the crisis of contemporary subjectivity appears to lie in the fact that today we no longer have a code, or an interpretative strategy to understand love. Love has lost both its mystery and its conviction. Which means that we cannot recognise love, or respond to it affectively. Our sickness, or homelessness, is caused by a lack of stable mirrors in which we can identify ourselves as anything other than 'empty dilapidated castle[s]'. (*Powers*: 186) This kind of narcissistic crisis is one that numerous analysts have also referred to,[44] and in isolating its nature, Kristeva is deliberately distancing herself from her earlier more unambiguous celebration of loss. However, the second order of the crisis is a trauma inherent in the very nature of love, as Kristeva defines it. Love is a 'narcissistic wound' which in putting us beside ourselves and for another, 'never dwells in us without burning us.' (*Tales*: 4) Here, the state of love is more connected with identity's abject disintegration than its harmonious resolution. In fact, the limits of love appear to be equal to the limits of subjectivity: when one loses oneself in love, an erased subjectivity 'achieves its point of culmination' ('SN': 11). It is most likely that the emergence of the first crisis: the death of God and the subsequent loss of a self supported by love has actually exposed a deeper, more permanent crisis where love's ordeal is a denaturalising experience that will always erode our ability to represent it coherently. When we speak of love, the 'object slips away'; (*Tales*: 267) when we speak of ourselves, we illuminate the transient being of subjects in passage from one state to another.

Whereas *Revolution in Poetic Language* had celebrated the instability of identity, Kristeva now wants to acknowledge that the maternal investments offered by the semiotic in language and the nuanced reading of the female analyst are not of a sufficient holding quality to support the subject in process. If love is about losing the self, it also presupposes the need for a stable, external support. Clearly, there are more than love stories at stake here. In offering to rework the topographic boundaries of loving speech, Kristeva effects a sense of distance from the body and its abject contents, and from the subject and object's mutual aggressivity. The experience of separation, she argues, is a problem for contemporary life. Separation from a primary caregiver is necessary for love not to fall into permanent abjection and if we fail to achieve separation, we will be unable to lovingly idealise others. The current sense of inhabiting empty speech arises because the subtle mechanisms of this idealising experience which are, after all, expressed in speech, have broken down. Her suggestion that we need to constitute new imaginaries, new 'baroque' kinds of seeming to make up for the failure of conventional structures, insists that this occurs within the provisional space of a loving, transformative relationship initiated by a redemptive third term: the Imaginary Father. Since Kristeva believes that conventional ideals of love and identification have foundered, the psychoanalyst will invent a new one. In this sense then, *Tales of Love* approaches the kind of comforting phenomenology rejected in *Revolution in Poetic Language*. There Kristeva had argued that Heidegger's 'care' ('cura') was ontological, effecting a band-aid mentality in the face of the subject's anguished confrontation with negativity. To the arrogant and self-confident critic writing in the early seventies, Heidegger's reading of love seemed redolent of a sentimental maternality. The violent metaphors favoured in *Revolution in Poetic Language*, the product of her emphatic new sublime, have by the publication of *Tales of Love* however, received a soothing coating in recognition that a revolution in language fails to take sufficient account of the *passion* of the subject. Perhaps too, the last decades have increasingly tended to produce wounded subjects in need of tangible care which the tendency to valorise a realm of pure theory in *Revolution in Poetic Language* was unable to register. Whatever the reason, and we must in passing also acknowledge again Kristeva's increasingly personal inflection in her critical work from the mid-seventies, the opening remarks of *Tales of Love* implicitly recognise the need to alleviate human distress, and in that sense are a radical departure from an earlier fascination with the estranging, *disembodied* power of negativity. 'No matter how far back my love memories go, I find it difficult to talk about them' (*Tales*: 1) is a statement announcing that if love is elusive, and if phenomenology must eventually discover its own limits within love, nonetheless the narcissistic comforts and gratifications of personal experience, and the factor of subjective experience generally cannot be entirely dispensed with. Love undermines being but fails to destroy its contours. This last point returns us to the second crisis: the nature of love itself, a state of affairs whose very *structure* interrogates stable distinctions between exterior and interior states, yet a structure now preserved from radical disintegration by the space of a necessary paternal figure.

The Imaginary Father

Kristeva tells us that her patients by and large appear to be suffering from a lack of psychic space. This lack which produces numerous painful effects, arises from the subject's failure to establish a sense of his own particularity and to direct it towards a loving Ideal. Idealising distance is a 'condition for the very existence of psychic space', (*Tales*: 31) Kristeva informs us. Or as John Lechte comments, 'love requires a Third Party (Other) whose role is to make possible the identification with another who is like oneself. Consequently, the other (object of love) is impossible unless the Other (Ideal) is also involved.'[45]

Where an ideal or idealising capacity is absent or frail, a person becomes ill – without love, but equally unable to receive it, or to recognise the existence of a loving other. In order to stabilise her patients, relieve them of abjection and offer them a ground on which to elaborate their love, Kristeva introduces the figure of the Imaginary Father.

The Imaginary Father is derived from Freud's 'father in individual prehistory' with whom there is a 'direct and immediate' form of identification.[46] In the essay 'Identification' in *Group Psychology and the Analysis of the Ego*,[47] Freud gives the example of the role model the father plays for his son's loving identification. The father is his ideal in a way that is different from his relation to the first anaclitic object he will love sexually, his mother. Identification of a non-sexual kind appeared before object choice for Freud, and as Kristeva remarks, this father invites an 'enigmatic, non-objectal identification'.[48] This archaic site harbours the first sign of primary repression, since when the little boy begins to identify with his father, he also has to learn to deflect his devouring, libidinal urges away from his parents and on to an acceptance of the sustaining power of words: a proto-symbolic relationship.

In actual fact, Kristeva interprets Freud's more empirical Father who at this stage contains the attributes of both parents,[49] as a Third Party, a factor that draws the mother's gaze away from the child, and prevents her from claiming the baby as her own Ideal, and thus part of her ego. 'He' is, as she puts it, 'the Phallus desired by the mother.' (*Tales*: 41) That the mother desires something Other than the child is what makes possible separation, absence, and hence the desire to give and receive love. While making use of the paternal metaphor to locate a Third Party, it is clear that Kristeva does not wish it to appear that this instance must inevitably collapse into phenomenology, becoming identified with a referential object: the real father. At one point she suggests that such a triangulation may be articulated by 'X' and 'Y' for instance.[50] Although this suggestion is quickly discarded, it does indicate the difficulties associated with using familiar (and familial) terms to illustrate something new and potentially estranging. It is even questionable that we can actually divest ourselves of the wealth of associations that we bring to the terms mother and father or man and woman, as I have already pointed out in relation to *Powers of Horror*. Separation prefigures emptiness, but it is an imaginary emptiness – in reality separation takes place in concert with an indwelling of presence. Thus we read the term 'Imaginary Father' as both gratifying our earliest object loves and going beyond them to a space that transcends, even problematises, all forms of object love. Curiously then, while the Other establishes the absent ground which is necessary for all subsequent identifications, its most important role seems to consist in calling the emerging subject out of itself to dwell in its loving presence. Its habitation thus offers space *and* intimacy to the journeying subject.

For the Imaginary Father is one who loves rather than judges. Yet in contrast to the pre-Oedipal incest privileged in *Powers of Horror* and 'Polylogue', the figure of the Imaginary Father in *Tales of Love* is non-libidinal, which suggests that the mother–child relationship in itself is too close and too allied to the libido to allow for differentiation. Perhaps this modification is also stressed because underlying the drives towards incest that were glorified in Kristeva's earlier writing lies the Oedipal contest: the struggle of the father against the sons where both were locked in destructive rivalry. Kristeva now wishes to redefine this first father not as a seducer but as the originator of Agape, and the precursor of a Law that does not recognise a phallic power struggle. Through agape we are drawn in to a primary identification that is 'always already ... under the sway of language.' (*Tales*: 27)

An 'always already' identification usually assumes the lack of a first cause and thus a mediated relationship to the other constituted by language as dialectics. But Kristeva additionally wants to argue that the appearance of the Imaginary Father occupies a qualititatively different space: one that is 'immediate' and *unmediated*. His enigmatic appearance occurs outside of, or on the edge of language. This is *not* the Oedipal space of Law and separation mediated by the Name of the Father. Rather what is being redrawn here is the subject's relation to space as transcendence or exteriority. In an attempt to distinguish the unique nature of primary separation, Kristeva turns to Hegel, who in his introduction to the *Phenomenology* speaks of the immediate as 'The absolute ... from the outset in and for itself beside us and [who] wants to be beside us.'[51] This Imaginary Other is in actuality not a metaphysical elsewhere, but a divine space or 'fold' which never left us – we are subjects always already inhabited by otherness.[52]

Hegel had argued that the Absolute is immediately present to us. This recognition is a founding moment for thought, since it confers presence on the subject. But the advent of the Absolute for the subject does not involve in the first instance a dialectical operation in consciousness, where the particular is sublated in and through the Universal. Reading Hegel, Heidegger observes that criticism 'can no longer consist in an assessment of the mediating capacity of knowledge ... [which] from the start ... cannot be a means.'[53] Hegel clearly wished to retain some form of appeal to transcendence (Spirit or Mind), but a transcendence that was 'immediate and therefore effortless' and thus in one sense, immanent. Such a procedure placed the Absolute *beyond* the consciousness, but still able to be registered by it. In *Revolution in Poetic Language* Kristeva had suggested that while for Hegel this 'first mysterious movement of "*immediate certainty*"' (*RPL*: 196) may have been theological, when placed alongside Kristevan semiotics its origin turned out to be yet another instance of the flux of material relations (that is, the presence of the drives). (*RPL*: 197) In *Tales of Love* however, the 'godsend' that the Absolute is has been recast in terms closer to those of Hegel once again. 'We are immediately within parousia', writes Kristeva, '"always already," before producing a relationship to it ...'. (*Tales*: 39) The relation between signified and signifier, particular and universal, subject and object, is, since unmediated, *indeterminate*, or in process.[54] There is a mysterious relation established then, between the flux of matter and the Absolute as loving Ideal that can neither be wholly universalised or dissected into discrete elements.

What this metaphysical inflection indicates is Kristeva's new recognition that a hypothetical exterior point folded *within the system* that will sustain the subject without overwhelming him, is the necessary origin and end of loving speech. The Imaginary Father figure *is* the journey that calls the voyager out of herself and into another place. Does this loving Ideal though merely leave us in the end with a restructured idealism? It is possible to read Kristeva in such a light, but for my part, I consider that the strengths of her analysis consist precisely in reconceptualising the relation of the subject (as interiority) to an exterior (transcendence or the Other). Quite simply, Kristeva's *Tales of Love* offers the subject a new relation to embodied space and its representation in language through re-reading the estranging effects of love on philosophy. Kristeva has turned her psychoanalytic lens to philosophy because it is the latter discourse that has had the most to say about transcendence, the ideal and the notion of the good, and it is philosophy that she wishes to immerse in the maternal folds of the semiotic's tongues of fire. The 'ego affectus est' is a subject mastered by love, the price paid for this 'knowledge', transformation and loss. Never stationary, the subject is a voyager in transit between one state (body) of love and another. Philosophy's subject, on the other hand, the ego cogito, persists in the conviction that knowledge is the sole prerogative of the consciousness. His speech as we have seen in 'Stabat Mater' is grounded in a hostile opposition between mind and body. Reading Plato's *Phaedrus*, Kristeva concludes that philosophy, in particular idealism, is founded on manic eros which may only free itself from the hold of physical passion and attain to the sublime (idealisation) through the discipline of rigorous contemplation. If eros finally gives place to the sublime it is simply because its desires have been transposed to a passionate encounter with the Other through rhetoric and dialogue. Language absorbs the conflicts of the soul within its own dazzling forms. Thus appropriating Freud's reading of primary identification as non-libidinal, according to Kristeva when libido is displaced on to the transference itself as structure, it allows the Other to orientate the emerging subject towards the other person who is loved sexually. But an identification based on emotional affection must come before and support a sexual identification, and this is so because of the sustaining presence of the Imaginary Father.

Narcissus

The Imaginary Father leads me beyond an autoerotic relationship with my mother into narcissism which always precedes object love, according to Kristeva's Freudianism. Narcissus is the central psychic character in *Tales of Love* and it is his tragedy, she argues, that is ours today. In Ovid,[55] the beautiful youth falls in love with what he takes to be an other, but which turns out to be a reflection of part of himself – his ideal. Incapable of granting interiority to himself and exteriority to an object (Echo), he reduces his own and another's subjectivity to ghostly refractions. Sound and image shimmer and captivate the 'watery prowler' but fail to lead him to a true, loving recognition of difference. When Narcissus perceives the object of his love to be in reality his *image*, he dies, unable to entertain the possibility that absence or loss of what one holds most dear is the prerequisite for joining in love with another. Interpreting the myth, Kristeva argues that subjectivity is grounded in love, and that confirmation of one's independence provides the necessary support for a subject to enter language and to construct sustaining relationships. When primary care is too close and too intense, there is either a shutting down of psychic development, or an extreme vulnerability to outside stimuli. In either case, the individual who experiences this kind of disturbance is in no position to elaborate a psychic space: 'home' and his 'protective [maternal] wrapping' enclose him too jealously. As Jessica Benjamin expresses it,

> at some point in the earliest struggle for recognition, the mother must actually remove herself from the child's omnipotent sense of control. She must establish her existence as another subject, as a person, so that the child, too, can have a sense of selfhood. If the mother is not herself able to tolerate this degree of differentiation from her child, to inflict this pain upon her or him, or if she is able to do so only by asserting her own total control over the child, the child's narcissism will either be unrealistically inflated or wounded.[56]

Of course the trauma of narcissism and separation wound us all: leaving home is a never-ending process and to a greater or lesser extent, we each suffer from an experience of separation where home and its comforts are either too close or too far away. But the psychotic person, while desiring otherness like Narcissus, cannot accept it. And also like Narcissus, what returns to his gaze as a scintillating exterior form is nothing but a hallucination: the product of imperfectly integrated drives. Because the drives have not been deflected away from auto-eroticism, the subject cannot accept a real object to substitute for the hallucinated one. Thus the ideal never becomes an external object, just as Narcissus was for his mother the phallic ideal (part of her body, her desire), and not a separate object, or a separate subjectivity over and against her own. Despite the popular notion then that Narcissus was preoccupied with his own love, we should rather recognise that the myth reflects a *failure* of self-love. Narcissus on the contrary, did not go far enough along the path of subjectivity.[57]

In a developmental sense, narcissism according to Freud is the product of a new psychic action supplementing autoeroticism; a turning away towards the 'imaginary father of one's pre-history'.[58] It can be seen as a fragile meniscus-like screen put up during the process that moves the not-yet ego to differentiate itself from the not-yet object. Kristeva suggests that paradoxically, emptiness inhabits the most intimate spaces of the human psyche. Narcissism can thus be read as the Lacanian *béance* or gap of the mirror stage which is also represented by the bar between signifier and signified, indicating that the plenitude of the first object, the mother, is forever lost. If this emptiness is not maintained, the psyche will be overwhelmed by a sense of chaos, the watery surface of Narcissus' world dissolving its subject in a scintillating play of forms and appearances.

Although the story of Narcissus has a cautionary aspect in one form or another, it serves for Kristeva additionally and contrarily, I feel, as the founding moment of intellectual activity and literature. Through metaphor, the wounded Narcissan subject transfers his longing to literature – signs replete with a multitude of possibility enable him to lace together a glittering, temporary habitation. The ultimate form of estrangement therefore is language and the limpidity of syntax, submersing the derelict subject in its shifting structures and obscuring his sense of loss by proffering a jubilant identification with signs. Writing by the subject of love thus proves to be the active means whereby the narcissistic exile loses himself and finds another place. And since it deals with images and reflections, Narcissus' action also founds specularity. His unique kind of psychic space is auto-referential, taking form itself for its object. As Kristeva recognises, because he fails to see the world of imagination and seeming for what they are – merely fantasy; because he is unable to distinguish between internality and exterior perception and master his perceptions through intellectual reflection, he dies. (*Tales*: 116) Nevertheless, to a degree any creative act involves a kind of Narcissan psychosis that falls in love with its own image. The literary experience inhibits separation's mechanism, destabilising the 'same through its identification with the Other.' (*Tales*: 279) If *Tales of Love* is concerned with providing a necessary psychic space through separation, I am intrigued to discover that what fascinate Kristeva throughout this text are those case-histories in the West where separation has frequently been a *problem*. Take the example of Bataille, for instance, whose meditation on incest confuses God, the sun, and his mother's sex. Or Stendahl and Don Juan, whose fear of a phallic, devouring mother far exceeded their amorous desire. These are figures who represent a precarious, even a failed narcissism. The artist *plays* with words until he does not know where inside and outside, self and other, discourse and the 'real' begin and end. Absence and differentiation therefore, despite their connection to an Ideal, never erase an autoerotic (abject) element that continues to find shelter for itself within literature.

Ego Ideal and Ideal Ego

Kristeva tells us that the lover is a narcissist with an object. To live, Narcissus must find an ideal from a space *outside* his own. But because today we can neither assuage the narcissistic demands of our *ideal ego* nor direct them towards an *ego ideal* we experience his suffering.

Because the old distinctions between inside and outside, and 'me' and 'you' have disintegrated, we cannot constitute ourselves as subjects. Needless to say, while I have argued that moments of ambivalence between conceptual entities are indeed privileged by Kristeva in philosophy, but equally in literature, it is also abundantly clear that where *all* is ambiguity, and where psychic space is radically lacking, abjection is the inevitable result. The relation she now establishes between ego ideal and ideal ego is symptomatic of an interesting turn to extol, against Lacan, the virtues of non-erotic, 'divine' love – which, incidentally, a woman may know more about – if we are to believe Kristeva. That at least is what I read as the challenge being extended to philosophy and psychoanalysis here.

The very first ego ideal, the site for what Freud later named the superego,[59] a site of proscriptions and ideals, lies in a transformation of early narcissism and the redirection of its energies towards another entity or structure within the self: 'man has here again shown himself incapable of giving up a satisfaction he once enjoyed,' writes Freud. 'He is not willing to forgo the narcissistic perfection of his childhood ... he seeks to recover it in the new form of an ego ideal. What he projects before him as his ideal is the substitute for the lost narcissism of his childhood in which he was his own ideal.'[60] In Freud's *Group Psychology*, love, hypnosis, and group identification all provide instances where the subject substitutes another person or persons for his ego ideal. By comparison, the ideal ego comes to have a different resonance. Bearing connotations of infantile regression, the term *Idealich* is suggested by Freud in 'On Narcissism' and 'The Ego and the Id', although he does not yet clearly distinguish between this term and that of the ego ideal. The difference between the narcissistic ego libido of the ideal ego and the new form of the ego ideal receives further clarification when in *Group Psychology* the former is related to the 'father one would want to *be*', and the second, to the figure one would want to *have* or be like. According to Kristeva, the latter position occupied by the ego ideal may contain the seeds of a loving, idealising identification that is ultimately superior to a hostile desire to take the other's place (that is, to be the mother's lover) which satisfies the needs of the ideal ego.

Other theorists have associated the omnipotence of narcissism with a primary relation to the mother more emphatically.[61] Lacan locates the ideal ego in the mirror stage of the imaginary, and it unquestionably has a tendency by many psychoanalysts to be viewed as more regressive than the function performed by the ego ideal. However, even the activity of idealisation involves narcissism: 'when we are in love a considerable amount of narcissistic libido overflows on to the object'.[62] Idealisation tends to aggrandise the object. In talking about the mating patterns of male and female sticklebacks, Lacan describes this 'closed world of two' as an intersection of object libido and narcissistic libido: 'Love is a phenomenon which takes place on the imaginary level, and which produces a veritable subduction of the symbolic, a sort of annihilation, of perturbation of the function of the ego-ideal.'[63] In love, this ego ideal configuration (the other who is not my ego) comes to be placed on the plane of imaginary narcissism and identified with the ideal ego, which is why love can seem like madness: 'That's what love is. It's one's own ego that one loves in love, one's own ego made real on the imaginary level.'[64] If separation and absence are primary conditions for loving identification, all the same, they are never free from an association with narcissistic *fusion* – a delightful or alarming sense of sinking, of being overwhelmed by the presence of another who can hardly be distinguished from oneself. In love we leave the space of one's own only to return by another route.

Agreeing that falling in love gratifies narcissism, Kristeva would however, stress the *non-erotic* ground of love. Her critique of Plato (and by extension, the wider discourse of philosophy) had led her to suggest that a violent, erotic urge to mastery inhabited thought. Unlike Luce Irigaray who calls for women to elaborate a new erotics of the divine through a language that would embody woman's 'flesh and blood',[65] Kristeva's relation to the divine – an affective identification with the Imaginary Father – is founded on agape, on a relationship that does not see the other as a sexual object to be possessed or devoured. The transference to the Imaginary Father makes us *strangers* in love where the path to the ideal passes through and sustains narcissism and the body, but does not make a permanent home there. Kristeva finds the mechanism to establish a *distance* from the more assimilating aspects of narcissism in a new perspective on the work of the drives. Considering this shift in representation where drives once read as destructive in *Revolution in Poetic Language* are now seen as requiring an attachment to a transforming ideal, the manner in which they are divested of libido is of great interest.

Along with incorporating a part-object of desire, the mother's breast, *Tales of Love* tells us we also incorporate a non-object, a model through the mother's orientation to an other. As well as gratifying needs then, the oral stage provides the first intimation of loving space. Thus the space of identification (*Einfühlung*) enables orality to be read by the child as having a prototypical form or pattern – it invests oral gratification with the potential for eventual transformation into a site for receiving the speech ('food') of the Other. Such an emphasis on a metaphorical non-object distinguishes Kristeva's reading of the nature of the love relationship from Lacan's, who by contrast reads the inauguration of the *symbolic* as establishing the ego ideal, identification and desire.[66] Kristeva's One, the Imaginary Father, is located *prior* to the mirror stage where my primitive desire to devour has been redirected through a metaphorical register on to a psychic level: 'In being able to receive the other's words, to assimilate, repeat, and reproduce them, I become like him: One. A subject of enunciation. Through psychic osmosis/identification. Through love.' (*Tales*: 26) Through metaphorical identification, drives have been linked to signifying ideals. We can see then that sublimation, where object libido is displaced on to a non-sexual aim, is at work at the earliest stages of narcissism. At this stage the ego ideal looks to be the superior locus for renewal and individuation within the psyche. But what is to prevent the ego ideal which Lacan links with sublimation and the Law (the symbolic) from becoming just as overbearing as the narcissistic demand for immediate gratification, driving the subject with an impossible set of goals and proscriptions? Besides, isn't all our idealising on love merely the rehearsal of an earlier narcissism? How can ego ideal and ideal ego ever be any more than an antagonistic couple? Finally, what is there about 'being in love' that could restrain the aggressive, incorporating path of the drives?

These questions lie behind Kristeva's attempt to rearticulate a third term that will reconstruct the ego ideal so that it satisfies the needs of narcissism and the body as well as redirecting that narcissism on to signifying its relation to the Ideal, the Other. Such a term would have to avoid simply reproducing the struggle for power and mastery that Kristeva found in Plato and that Hegel believed to be fundamental to creative existence. Thus when we begin to place all-consuming narcissism and a demanding ideal in relationship, what emerges in the human psyche is 'lovesickness', where the subject does not yet know how to be, because he defines his existence as '"I" *is* because *I love*'. (*Tales*: 169) '*To love* comes in here in the place of *to be* and *as*: copula and comparison, existence and image, truth and deception. A drifting together of the symbolic, the real, and the imaginary.' (*Tales*: 162) 'To be' and 'to have' need to be mediated by a missing third term (that of the imaginary): to seem, or to be like. We know that the Oedipus complex is characterised by having the phallus ('Who has it?'), and that the pre-Oedipal stage of primary narcissism defines itself in terms of being the phallus ('Who is it?'). (*Tales*: 47) 'Being like' by comparison, may well be a condition that challenges the fixity of both possession *and* narcissism, particularity *and* fusion, ego ideal *and* ideal ego, since it introduces the desire for 'unbeing' into identification through defining love as a non-objectal, non-verifiable (imaginary) transference. The drives are cathected on to a form or metaphor. Being in its most primitive form for Kristeva is being as form, act or metaphor: 'being like', in other words. In this sense, neither Freud nor Lacan's categories ('the father one would want to be'; 'the father one would want to have') appear capable of articulating the *unhomeliness* that love is.

For it is only when love is regarded as a state of *unbeing* that the permanent sense of mystery we have of each other when we love may be preserved. Neither becomes an object to be mastered or fully known by the other since love restores an enigmatic form of appearance to its subjects and their speech. While we are never completely at home with ourselves or each other, transference love effects a rearrangement of psychic and discursive space to provide a temporary resting place from which we depart once more, refreshed and transformed. Nevertheless such a deconstruction of being does not valorise separation. As Kristeva comments, the kind of love under discussion is something absolute into which the subject falls and is 'without doubt the maximal defence against castration: "If I love like this, nothing can happen to me; I will neither see you, nor be seen."' ('SN': 10) Who/m do I love when I am (in) love? Myself, or another? Metaphor, like being in love, 'oscillates between a full and an empty sense'.[67] Its fusion of semic fields mimes, even as it calls into being, amorous fusion. True agape is a confused struggle between flesh and spirit, just as Bernard of Clairvaux's battles with the flesh still depended for their spiritual intensity on the flesh's existence, and therefore on the continual passage between ideal ego and ego ideal. Love like abjection is an ambivalent state, yet without its permanent dejection. Its uncertainties are also what make it 'feminine'.

I find a number of intriguing differences in the positions taken by Lacan and Kristeva on love. For both theorists, identification propels the subject to take up a place in relation to the signifier of the Other. (*Tales*: 37) Whereas Lacan puts the agent responsible for identification of the ego ideal in the metonymic realm of desire with its 'phantasmatic *narrative*' (*Tales*: 30) and hence in submission to the symbolic and the object *a* (in essence the part-object), for Kristeva, the object of identification lies not only prior to the mirror stage, but is also in process, thereby avoiding a situation where idealisation under the Phallus can become tyrannical. This manifests itself in the analytical situation where the analyst is still seen as a desiring subject, yet as one who also stands in the place of a 'non-desiring but loving father [who] reconciles the ideal Ego with the Ego Ideal'. (*Tales*: 30) And it is the analyst's 'temporary' but 'effective mergings' which precipitate the splitting that will establish the psyche in permanent relation to an other. (*Tales:* 31) Thus Kristeva retains Lacan's 'spaltung', but redefines the object as one of transference and love rather than desire and fantasy. Desire as we know privileges lack, whereas affect, which comes to the fore in any consideration of the non-object, 'while acknowledging the latter [lack, absence], gives greater importance to the movement toward the other and to mutual *attraction.*' (*Tales*: 155) That is, the impetus to merge *without aggressive capture of one by the other* rather than separation as such is of primary importance in the constitution of a loving subject.

Kristeva's critique is once again directed at what she noted in *Phaedrus* as 'the male rush toward phallic domination'. (*Tales*: 62) While the analyst is still desired, she is also a site that draws and attracts metaphoricity. Here, the subject not only desires the other, he *identifies* with the Other (the subject's ego ideal); he *belongs* to it.[68] Such a sense of belonging, however transitory, distinguishes Kristeva's 'feminine' reading of love as founded upon a drive that in the first instance relinquishes sexual conquest in order to gratify a new kind of intimacy, from Lacan's. *Tales of Love* is not arguing that women are better able to love than men or that women have not been loved as they should. What is being suggested here, I think, is that women have superior rhetorical force as philosophers if, and only if, they refuse to privilege an *erotic* relation to the body. That is, if they read language as a love affair with metaphors rather than objects and bodies. What is required is a *feminine* conflation of narcissism (ideal ego) and idealisation (ego ideal), a transference relation to the Imaginary Father whose impetus defuses the body's libido into words embodied with affect that *women's* predisposition towards narcissism enables them to represent. The topography of love crosses masculine and feminine bodies seemingly indifferently, but in the process leaves behind an obscure, imaginary thickening which the female voyager may possibly be better placed to 'see'.

Women and Feminism

Kristeva is anxious to find a place for the female theorist within her own synthetic reconstruction of philosophy's material base: that is, within philosophy as amorous, as opposed to erotic rhetoric. To repeat, her subject generally speaking is universal, his speech parcelling out masculine and feminine through the play of signification. Kristeva believes that if language let itself be transformed by affect as the new space afforded by love, the violence and mastery implicit in the will to knowledge would be subdued. Universality in discourse would then reconstitute itself as a genuine play of sexual differences within and between subjects. Masculine and feminine are thus closer to a notion of positionality than they are to discrete identities, even imaginary ones. Yet in order to be consistent with a concomitant emphasis on woman's different relation to the Phallus (to meaning, power, and discourse), Kristeva's enunciation carries a marked *surplus*, a 'discreet trace', which privileges the position of a female intellectual and philosopher whose ambitious exploration of the unknown aims to take her to the boundaries of critical thought. For she also believes that once language truly learns to be at home with affect, women will no longer have to be the repressed other of speech. Their understanding of the feminine may in fact then make them more acute listeners than men. The utterance of *Tales of Love*, its content, offers a history of the discourses of love in the West. Its enunciation by contrast, offers an implicit feminine commentary on that history.

At one level however, Kristeva's discourse has still internalised a conventional anxiety about the female body and a conventional longing for a realm of amatory and spiritual ideals where feminine sexuality is excluded. When she sets up the terminology for what she regards as a necessary triangulation, it is perhaps unfortunate that the third should be a loving 'Father', but also a reflection of the fact that mothers still maintain much greater investments in primary care and bonding. The father in this sense is both form and something more empirical: a parent to whom is addressed a discourse of love that will situate the child in a place not too far away from home, but not too close either. Kristeva's attitude to women in the text is predicated less on an oscillation between hostility and fascination than a recognition that if we are to avoid the condition of perpetual prematurity, in order to become subjects of speech and love, in order to speak about love, we need to leave home. Irrespective of gender a fundamental difficulty in achieving subjectivity is isolated here; a difficulty that seems to be more acute today than ever before. Even worse, Kristeva maintains that separation is more difficult for women than men: 'the dramas of individuation demand of her such a violent rejection of the mother, and by the mother, that in the hatred of the loved object a woman immediately finds herself in a known and intolerable country.' (*Tales*: 373) Might not the hostility we see revealed in her writing towards unrepresentable maternal identity be a reflection of the difficulty any woman has in separating from her mother, and the lifelong ambivalence she often feels for her? Separation from the maternal home is what enables us to construct our own ego ideals in relation to an Other; we cannot recognise self-reflection as such until we have ceased to be ideals for our mothers (or fathers).

Again though, it is the nature of separation that is in question. Separation is not the unproblematic experience we anticipate because it comprehends both intimacy *and* absence; oneness *and* alterity. It is surely not the radical separation from the body that Platonic discourse struggles to achieve. That is why I cannot entirely agree with John Lechte who argues that in *Tales of Love* the fundamental question is separation, defined as absence or emptiness. While recognising the primary drama of separation undergone by the subject and the need for a new understanding of space and its relation to affect and the body, I feel there is a further aspect of this drama that Lechte does not discuss, which is the text's emphasis on fusion. Lechte's reading by contrast appears to represent the kind of separation implied by primary narcissism as a new form of Absolute Ideal. What I hear equally clearly when I read Kristeva is another voice that knowingly privileges femininity or, more precisely, *a feminine relation to the theoretical object*, despite appearances to the contrary. I have the impression that Kristeva believes the female analyst may be better placed to play the role of a loving Other to her patients precisely because of her recognition of the intense difficulty a woman experiences in separating from her mother. Conversely her possibly greater narcissistic attachments to an autoerotic space may make her more receptive to the narcissistic investments of loving speech, as well as more determined to sublimate that narcissism through transference to an Ideal. The register in which Kristeva has chosen to write demands a high degree of sublimation or abstraction, so the challenge becomes one of finding an inflexional mode through which to express this contrary voice: a voice, moreover, which must somehow take the question of woman and love 'beyond the looking glass' even as it will continue to inhabit the whole range of associations that the looking glass brings to mind.

Tales of Love spends very little time ostensibly discussing women. Kristeva's history of amatory discourse in the West runs from Plato through Shakespeare and the troubadors to Bataille with only a handful of female names: Diotima, Metis, the Shulamite, the Virgin

Mary, Juliet, and Jeanne Guyon. Metis is described as 'a wily agent of the symbolic within the maternal continent ...'; (*Tales*: 73) Jeanne Guyon's silence is linked to archaic narcissism; (*Tales*: 307) androgynes, like lesbians, refuse to recognise difference, fusing heaven and earth together.[69] (*Tales*: 70) Only the virginal Diotima and the Shulamite woman are held up as examples worthy of emulation and identification. The shepherd and his love in the Song of Songs are the first two autonomous loving subjects in the history of the West, in Kristeva's view. Subject and addressee of the utterance of love, they are never united, but always separated by a distance: now pursuing, now in flight, it is the other's absence that they desire. The Shulamite woman is thus 'the first woman to be sovereign [and subject] before her loved one.' (*Tales*: 99) The priestess Diotima in Plato's *Symposium* by contrast, is rather like the Virgin because she presents love as both desexualised and idealised.[70] (*Tales*: 72) For Kristeva, she has a uniquely feminine attitude to philosophy because her love is based not on immediate fleshly gratifications, but on 'the production of ... works aiming for immortality.' (*Tales*: 72) Diotima's vision of sublime beauty is passed on to the male philosopher, but not before Kristeva has insisted that the feminine desire for procreation, sublimated in the quest for knowledge and beauty, is the privileged receptacle for a particularly jubilant vision of philosophy's object: 'Is the amorous philosopher a disciple of a visionary daughter? The idealist is the daughter of the dazzling, invisible father.' (*Tales*: 75) A woman is here given the privileged role of intermediary between ideal and eros, where eros is read on the side of the masculine, not the feminine. The cost of this role is undoubtedly a loss of sexuality for Diotima, but she has established nonetheless a unique relationship to knowledge. Kristeva could well have Diotima (or the female philosopher) in mind when she refers to Plato's figure of the 'daemon': 'This yearning for fusion with the supreme Good, a yearning at the same time for immortality, this desire for that which is lacking and sends its emanations through the body of the young man is considered an *intermediary*. Plato calls it a "daemon," by which he means the messenger, the go-between, the medium of synthesis between two separate domains.' (*Tales*: 63) Ostensibly a commentary on the nature of the search for the Good, we can read the desire which animates the young man akin to the way Kristeva perceives desire operating in the woman who philosophises. She is a privileged figure who mediates between the domains of semiotic and symbolic, drawing on the multiple range of subject positions (aggressive, restorative, penetratingly analytic, coolly remote, narcissistic, passionate) to articulate the multiple reflections cast by her theoretical object: an object for which she has a more than passing affection!

So to suggest as does Kaja Silverman that language acquisition is 'now completely under paternal jurisdiction' and that the semiotic 'seems to have fallen by the wayside'[71] is to ignore the feminisation of philosophy and language that *Tales of Love* declares. Kristeva is quick to criticise the phallic master/slave struggle that eventuates under any repressive system of thought: that is, wherever a discourse on idealism or metaphysics ignores its investments in the mother-tongue. This is why her emphasis on gratifying both ideal ego and ego ideal is so compelling because it represents the perpetual oscillation between narcissism and identification (sublimation, in Diotima's case) that identity and *reading* is. Foregrounding the notion of a loving father or reinstating the paternal metaphor is the most obvious narrative in *Tales of Love* and fundamental to its thesis, but surely not the only narrative. Kristeva may not valorise woman as phenomenal identity in this text, yet we can hardly attribute the force of the following suggestion to a theorist who turns a blind eye to her *own* feminine investments:

> It is far from certain that woman be more narcissistic than man, as Freud maintained. But for a woman to be able to redirect the insatiable craving for a fine distinctive image toward her inner bosom or, in more psychological terms, her inner solitude, in the exquisite pain of contemplation, daydreaming, – or even hallucination – that amounts to a true resolution of narcissism that is not at all erotic (in the Greek sense of the word) but is, quietly or fanatically, wholly amorous. Dissipation of the glance within itself, fusion and permutation of the one and the other, neither seeing nor seen, neither subject nor object; love in the feminine, against which mystical experiences stumble, coils up around the mother-child's tight embrace, the blurr of images prior to the 'mirror stage.' A swallowing up of the imagination by the real, the emergence of the imagination under the aegis of the symbolic, the beginning and absolute of the ideal – this feminine facet of love is perhaps the most subtle sublimation of the secret, psychotic ground of hysteria .... (*Tales*: 112–13)

A narcissism without calling itself as such: here we have displayed the narrator's feminine signature, her personal investments staked out yet *mediated* through a comment on the way intellectual reflection constitutes itself *per se* and additionally, how it constitutes itself most fruitfully in certain women. For it seems to me that this particular focus on amorous reflection as problematising subject and object, and as composing both fusion and dissipation, is not merely linked to a female resolution of reflection and therefore something optional, but is constitutive for Kristeva of *all* reflection. The 'beginning and absolute of the ideal' locates the feminine at the very heart of love and knowledge; a feminine that places *some* women (especially herself) in a potentially advantageous position. Just as the hysteric is able to take herself for someone else, just as she is able to establish a relation to an idealisable object even if she tends to deny her difference from that object, the female intellectual is presumably in a better position to speak of love than anyone else: provided of course that unlike the hysteric, she 'move away'; that she sublimate her narcissistic longings through contemplation of an other/Other.

I do not think however, that Kristeva is a feminist. She is clearly hostile to the feminist assumptions regarding group identity (even if critical theory has pluralised the question of identity), political projects, and the continued emphasis on oppositional narratives. She does not set out to explicitly privilege women in her research, although a very strong implicit discourse in the text does reveal a surprising degree of enthusiasm, even commitment to fashioning a distinct and valued place from which a female intellectual may ask questions about theoretical thought. Kristeva appears to affirm the particularity of feminine experience while insisting that it accept the constraints of language. Hence the topography of this special place of reflection still rests on many of the exclusions and preconditions of a Lacanian discourse on subjectivity: namely that castration (loss) is universal and that women assume a different position in relation to the phallus, which then makes them in Kristeva's eyes, *potentially* the most qualified to interrogate and displace truth. Yet in conforming to the terms of the psychoanalytical narrative, she also manages to critique them, to make them strange. I cannot tell whether ultimately she finds privileging the feminine, or estranging our domesticated habits of thought the most compelling. Suffice it to say that *Tales of Love* is comprised of two imbricated discourses: the first, an explicit formalised narrative on amatory styles which reveals the fragility of all identity and which strips love of its culturally normative representation even as it renegotiates a path to the Ideal; and the second, a more surreptitious and personally engaged commentary. Love problematises the referent and leads me out of habitual patterns of speech into a place where my identity founders but is also renewed. I can claim a limited position of privilege for the female intellectual, but only if this position is in constant transformation towards an Other. When the non-objectal nature of transference is forgotten and the female intellectual or the body is elevated to the position of a Universal category, it becomes as oppressive and phallic as any other representation. Thus in reading Kristeva on love, the demands of my ideal ego and my ego ideal are gratified in this complex kind of textual doubling. And if I submit to the terms of her discourse, through transference I find my subjectivity revived; not through a transcendent experience (or at least as it has traditionally been represented), but within 'the infinity of the signifier.' (*Tales*: 277)

Conclusion: Love as Transference

In the final analysis, it is love (and being) we are *talking* about: the utterance precedes the propositional act. (*Tales*: 268) Where subjectivity is set in motion with the Other through utterance, modifying my speech and my being, the transference relation becomes the privileged site of exchange: 'The univocity of signs undergoes equivocality and is resolved in a more or less undecidable connotation when the subject of the utterance, in a state of transference (of love) toward the other transposes the same process of identification, of transference, to the units of language – the signs.' (*Tales*: 275) Spacing is here redrawn to accommodate a sublime, loving immanence/'transcendence' always already folded within the subject, whose enigmatic witness is the semiotic fire of tongues.

It is for that reason that Kristeva characterises transference as the most costly form of love relationship possible. Love in analysis is a transference that Freud in *The Interpretation of Dreams* initially called *Verschiebung*, a displacement of meaning and intensity, and later *Ubertragung*, a displacement of love toward the analyst.[72] Kristeva's understanding of the role of the analyst in psychotherapy has less to do with mastery than a passionate involvement and openness to self-transformation: 'The analyst is within love from the start, and if he forgets it he dooms himself not to perform an analysis.' (*Tales*: 13) I personally find these comments on the role of transference to be the most humane and satisfying aspects of the Kristevan corpus. What often read as Manichaean preoccupations with re-reading metaphysics on the one hand and privileging femininity on the other are to some extent mitigated by the author's tribute to the mutually transformative role played by speech in analysis. Although her Freudian-based psychoanalysis does not advocate the kind of identity for men and women that I still consider to be necessary for survival, she does insist that the analyst assist in alleviating suffering, and helping analysands to build imaginary spaces which they can inhabit: 'Help them not to suffer from being mere extras in their lives, or splinters of parceled out bodies carried along by the spate of their pleasure [or pain]. Help them, then, to speak and write themselves in unstable, open, undecidable spaces.' (*Tales*: 380) The world of seeming, when associated with a primary metaphor that calls us to life within a discourse of love for an Other offers the only possible shelter today. In light of which the strange landscape produced by poetic language and the horror of the body's uncontrollable interior find themselves accommodated within a new dwelling where Kristeva's fascination for estranging language and identity is tempered by a genuine recognition of human suffering and desire.

The ideal model of subjectivity affirmed here is that of an 'open system ... capable of innovation'.[73] Open systems presuppose a mutually transforming interchange of information where neither party is closed off to the other. The outside is not seen as a threat to be mastered or feared, but rather as a difference to remain in dialogue with, perhaps even eventually to be introjected by the psyche without excessive naturalisation or amputation of its intrinsic alterity.[74] It is at this point that Kristeva's critique of narratives of appropriation and desire, particularly when those tendencies remain unacknowledged by psychoanalysis and philosophy, becomes most acute. When there is genuine exchange beyond the pain of separation there exists a space of play, where we indulge in games of seeming and imagination. Lacan had taken Freud's *fort/da* game as the prototype of playful desire, yet clearly, even while the infant experiences loss and translates that loss through play into a primitive binary language, he is *master* of his own game. Like play, the symbolic masters presence and absence.[75] Kristeva reads play as something more costly. 'Imagination succeeds,' she writes, 'where the narcissist becomes hollowed out and the paranoid fails.' (*Tales*: 381)

The process of imagination or seeming that underlies the analytical act of love, unlike pathological narcissism or paranoia, gives the object, the other, a subjectivity. Paranoid thought as we have seen in Kristeva's reading of Hegel in Chapter 3, amputates the object and attempts to master it through analysis. It rests on a fantasised *petit objet a*; a part object which we both desire to fix forever and find elusive. Here the superego rules, and idealising sets its stakes so high that the desired object faces silence or erasure. Paranoia is an ossifying of narcissism. The narcissist recognises his specular reflection alone, therefore he can only know emptiness; his emerging love turns to paranoia and mistaking himself for the other, he dies – literally or spiritually. Freud too couldn't recognise his desire, and substituted his fantasy ('Dora wishes to give me a kiss') for the narrative of transference and counter-transference. Thus what remains according to Kristeva is the imagination; not unanalysed so that it comes to echo Nietzsche's power to the imagination, but as an endless series of creative illusions, redemptive works in progress constructed jointly by two loving, speaking subjects. He and she? Me and you? Ego and ideal? Ultimately transference love renders such distinctions meaningless. I could suggest that privileging a dialogical interactive relationship reflects a profoundly feminine inclination, but to do so in any final sense would be to surrender to a sentimental, romanticised reading of woman. Kristeva's later writing on the place of woman is undoubtedly more 'racist' than in *Revolution in Poetic Language*, but even when we discover an insistent feminine voice that has managed to withstand a horror of the maternal, its claims to identity are immediately challenged by the provisionality of interpretation. When the analyst chooses to write about love, she becomes fully implicated. Drawn in through transference, she temporarily loses her female specificity and becomes engaged in a more generous, co-operative venture between two subjects who confront each other face to face, passing through the silvery pool of Narcissus to a place whose form we perceive arising out of our wake to greet us.

5

Changing the Alphabet: Event as Revelation

At every turn Julia Kristeva has attempted to articulate new forms that will host the human experience of exile. Whether traversing the subjective body or plumbing the interiors of speech, her writing probes those territories that gleam on the edge of consciousness. The fire of tongues that ignites in every speaking being when the resources of the unconscious are imaginatively translated into signs expresses Kristeva's belief that although becoming a subject requires a journey away from our maternal origins, these can be reinvoked in incandescent fashion through representation. However, despite a readjustment of focus in recent years, Kristeva still argues that whatever the ecstatic illumination afforded by the material richness of signs, it is always played out against a backdrop of emptiness, violence and death. In Chapter 1 I used the image of the unreadable map to illustrate the way literature and poetic language intensify the experience of separation and rebirth. Without experiencing a sense of disorientation, of dislocation, we remain prisoners of banality. Kristeva seems to believe then that even if all subjects must undergo separation, to experience it as a perpetual state of life makes one vulnerable to a superior form of knowlege. It opens us to a new, imaginative reconstruction of 'speaking in tongues'. But although she makes use of Christian terminology, Kristeva does not view speaking in tongues as an encounter with a *real* Sublime Body. The resources of the unconscious dissolve all forms of personality and identity and sweep us up into a dazzling *void* in which we hear not the tongues of angels but 'foreign words ... [that] play the part of seraphim ..., flocks of angels ... [that help us] soar through secret skies.' (*TOM*: 166) God is the logic of the unconscious that produces an 'infinity of languages'. Thus Kristeva privileges the unhomely nature of subjective existence, where the primary grounding in identity is represented as an estranging encounter in language that indelibly wounds the subject.

Curiously though, what will sustain this wounded being is language itself, because language can translate subjective estrangement from a maternal body into a host of signs. We can *speak* about our exile. Language therefore, as Derrida would say, is *pharmarkon*, both salve and poison, agent of estrangement and comforter. However, there is a further twist to Kristeva's argument, because she also argues that the most affective kinds of language can actually intensify estrangement. Poetic language maximises the homelessness of the subject by exposing him to the void that supports speech and identity. More than the language of social convention and communication, it dramatises the origins of subjectivity. So it would seem from Kristeva's point of view that writers and artists whose task it is to be permanent travellers lead a precarious existence on the edge of meaning. That the creative person frequently experiences instability or alienation is hardly a new recognition, but it is new to suggest that through an immersion in signs, the artist both encounters emptiness and punctuates it. Thus art and literature bear witness to a deeper kind of exile, but just as the ordinary individual is able to express himself or herself through the resources of language, art and literature offer us a catharsis too, only this time a more sustaining one.

In Part I of this book I drew a distinction between the kinds of estrangement that occur within language and those forms of estrangement that present themselves as occurring when language fails. Lacan and Kristeva argue that the entry into language is always marked by estrangement; Kristeva further believes that this traumatic entry into speech is intensified yet somehow relieved by poetic language. Both are theorists of modernity who assume that those moments when language fails, or seems to fail, can lead to madness. The visionary remains isolated in the vision (which for Kristeva is illusory anyway) unless he or she translates the experience into words. Likewise, unless those marginalised by culture *speak* their marginalisation, they remain trapped in narcissism. Women and aliens for instance have the potential to enrich cultural life because they stand for difference, yet without the resources of language creatively or analytically disposed, their potentially subversive signs of difference melt away. Neither Lacan nor Kristeva accept that the world of the book closes at the end of the day; that there are times when language rolls back to reveal a world of forms and objects which lovingly draw the watcher into their apprehension. For modernity, whatever exists outside language is inexplicable and life-threatening. It is Lacan's Real, Kristeva's semiotic without the mediating symbolic, Freud's drive of the organism towards extinction.

Yet what intrigues me about Julia Kristeva's writing is that it is sometimes contradictory, apparently advocating an encounter with the very mode of experience its assumptions had ruled out. Kristeva advocates a subjectivity always already bounded by language, but she is just as drawn to examine states where language fails: in fact she is fascinated by them. She studies forms of writing where people have teetered on the edge of meaninglessness or where the somatic has become the only medium to express affect. Dostoevsky, Nerval, Duras, Baudelaire, Madame Guyon and Narcissus are figures who were all infatuated with the enigmatic, the inexplicable. Despite the fact that excepting Narcissus they also survived their infatuation with something outside language, translating it into signs, their stories equally indicate the limits of a theory of language that claims everything belongs in its world. Instead, we recognise that what is being dramatised here is a confusion between states of experience within language, and states of experience outside it. The notion of a boundary confusion is not limited to our modern life of course, but Kristeva along with other contemporary theorists has made a point of celebrating the impossibility of ever distinguishing inside from outside. However, when she collapses the distinction between inside and outside, her ultimate intention is to site this collapse within the unconscious, which as Lacan has told us, is language, and as Kristeva has added, is the semiotic coursing through language. If we are still like Yeats forced to ask how we can tell the dancer from the dance, our suspense according to Kristeva derives less from a recognition that the self can be both in language and swept up into a moment outside it, and more from assenting to the linguistic hegemony of the unconscious. Her fascination with moments where language fails is thus rescued at the last moment by an appeal to the always already linguistic nature of the unconscious.

In the second part of the book, I have explored the effects of the hegemony of the unconscious. Underlying my exploration is the assumption that although language stretched beyond and through its limits is necessary for any renewal of thought, creative or intellectual, in order for the full resources of speech to be accessed, language still needs the idea of an exterior. Kristeva's revolutionary conception of space which I discussed in Chapter 3 is a remarkable appropriation of a metaphysics of presence to Freudian drive theory. Seeking after moments of transformation but resistant to their metaphysical context, Kristeva argues in *Revolution in Poetic Language* that language and subjectivity are renewed through the semiotic processes engendered by the drives. Meaning is thus initiated through the infinite movement of the drives, which by their very action radically reconquest space. A poetics of language therefore is the corollary for a poetics of space, since the action of spacing now becomes the agent of transformation that was once owned by God (or the notion of the transcendent). Yet as I have also shown, when this theory is interpreted literally, it reduces Mallarmé's poetry to a heap of rubble. The impulse that compels poets to explore the unnamable just doesn't sit easily with Freudian psychoanalysis, and all the more so with Kristeva's accommodation of poetic language to the sex drives.

Furthermore, when the sex drives are viewed as inseparable from the death drives, and when the death drives are the agents of the unrepresentable real, there is a hostile confrontation between an interior always under threat from a destructive exterior. This sense of aggression towards the outside suggests that Kristeva has overdefined the real as unrepresentable and the symbolic as its only restraint. In her schematisation, the semiotic tends to merge with the real as a seductive danger for the subject whereas the symbolic appears as the oppressive but necessary structuring device that helps the 'murderous' body pass into language.[1] It is interesting that in later work Kristeva attempts to address this confrontation by giving a larger space, indeed a redemptive role, to the imagination. Kristeva's understanding of the imagination though is still consistent with her ongoing commitment to semiotics and to Freudianism. That is, for her it is the drives represented in the unconscious through semiosis that enervate language and language of the imagination most especially. There is no exterior reservoir which may wash the imagination with an unexpected freshness, no surprise, wonder, or even estrangement that drive theory cannot account for.

Nonetheless, while I feel sceptical when a direct and immediate causality is established between the sexed body and the imagining, or dreaming body, I share Kristeva's interest in the relation between eros, language and the devouring body that I have studied in Chapter 4. No theorist has explored more intimately the antipathy towards the material body that we discover represented in texts ranging from 'Stabat Mater' to *Powers of Horror*. It is to her credit that while presenting a disturbing picture of widespread hatred towards the figure of the mother, Kristeva attempts to argue that the many forms of cultural abjection aimed at femininity in fact are due to a more profound psychic struggle which arises when a boundary is being established between the subject's inside and outside. An interesting illustration of this disjunction appears in Céline's *Voyage to the End of the Night*. When Robinson expresses his contempt for love, Madelon assumes it's because of her body, or because she doesn't keep her house clean enough. But Robinson says no, his indifference arises from something far more profound that comes from 'everyone, everything'. Unfortunately Céline combines a representation of boundary confusion with a hatred of women, and Kristeva equally finds it difficult to separate the two experiences, since she believes that for matter to become 'porous' rather than devouring, language must pulverise the female body. Only in this way are the Robinsons and Madelons able to merge, 'she and him, him and her, neither nor, in a counting process'.[2]

In order to allow a support for this strange kind of merging, even metamorphosis, of identity, Kristeva found it necessary to stage the reintroduction of the imagination. The Imaginary Father represented in *Tales of Love* reflects Kristeva's attempt to tie the imagination to the drives and thus lessen their capacity for destruction. But although she may well have assimilated a romantic view of Art as predicated on suffering and loss, Kristeva reinterprets the work of the imagination or the imaginary as being one of learning to incorporate a form or model *before* an object. In this way she is able to intervene between devouring eros, ultimately derived from a hostile real, and the austerity of symbolic law by means of a redemptive third term. The world of *seeming*, of luminous appearances, appears before the sense of an object separate from and exterior to myself, and because I learn to incorporate a form along with my mother's milk, I am prepared for the eventual identification with non-objects (words) I must make in order to survive as a subject. Additionally, the term of Imaginary Father recognises that there must still be a privileged founding moment around which language and identity cohere, a mysterious externality that preserves a distinction between inside and outside even as it dissolves boundaries and borders between one identity and another.

It is significant that the moment of dissolution initiated by a loving father-figure is articulated by a woman, and throughout this book I have suggested that the various forms of confusion of identity that Kristeva frequently refers to may in turn be viewed as a kind of trope for the woman who wishes to be an intellectual. Woman's different relation to her body and her unique capacity for bearing children have afforded her a different relation to cultural and social discourse. So when a woman wishes to both participate in intellectual discourse and to retain a sense of her female singularity, she finds herself, in Lacanian terms, both wanting to have and to be the phallus. In Kristeva's case, this problematic seems to shape itself around wanting to argue with the master thinkers of philosophy while retaining a feminine autobiographical signature. What results is an almost unthinkable paradigm that only avoids out and out confrontation between 'masculine' mind and 'feminine' body by appealing to a transference or metamorphosis that is non-objectal, or linguistic. Yet it is precisely because of its unthinkable nature that the figure of the female intellectual may be able to illuminate the contemporary experience of the collapse of boundaries and limits precipitated by the death of God and the failure of the notion of the transcendent.

However, although being different obviously affords a unique perspective from which to describe it, performing an enigmatic identification with the condition of estrangement alongside speaking about it also raises serious questions about the analytical reach of Kristeva's discourse. In Chapter 3, I showed how Kristeva's critique of the State, in opening it up to the infinite, privileged a mode of explanation where the *énoncé* could not be clearly separated from the *énonciation*. That is, the speaker becomes crucially implicated in the object spoken about to the point where it is impossible to distinguish one entity from another. Modernity has made a point of acquiescing to just such a truth when it endorses the shifting point of enunciation and its effect on the object, but Kristeva, while performatively endorsing this 'truth' in her own work, finds herself in conceptual difficulties when she is lead to state that the dissolution of boundaries is equally a problem for contemporary life.[3] Many of the patients she sees are so-called borderline cases, people whose failure to gain a sense of stability manifests itself in somatic and relationship disorders, or those in whom boundaries fail altogether as in psychosis or schizophrenia. But if the analyst is fascinated with marginal experiences, indeed makes them a crucial point of reference in her work, how then is she to help those who are made ill because of them? What analytical concepts have the efficacy to cure when the analysis is infused with a performance of disease? Furthermore, if the analogical is equated with the ontological as Kristeva states explicitly in her study of Proust, how does the analyst or intellectual discriminate between the transformative impulse towards open systems expressed in *Tales of Love* and the destructive effects of primary hatred we find in her most recent novel, *The Old Man and the Wolves*? The possibility of endless regression is a real one, and in what follows I will examine some of Kristeva's strategies that without fully avoiding this danger, may go some way towards alleviating it.

The Old Man and the Wolves: 'I loose my secret sorrows like packs of hounds against things and people'.

In a city somewhere in Eastern Europe named Santa Varvara (Santa Barbara in the French original), an old man is watching the invasion of his country by packs of wolves. Septicius Clarus is a boundary creature, a watcher whose visionary powers give him a heightened awareness of the destruction that threatens his society from within and without. For the wolves are not merely real creatures who devour people and animals; they inhabit people from the inside too, ravaging their psyches and turning them against each other. A journalist, Stephanie Delacour is commissioned by her editor in Paris to write a story on the invasion of the wolves, but as she discovers the complexity of evil in Santa Varvara, Stephanie's reporting turns into a mourning for the loss of her father and the Old Man, and ends with a challenge towards all forms of corruption: 'I turn my key in the door with the alert assurance of a detective. Expect no quarter. I hate the wolves, and now I've got their measure.' (*TOM*: 183) *The Old Man and the Wolves* is about the experience of death and loss that confronts the modern world. In Kristeva's second novel, first published in French in 1991, the writer asks what exactly is it that binds us to one another? Is it the sex drive which turns into hatred after it has trapped people together, or is it rather a desire for connection that persists beyond the impulse to hate? And if today we live at the end of an era and the beginning of a new one, what will this new world look like? What is the function of metamorphosis today?

'I resolved to tell of creatures being metamorphosed into new forms', writes Ovid beginning his *Metamorphoses*, and Kristeva chooses his words to open her modern version of the dramas of transformation. Ovid's stories are full of passion, pain and joy, but his life-affirming narrative, precisely because it is a narrative, preserves the integrity of the original moment of transgression as well as the new form attained through metamorphosis. As Kristeva writes, 'faced with the power of any divinity, ... human beings are helpless and, in their helplessness, change shape. And their transformation produces a story, and time strikes out henceforward in whatever direction is required of it.' (*TOM*: 182) Metamorphosis is a universal experience: even outside the parameters of fiction we see its effects in the capacity of language to enrich and extend the resources of the sayable, and in the psychic transformations that are possible when people begin to love, or when they translate a random series of events in their lives into a more complex kind of 'revelation'. The trouble is though that living as we do at the end of an era where particularity is being effaced by the complex nature of post-industrial life, the cutting power of Ovid's generous vision is losing ground as identities merge into each other without leaving so much as an imprint of their previous existence. So today we experience metamorphosis without meaning, sense or memory:

> But we belong to a different world: one shape is replaced by another, every image blots out its neighbour, and man degenerates into beast through sensational tales, thrillers that don't have the time to tell an original story but merely solve a mystery, a murder tracked down by a modern detective, the Ovid of our modern metamorphoses. (*TOM*: 182)

The wolf stands for the impulse in society to savage the outsider who is different even as it implies a society in the grip of torpor and meaningless transformation. When man 'degenerates' into beast, the forms that structure human experience and connect between one time and another, one form and another, become subject to impossible stress. Our 'different world' forgets to remember those forms which once inhabited it, and in so doing, Kristeva believes, consumes itself in destructive fashion. Even our narratives pander to the popular demand for sensation without analysis, for events without revelation.

In *Civilisation and its Discontents*, Freud tries to explain the preservation of the memory-trace through the image of ancient Rome. If pictorial space could somehow be made to show the different buildings that have occupied the same position in Rome since time began, we would be able to give visual emphasis to an important truth about mental reality; namely that the psyche is an entity with a 'long and copious past… in which nothing that has once come into existence will have passed away and all the earlier phases of development continue to exist alongside the latest one'.[4] But Freud belonged to an era with a different conception of psychic space, and while Kristeva follows Freud in many things, she believes that the peculiar nature of life today is working to erase the memory-trace and hence, psychic depth. If people still bore within themselves the inscriptions of the past, Kristeva argues, they would be less susceptible to the kind of bestiality she sees present in contemporary life. But by and large postmodern society appears indifferent to the wisdom offered by another time. Alone in Santa Varvara the Old Man studies Ovid and Tibullus who wrote from the edge of the Roman world, their poetry turning 'a brutish cacophony' into 'the most marvelous sounds'. He compares the decay that surrounds the magnificent writing of the Roman poets with his own society's slide into hypocrisy and compromise, but his visions of brutality unleashed by the wolves only embarrass others and isolate him.

Kristeva's critique here seems to be directed to the universal banality which she feels is growing today, fed by the increasingly sophisticated powers of the media to disseminate a shallow, pleasure-seeking discourse. 'When something is ordinary it is nondescript, devoid of all specificity ... It swallows our humble attempts at originality, grinds up our follies with an implacable "That's life," which makes any disturbance seem dull.' (*TOM*: 45–6) Although Santa Varvara's history concerns the stranglehold of totalitarianism, the city's problem is a global one, the Professor's warnings universally applicable:

> Keep on holding aloof. Persist against the ordinary. Mistrust arrangement. Confront the permanence of compromise with the constancy of refusal. Exaggerate! Perservere! ... On the basis of your ordinary despair, that weak yet enduring foundation, rise up continually, all of you, against the pact of domestication! Disunite against the ordinary! (*TOM*: 46–7)

Even the Professor's favourite pupil Alba Ram lapses into inertia when she marries Vespasian, forgets her teacher's injunctions and settles for a life of deadening hatred that comes from 'playing at the ordinary'.

In a sense Kristeva's novel is an allegory of postmodern society and recasts the same question posed earlier by Alice Jardine: is there a chance for something new to arrive in the postmodern era that will escape the 'boredom catching up with everyone'?[5] *The Old Man and the Wolves*, then, rearticulates Kristeva's persistent concern with the need for innovation in personal and collective life. Unlike other earlier texts however, its final message is more pessimistic. There is no way to avert the Old Man's murder and the inevitable normalisation of wolfish behaviour. Even more problematically, Stephanie Delacour, the detective who attempts to track down those responsible for his death, is not herself immune to the wolves' invasion. She may see their behaviour as criminal, but she too is a wolf: 'Let them do whatever they like. I shan't lift a finger any more. The murder has left me unscathed. I'm one of them. A wolf. A female wolf who knows what's behind it all and is prepared to talk about it. That's the only difference.' (*TOM*: 183) So if Stephanie is herself corrupt, how can we trust her? What hope is there in the struggle against ordinariness, as Kristeva puts it?

Here we see reiterated the same confusion of the subject with the object of her investigation I noted earlier. Stephanie has her own corrosive ordinariness to contend with: she knows Vespasian is a brute, but is captivated by him anyway, and although she despises Alba's compromises, is as implicated as Alba in her neglect of the Old Man before his death. At the close of the novel Stephanie realises that what really killed her old Professor was his recognition that evil and good could no longer be kept separate but dwelt in loved ones and enemies alike: 'He cracked up when he realized there was no longer a Berlin Wall between the wolves and those he loved. This interpenetration of two worlds seen from his own essentially moral point of view as irreconcilable, must, it seems to me, have been the real cause of his death.' (*TOM*: 177) If his aestheticism had kept him from submitting to criminality, the Old Man's favourite pupils by contrast embraced the ordinary along with his teaching and so much more than him became divided beings: people who struggled against corruption but frequently failed to rise above it.

Stephanie's mourning for her own father's death, prompted by the Professor's, follows a similar course, as it transpires that the two men not only knew each other, but held similar visions of the true and the good. Stephanie shared their intellectual worlds and recognised their spirituality, but could not wholeheartedly live out their otherworldliness. In tones reminiscent again of the reading of Bellini's Madonnas in *Desire in Language*, Kristeva represents their distant gaze as a strange mix of passion and pain, as compelling as it is remote. Stephanie's father's face is so vulnerable that maintained 'in permament prayer', it is, like an all-consuming flame, 'unbearable to contemplate'. Here conflating representations of the Virgin and the Imaginary Father from *Tales of Love*, Kristeva's father-figures, 'men of sorrow', are infusions of maternal and paternal, comforting, unutterably sad, but untouchable. Over and against their sexlessness is Stephanie's perception of herself as earthbound, 'a diabolical counterpart to [their] ... angelism', or as struggling to reach an impossible ideal.

The detective then, must assume some responsibility for the crime. She too is guilty for the death of the Father. It is true I think that one of the emotions inhabiting this philosophical parable of Kristeva's is a sense of guilt. To have loved and been loved by an immeasurably unattainable father and to have watched Septicius Clarus transported in spiritual ecstasy leaves a powerful residue of failure in the daughter. Stephanie cannot readily reconcile invisible heights with earthly depths, and for that reason makes herself vulnerable to guilt and depression. For if the Old Man's world that separated good and evil is failing, whatever the novelist or detective now wishes to say about criminality is tainted by an awareness of complicity. How can we separate the dancer from the dance? the speaker from the spoken? The wolves must live inside, as well as outside of us, and no sacrifice is large enough, Kristeva seems to say, to remove the burden of that knowledge. The grotesque fountain playing beneath Alba's apartment, Vespasian's seedy bar, Billie Holliday's voice, the tongues of fiery leaves that Clarus momentarily becomes, the innocent deaths: all, all are of a piece, part of the world's 'unbroken flesh'. All of us are passing through on the way to death, bound to each other out of necessity, whether from hatred or love, and all in tearing the world's flesh tear our own. In order for that vision not to crush us or leave us dying of despair however, we must arrive at a new kind of saving grace. To me, there are two options open. Kristeva explores one, but not the other. *The Old Man and the Wolves* is coloured by a melancholy acceptance that we soil our neighbours as we soil ourselves, but while Stephanie admits the inevitability of 'unconscious excretion', she moves away from abjection by metamorphosing the memory of her men of sorrow into poetic language and myth. In doing so, she translates the tragic events that dominate Santa Varvara into a kind of revelation that through fractured narrative and poetic reverie makes a lasting space of imagination and energises her in her determination to keep on fighting against crime. This space, incidentally, allows the novelist to keep on posing the questions that have always preoccupied her: what happens when spirituality inhabits an erotic body, or when a delight for the illuminating truths offered by language is mixed with universal crime? There are no final answers offered, but because these questions are always asked against the backdrop of a perfect father, they still leave a lasting feeling of pessimism and regret. A second option which Kristeva does not explore in this novel may have moderated her pessimism, and could have lead her to develop her study of the relation between external and interior space somewhat differently.

Stephanie's view of Clarus and her father is constructed around an absolute opposition: herself and her mother both earthbound on one side, and the two men on the side of the angels, holy and incorruptible. Yet if she had been able to see her father for all his visionary qualities as inhabiting a fallen world, she would not need to feel responsible for his death.[6] Or put another way, recognising her father as being in his body for her mother, as lover as well as father, may well have enabled her to view the ordinary with less suspicion and to have correspondingly tamed the intensity of her investment in language. I agree with Stephanie that new forms and images will appear out of the present chaos and may indeed revive us, but I do not concur with Kristeva's attribution of agape to a loving Father and eros to a devouring (or ordinary) Mother. For if language now has to play for Stephanie the part of a loving maternal father, then presumably people and objects are other: that is, wolfish. The outside still threatens, even as it seduces, and in many cases the holding power of language may not be sufficiently great to restrain our psychic boundaries from collapsing. And with inside and outside no longer differentiated, our capacity to be sustained by life in all its minute balances and variations will be depleted. A different vision of the relation between interior and exterior space would have grounded the path to subjectivity and individuation in loving recognition rather than estrangement and alienation. Such a recognition would still have accepted difference and division within the subject, and even within the speech act, but a division cradled by a mother's (or father's) erotic *and* spiritual love.[7] In which case the exterior world need not be seen as either inhabited by destructive forces or as a terrifying void or blank, but an externality supporting and in turn supported by a psyche that plays with its boundaries without fear of their ultimate dissolution.

It would be unfair and inaccurate however to suggest that Kristeva fails to explore the relation between play, transformation and love. The tone of her novel is bleak, but while her female protagonist remains incarcerated within an estranging body and society, Kristeva indicates that her femininity may offer a different vision to the Old Man's that in the end is more salutory, even more 'true'.

'A she-wolf. Who understands logic and speaks it.'[8]

The closing lines of *The Old Man and the Wolves* are ambiguous. Barbara Bray's translation for Columbia Press reads the above as 'A female wolf who knows what's behind it all and is prepared to talk about it'; Anny Brooksbank Jones in *Textual Practice* follows the original text more literally as I have done too.[9] Doubtless both readings are valid, but each have a different resonance. Bray's indicates Stephanie's simultaneous awareness of the reasons for the current invasion of wolves and her complicity in it; the latter emphasises the discrepancy between animality and logic but brings the two entities together in the image of the she-wolf. Stephanie is the female wolf who at least knows about her investment in life's banalities, and will use her knowledge to fight against the absolute corruption that follows from indifference. But the kind of knowledge we see privileged in Brooksbank Jones' translation is an understanding of 'logic'. Stephanie knows how the universal logic of crime is constructed, and she knows both analytically and empathically. She knows analytically because she is a detective and a journalist in search of the truth, and thus attuned to those inconsistent flickers of insight and evasion that pass in ripples across the surface of the world's flesh. She knows empathically because she takes part in banality and ordinariness herself. Her capacity to understand thus springs from her assimilation of both the wisdom of the Old Man and the inescapably soiled nature of human existence. Together these attributes lend her a purchase on a life in which she is fully implicated: in other words, the fusion of suffering and its analysis creates a new psychic space in the midst of its collapse. Remembering her father's occupation, Stephanie calls this privileged moment a 'reversible space, the essence of ambassadorship, of mission' that moves between 'compromise and revelation.' (*TOM*: 141-2) By contrast, the Old Man's visionary kind of suffering was 'the banner of the weak, a radiance that wards off degradation', (*TOM*: 12) but we remember him as a man never fully caught up in the fabric of life who always watched 'from the window', and his last pupil needs more than his separatist visions to help her speak 'logic'. She needs to be able to experience and understand suffering from *within*. The space of this experience which is for Kristeva the one form of truth today, is absolutely minimal and remains under threat from powerful exterior forces as well as the writer's own melancholia, but it is the only position that is available, Stephanie recognises, from which to unleash her 'secret sorrows' against the malaise which appears to be getting worse. For Stephanie believes that although she is a wolf herself, she can still fight against the forces of hatred before they make criminality and violence the *only* way of life.

It is difficult to decide how much redeeming status to give to the crime writer's knowledge of herself as a *female* wolf. Is it true as Kristeva suggests in conversation with Bernard Sichère that Stephanie's personally vital space of love and memory plays a part in holding off universal corruption? Are her subjective investments as woman, lover, pupil and child the antidote to the hatred we see in Alba and Vespasian? The answer to these questions must be sought in the structure of the novel's enunciation. The moment Stephanie begins to write, as Kristeva explains to Sichère, the change in narrative perspective signals a change in tone, and the confusion and polyvocal nature of the first part of the novel metamorphoses into the speech act of a woman who can be both passionate and disengaged in her search for what remains of truth. Against death, Kristeva pits her protagonist's 'vigilance, which is the resistant force of life, if not hope'.[10] Moreover, Stephanie's quest is given further depth by the personal nature of her reflections in the third part of the novel which takes the shape of a 'personal journal'. Female experience throughout the ages has often been expressed most vividly through the medium of letter, journal or diary, counterweights to more public forms of discourse. Transforming the space of enunciation into a personal confrontation with the death of her own father actually enables Stephanie to understand the full significance of the Old Man's death, and thereby to open the narrative to new forms of transformation and revelation.

Thus what gives the novel its revelatory thickness and gives it a shape resistant to the crushing forces of media-fed banality is the personal act of mourning, and in particular, the act of mourning a father. In the same interview with Sichère, Kristeva admits that part of the motivation for the novel lay in the death of her own father in a hospital in Bulgaria, so the enunciation carries a double burden of grief. The fragile interior space that generates the novel's thickness grows out of these very acts of mourning because the unique fusion of cruelty and love recalled through a father's death is, according to Kristeva, 'an eroticism all in folds'. And it would seem from the linking of 'the sensibility of a woman, child and a lover' with mourning that Kristeva regards a woman's subjective experience as being of great importance in constructing this space. Not every woman's experiences are privileged though: witness the example of Alba Ram who swallowed her own hatred and closed her eyes to murder. As Kristeva says, 'We have become unmoved by evil just as we have been unscathed by love.'[11] Stephanie's performance of female identity is different because she recognises the nature of the wolves within and this recognition when coupled with a personal enactment of grief and love maintains, even deepens, her introspective capacities. But why should this be a distinctly feminine experience? There is no immediate reason to suggest that men cannot clear a space in their own work and lives for personal affect, nor that the female detective is in a similar privileged position to the female analyst that Kristeva hints at in *Black Sun*, for instance.

In *Black Sun* we read that for 'those who are racked by melancholia, writing about it would have meaning only if writing sprang out of that very melancholia.' (*BS*: 3) And further, as I argued in Chapter 1, women analysts who remain partly bound to their mothers but are able to sublimate their acute form of melancholy by putting it into the speech of the transference may express a unique relation to the object and a unique configuration of *énoncé* and *énonciation*. A similar form of identification appears to be occurring in the novel although here it is the relation to the father analysed through the eyes of the detective/journalist. Kristeva maintains that what distinguishes her novel from contemporary texts which frequently begin by 'profaning' the father, is her commitment to a 'sympathetic father' who loves and is loved.[12] Stephanie is mysteriously enervated by her memories of dead fathers now metamorphosed into a teeming mass of sounds and images. Kristeva is anxious that at this era which she views along with Heidegger as the twilight of the gods, people do not replace the Professor with a new hero, so she advocates 'parcelling out' the notion of a sacred passion by replacing it with new 'atheistic figures', but at the same time, she cannot dispel her obvious fascination for a Law that her intellect tells her 'no longer exists'. And in essence, that fascination is one of a loving if sceptical daughter. 'It's said', confesses Stephanie, 'women don't go in for atheism because they're always in search of an illusion, namely that of a lover who will be both father and mother. But atheism may be a solution for women living in the wilderness bequeathed to them by a dead father.' (*TOM*: 175) Stephanie's atheism is radical because unlike other women she has ostensibly refused the comforting illusion of a maternal/paternal God and replaced her need with the consolation of an infinitude of tongues. This does not make her a 'man', as Kelly Oliver suggests of Kristeva in another context,[13] for it is precisely because the daughter's passionate connection with her father allows her to grieve for him that a non-corporeal but erotic psychic space is opened. Stephanie's unique capacity to move between a private exploration of grief and its dissolution (or sublation) in language as Ideal is theoretically compelling and undoubtedly lends weight to the sense that the notion of the reversible space is feminine. Sons, Kristeva seems to imply, are still too busy trying to put the father to death, but women keep on believing and investing in the personal. Fanciful or not, this is how Kristeva the Freudian reads the sexualised investment of the father–daughter relation and its potential for psychic transformation (or, more crudely, sublimation).

Now although *The Old Man and the Wolves* makes use of various narrative strategies to illuminate the special relation between father and daughter which quite clearly doesn't end at death but can be metamorphosed, for me some unexplained but familiar complexities remain. What guarantee is there, for instance, that Stephanie will not become as anodyne and wolfish as anyone else? Even if women as a whole are the last believers in the 'personal', Stephanie's femininity is as vulnerable to invasion as is her capacity for atheism (which judging by the way she mourns her father and the Old Man, could be more imagined than real). And how do we reconcile the attack on ordinariness in the first part of the book, and a veneration of it somewhat later? Earlier, Septicius Clarus had denounced 'lousy old ordinariness', but when Stephanie remembers the Professor's wisdom, she concludes that:

> men and women have become indistinguishable from wolves through despising the very thing whose memory I'm trying to preserve: the *quodlibet*, the being that matters no matter what. I kindle my feelings through minute details, meaningless dreams, insensate crimes; I gather up the quodlibets, the quips of ordinary loves. Father and the Old Man both had the simplicity of ordinary men, no matter who, and that was why they mattered, no matter what. (*TOM*: 146)

At what moment and at whose instigation is the wolfishly ordinary person redeemed by being an ordinary man or woman who matters 'no matter what'? What is the difference for Kristeva, and if there is no longer a wall between good and evil, how can this difference be maintained? For me, Kristeva has intellectual virtuosity and considerable inventiveness. Lacking the dexterity of the truly gifted novelist, her book is nonetheless an attempt to embody a contemporary allegory with quite heart-rending personal experience, but she appears to be confused when it comes to distinguishing evaluatively one kind of experience from another. Additionally and interconnectedly, because of the reversible nature of the psychic space inhabited by her female detective, Kristeva cannot decide when it is that animality gets out of control and becomes a problem. At what point ought we to start worrying about evil, and naming it as such? Is the soul-death of our age which *The Old Man and the Wolves* announces a critique or a performance of postmodernity? These questions which return once again to the nature of space and its ethical reach direct us to Kristeva's study of Proust, a novelist who from his cork-lined bedroom wrote about more evil than Stephanie Delacour could ever experience or imagine in a lifetime.

Proust and 'the look'

According to Proust, reality perceived unmediated by the past is a disappointment, and fails to bring satisfaction to the narrator. Part of his explanation for the shortfall in reality is due to the shallowness of social life which reveals itself in the way the glittering masks of his characters falter and crumble under the impact of time. Time effects the reader not merely as the experience of temporality, but as the time of the narrator's gaze which directs a withering look at the society in which he moved. As Proust writes:

> So the apparent, copiable charm of things and people escaped me, because I had not the ability to stop short there – I was like a surgeon who beneath the smooth surface of a woman's belly sees the internal disease which is devouring it. If I went to a dinner-party I did not see the guests: when I thought I was looking at them, I was in fact examining them with X-rays. (Proust in *PatS*: 65–6)

Kristeva likens the investigative qualities of the Proustian narrator to a scalpel or ray which reveals at one incision his own ironic disillusion as much as the internal disease of the guests. Proust's society suffered like our own, according to Kristeva, from a lack of depth in which the 'spectacle, made up of appearances juxtaposed or set in contrast to each other [was] its only reality[,] springing from the ephemeral decrees of public opinion.' (*PatS*: 69) Social discourse is one of conformity and hence artificiality, a gloss that dissimulates secret depths in which the characters' narcissisms are reflected as shameful illusions. Rather than discovering an essence or truth behind these illusions, however, Proust finds only more appearances: 'a demonic array of transferences and metaphors' (*PatS*: 70), which Kristeva compares to our present-day 'society of the spectacle' that 'transforms its supposed protagonists into mere apparitions, into "looks".' (*PatS*: 70–1) Maintaining his protagonists in a state of constant dissolution therefore, the writer goes even further and strips the mysterious depths from God and Being in order to show the essential artifice that subtends our entire existence. And like the author of *The Old Man and the Wolves*, Proust knows that his narrator is not immune from appearances either, that he too is touched by 'the omnipresence of artifice'.

Kristeva had already made reference to 'the look' almost ten years ago in conversation with Fabienne Leleux.[14] In this interview for *L'Infini* she examines the nature of the crisis in the human sciences which for her is due to the difficulty she believes some have in accepting both the end of metaphysics and the consequent need to construct a new kind of ethics. The death of God has left in its wake a 'state of abandonment and dereliction' which has inspired people to assume an endless number of roles and identities and explore the world of seeming. However, Kristeva adds that although she admires these games, they can be purely hallucinatory unless accompanied by a form of linguistic analysis. The subject-in-process welcomes the look as a sign of freedom from the censorious gaze (which Kristeva links with Lacan and the Law) but unless the subject's multiple games with identity hold on to a sense of particularity or subjective limit, they will fail to withstand the death drive. Again, though, while insisting on the need for naming and analysing our 'private cinema' shows, it is clear that the analyst is as drawn to the spectacle of the look as Proust is drawn to the looks of his society. In fact, it seems that the writer *is* the look whose capacities to put himself in the place of his characters involve a transfusion of identity, a loss of his unique particularity at the moment of identification. For Proust and Kristeva this moment is pleasurable, especially when cruelty is involved. So the illumination of evil is inseparable from its enactment, and even Proust's lined bedroom is too fragile a limit to prevent his enjoying evil at the moment of representing it. What then distinguishes Proust (and Kristeva) from the society they find so disappointing? The answer is certainly not to be found in Stephanie's *quodlibet*, because ordinariness fails in *A la recherche*. Even more, other people whom one loves are hell for us, because they have the power to hurt us: 'And it is because they contain thus within themselves the hours of the past that human bodies have the power to hurt so terribly those who love them.' (Proust in *PatS*: 25) In retaliation the narrator can murder those he loves or expose them to the cruelties of the passing of time, or his relentless X-rays, or he can gather up what remains and compress them into the peal of a cathedral, the noise of a spoon, the texture of the madeleine, but he cannot and does not celebrate the simplicity of ordinary loves as Stephanie attempts to do. On the contrary, Kristeva believes that the sole difference between Proust and his society was his belief in the unordinariness of art which even as it extracted eros from human bodies (and so, I would argue, actually contributing to the depletion of Being), reinvested it in signs and images.

The artist does not merely represent what he sees in the shape of innocuous narrative events and commentaries, but arranges his effects before finding a cause: his mother's essence impregnates the madeleine and the 'ferruginous' bell at Combray; a woman becomes as insubstantial as a perfume or a piece of music: these transformations redeem art, but excavate the ordinary *before* allowing Proust to be disappointed with its lack of secrets. Thus Proust is a melancholy writer, but one who cheats the passing of time by joining the future and the past through bringing metaphor to the present. Through the agency of metaphor, the only truth that Proust could support is set to work on people and things to show that Being is nothing other than their analogical connection. Metaphor lies at the heart of experience: it *is* experience. Kristeva understands this Proustian moment as twofold, where one is both 'devoured by the World, devoured by the Work ...', but simultaneously brought to life in the writing of the work which becomes a kind of 'transubstantiation'. Proust's (and his narrator's) kind of criminality therefore seems to be of a different order say, to Albertine's or to Morel's because while the former equally belongs to the world of appearances, as the writer he additionally steals being from one identity to invest it in another. The analogical is ontological, and its equivalence gives us exquisite pleasure as readers for the words of the text reopen the vessels of our own unique memories and deliver them back to us englobed within a different and surely more complex world of perception. Yet at what point does our receptiveness to Proust which has the tendency to cast us back once more into a private theatre of subjectivity inevitably give rise to a crushing of any impulse towards the good beyond subjective pleasure? Or equally to a contempt for the irreducibility of the particular? May this equivalence between analogy and meaning be the same kind of negative transformation effected by Kristeva when she uses the wolfish remnants of Vespasian and Alba to explain the failure of morality and the illusion of the social bond? And when Stephanie finally translates her personal requiem and loyalty to the *quodlibet* into a fire of tongues is she not in some measure expressing her distaste for the very social herd of which she is still a compromised part? Kristeva uncompromisingly associates the herd mentality of social groups with a lack of freedom which must be fought for through relinquishing the 'disillusioning spectacle ... of mimetic processes and foolish beliefs'. (*PatS*: 94) But in diagnosing criminality and the society of the look, Kristeva and Proust hardly remain isolated from their analyses. This empathic identification with evil on the one hand and semblance on the other is one reason why both writers move us because they dramatise an irridescent if tragic truth about humanity, but the question remains: do irony and metaphor (or metamorphosis) preserve us from psychic and social disintegration?

I would like to examine more closely Kristeva's reading of Proust's narrator on the edge of society. Swann 'as a Jew and a writer, views society as a stranger only in order to see it as it is, in its falsity', Kristeva notes and further, quoting Proust: 'Our social personality is a creation of the thoughts of other people.' (*PatS*: 95) Kristeva appears to be at one with Proust in his scornful fascination for collective life. Social discourse is a scintillating play of surfaces that appears all the more alluring when it gestures towards a depth it cannot deliver; its propensity to drown its protagonists in a ceaseless exchange of properties and roles appeals to that part of a person that longs to be a part of the 'world's flesh' where '*I is Everything*' (*PatS*: 95) – and conversely, where I is Nothing. But this kind of merging does not seem to be the prerogative of social life alone, in fact Kristeva views the instinctive need to dissolve one's singularity as best met through the disabusing powers of art which she believes 'shreds the social order into little pieces.' (*PatS*: 96) The social order actually ends up depleting people of inner being and eliminating their opportunities for joy, she argues, because it cannot admit a sensibility at odds with the will to power. Now this view of society is certainly a familiar and frequently true vision of much social behaviour today, and reflects the kinds of destructive group relationships studied by Freud in *Group Psychology and the Analysis of the Ego*. But if social life can manifest a thirst to dominate others, it can equally provoke and extend people's capacities for creativity and thought in a way that solitude can never do.

I wonder if such an ambivalence towards the social springs from an acceptance of Freud's belief that because the organism constructs itself initially as a defence against external stimuli, hatred is the primary affective response, and so the social group will always have a tendency to be represented negatively by Kristeva. Because the analogical is ontological, the other is *always* a wolf. The unconscious threatens to drown us in its watery depths; others will inevitably seek to enslave us in their pitiable mediocrity. What is art, or the infinity of tongues in this case but a phobic symptom to ward off an invasive and hostile outside? Clearly sympathetic to this view and citing Proust's philosophical sources, Kristeva suggests that under the German romantics the resources of psychosis which both assisted and limited the passage of the psyche between the self and the world, the inside with the outside, had been appropriated to social hostilities between people and groups. (*PatS*: 97) Could we not argue rather that the collapse of the balance between one entity and another into either complete loss of psychic space on the one hand or a freezing of boundaries on the other has arisen precisely because of a failure to open up our limits to people and things beyond a very private, and narcissistic 'look'? After all, the aesthetic is heavily dependent on the social. Take for instance the example of Proust himself, who when critiquing society describes it in the following terms: 'Our social existence, like an artist's studio, is filled with abandoned sketches in which we fancied for a moment that we could set down in permanent form our need of a great love.' (*PatS*: 95) Who is to say which is the better representation of love, the least false? That which is lived or that which becomes Art? Probably the intellectual will assent to the latter, and certainly Kristeva has consistently and rigorously called for an analytical discourse that will thicken and resist the impulse to live without reflection. Why then does Proust use the image of the artist's studio to illustrate the social? Only if to show the superior means of representation available beyond 'abandoned sketches' to the real artist, yet in opening the social to the artist and the artist to the social, far from demonstrating the irreversibility of the process, he has unwittingly shown us the interdependence of two modes of experience where each draws from and sustains the other, not in hostile opposition, but in a process of mutual openness and enrichment. In such a situation Art would not need to pose as the agent of revenge over a punitive parent or disappointing social group; nor would social discourse be obliged to remain so closed to personal innovation and difference.

But would the scene I have outlined above take us any further in understanding the source of evil, and in discriminating between our implication in universal crime and the moment when it becomes a contagion that makes life and analysis impossible? For the truth of postmodernity is the general loss of limits and boundaries, a truth in which we can experience a joyful kind of estrangement, but if entirely unchecked can lead to psychic pain and permanent exile. The other is good, as well as hell for me, notes Kristeva, and recommends the model of the open system as the means of allowing access to innovation and change from the outside.[15] By this means she feels that the minimal psychic space which as we saw with Stephanie Delacour was composed of a personally committed vigilance based on loss and its knowledge, will be preserved, and the destructive tendencies already resident in the psyche resisted. The individual has idealisation capacities that may enable him or her to withstand the forces of death, capacities that will 'move against death and ... create something new *from that very place*'.[16] Thus for Kristeva the postmodern condition which implicates everyone still permits a kind of contaminated resistance, just as Septicius Clarus resisted the external invasion of the wolves by battling them within his flesh. In other words, she believes that *naming* these subjective limit states will assist the person to avoid tipping over into violence or self-destruction more effectively than any form of antidepressant or socially imposed ethic. The outside then must be an ambivalent place since it can both lead the psyche into complexifying itself as an open system, and also invade us in the form of hallucinations or a deadening round of events.

CHANGING THE ALPHABET: EVENT AS REVELATION

When I am in a state of heightened awareness towards things and people in the world, I imagine that the texture of my skin changes. Its waxy lining loosens, begins to melt and becomes porous. Objects brush against my skin like silk, or knock against me, some with movements langorous and restful, others with incredible velocity. Synaesthesia begins its work and I imagine the smell of pines in a hot stuffy room, or a stifling odour when watching a movie. Each sense accommodates and transforms the messages from the other, and in this way the exterior world comes to inhabit the interior, infused with passion and immediacy. Perception is a mysterious process, and the effects on the human body system as a whole have never been charted with exactitude, perhaps because the response to stimuli is individual, calling simultaneously on a host of unconscious memories and sense impressions traced on our nervous systems long before we could speak. When I see the light gather and clarify itself around an object, I am not seeing either a light from another time in my past, or, strictly speaking, the light on the present object, but a transfusion of one into the other. Memory moves ineluctably, scrolling perceptions and memories of perceptions into its bolts of shimmering flesh, unrolling and gathering where it will, imperceptibly rearranging and transforming the stuff of the world and the psyche until I become literal host to a joyous cloud of witnesses, fragmentations of self and others that immeasurably enlarge my experience of life.

But in this situation of heightened awareness, objects and events can also burn and bruise the person who has surrendered their psychic boundaries. An alteration of disposition from an unpleasant experience acting on a revived painful memory, and the exterior becomes baleful, its objects hostile, invasive, aggressive or indifferent. The former rapturous accord between self and world disappears, replaced by a sensation of disintegration or painful desiccation. Virginia Woolf is one artist who has recorded these shocks of perception which have left her in anguish. In *Moments of Being* she talks about the 'purest ecstacy' of hearing the waves at St Ives break on the beach and watching the acorn knob on the blind move across the floor, but later the joy of this childhood memory is replaced by the feeling she has when fighting her brother which is one of 'hopeless sadness' which she describes as a 'sudden shock' as if from a sledge-hammer.[17] She observes that it is the feeling of hopelessness in the face of some suffering beyond her control that causes these shocks, and concludes that when she begins to write about the shocks in an effort to understand them the feeling of hopelessness is alleviated. This capacity to receive shocks, she believes, is what makes her a writer, and it does because it brings with it the urge to understand and explain:

> I feel that I have had a blow; but it is not, as I thought as a child, simply a blow from an enemy hidden behind the cotton wool of daily life; it is or will become a *revelation* of some order; it is a token of some real thing behind appearances; and I make it real by putting it into words. It is only by putting it into words that I make it whole; this wholeness means that it has lost the power to hurt me; it gives me, perhaps because by doing so I take away the pain, a great delight to put the severed parts together.[18]

Proust too talks about the relation between pain and writing, or 'the idea'. He calls thought 'sympathetic ink' which translates the suffering others cause us into an idea or a 'divine form': 'if a particular grievous event that deeply affects my feeble self enables me to discern a general law governing both beings and the world, I rejoice in my discovery which is the very same thing as my art', writes Kristeva, thus Proust's 'Ideas come to us as the successors to griefs.' (*PatS*: 79) When impressions are translated into signs, time becomes sensuous, experience extends between sensation and understanding, and the sufferer turns into a writer who enriches the space of the book with his world of intensely rendered perceptions. Without writing about or verbalising the events that shake them, Kristeva argues, human beings pass up the opportunity to develop more complex psychic interiors.

In her essay 'Place Names', she discusses the event of childbirth as one which draws the narcissistic couple out of themselves through their new born love for the child. The child is the factor responsible for complexifying human relationships and speech, and in a more recent essay, 'Evénement et révélation' ('Event and Revelation'), she again takes up this idea of the infant as 'revealer' or 'discoverer' (*révélateur*) between analysand and analyst to explain how the 'event' can signify not only the birth of the child but the birth of the subject; in fact his or her continual rebirth. Kristeva uses the illustration of the child to probe the nature of psychic complexification because she views the child as a 'crossroads being' on the edge of the biological and the symbolic, thereby prompting us to reconsider the relation of the inside of a structure to its outside. More particularly, she asks us to consider how human beings may remain accessible to the notion of a 'revelation' that will maintain them as open systems, capable of acknowledging variations in the external environment through an innovative psychic response. Contrary to popular understanding, Kristeva tells us that revelation is not mystical quietism and implies neither wisdom nor the unveiling of truth. ('ER': 3) For the analyst, it is a truly revolutionary moment when the outside of an organism rears up and disturbs the habitual patterns of interior organisation, thus it carries a risk, or danger, delivering 'a staggering blow to narcissistic stupidity' ('ER': 4), but if the organism is able to appropriate this risk, it will emerge more resilient and better able to confront an unpredictable future.

Founding her essay on revelation with its traditional resonances of apocalypse and hidden spiritual mystery is a strategic coup that demonstrates once again Kristeva's commitment to deconstructing metaphysics while accommodating its resonant vocabulary to the plain of language. In theological terms, the grace of God revealed itself to the prophets and apostles and thus forged a unique opening of the interior of humanity to the workings of a divine exterior. Even though Protestantism placed more emphasis on the individual creativity of its saints, both it and Catholicism assumed the idea of a First Cause. Since language has taken over the idea of an exterior cause, even if its externality is now to be found in its immanence, Kristeva tells us that the only means to retain the idea of an exterior still able to bring something new to experience and speech lies in maintaining an openness in the psyche to change. Thus the weight of revelation passes from the intervening hand of God to the autarchic initatives of the psyche. And since, if Kristeva is to be believed, the heavens are now empty (*le ciel vide*) and the representational truth of theology exhausted, its valuable aspects therefore need to be grafted on to other kinds of discourse. Thus the events she describes in her essay are equally derived from the language of contemporary biology and logic which suggest that a change to the environment outside the organism can either be interpreted as a disruptive noise, or as the potential for structural innovation whereby a rearrangement in the genetic code or 'alphabet' occurs. An event therefore has a potentiality for transformation, but only if the organism's system adapts itself, otherwise it ends by merely repeating the disturbance without modifying it. In the speaking being who is able to respond to noise as event, and who is furthermore able to complexify his or her psychic apparatus, this leap of innovation Kristeva terms a revelation. Although innovation must be accompanied by the grafting of a word or sign which amounts to the same kind of '*idealisation of the word* of the other' ('ER': 5) that occurs in love, what radically distinguishes revelation from the transference that occurs in love and analysis is its ability to result in an 'intrapsychic modification which opens the scene of transference to *extra-analytical reality* and to the *real* of the drives ... which can remain untouched in a cure.' ('ER': 6) A revelation is not the same as an interpretive word; its effects are more radical and Kristeva associates them with the kinds of potential crises experienced by narcissists and other limit-states individuals. A revelation is sustained by its source in the real, so in one sense it still retains a connection to hallucination and ecstatic experience (or at least to their energies).

Indeed, there are moments in this essay when Kristeva in a double movement familiar by now seems to identify with the prospect of a crisis on the edge of the real where there is an overwhelming desire attached to losing all hold on meaning, and to simply live the event without analysis or understanding. Those patients who suffer from narcissistic wounds, she tells us, either lose their inessentiality in the experience of God who bears the weight of meaning, or they absorb the events of the outside undigested into a series of false selves. I recall that Stephanie turned herself 'inside out like a glove' in Santa Varvara society, and that Kristeva elsewhere celebrates the loss of identity that occurs when the theorist loses herself in the theory, and when the lover loses herself in love. But her temporary fascination with neither seeing nor being seen and embodying the event without analysing it passes, and she reminds us, as well, doubtless, as herself, that permanently losing oneself in God or turning one's self inside out like a glove ('ER': 8) is to be trapped in an unbearable world of shattered mirrors. So her notion of reversible space is strategic, apprehending a loss of limits, but eluding permanent compromise through revelation and analysis. Thus an encounter with the real must be distinguished from its private extra-linguistic nature by its facility for adding to a subject's symbolic and imaginary resources which are fundamentally linguistic. In fact, unless the visionary, artist or borderline person translates their perceptions into a signifying discourse, it is likely that Kristeva would view their hallucinations purely as symptoms,[19] events *devoid* of revelation! Revelations exist to thicken the language of the subject and enlarge his or her world ('L'événement, c'est le livre', 'ER': 10); unanalysed they remain a joyless procession of events chained together that the subject actually uses to resist the impulse to accommodate what is exterior to itself. For if, as Spinoza once said, that love is 'the joy that accompanies the idea of an exterior cause',[20] through revelation language now embodies the idea of this external cause and so leads us, if we believe Kristeva, into love. Language thickened with affect becomes the loving arms which sustain us and carry us away to an apocalyptic encounter on the edge of being. In such a way men and women may live as open systems, permanently accessible to the interchange that takes place between one mode of being and another. Through verbalising an event or an encounter with the real, Kristeva believes that subjects enter into a form of transubstantiation where the 'alchemy of the word' so irradiates the resources of the alphabet that it brings bodies and language together in a state that approaches a 'mystical metamorphosis'.[21]

CONCLUSION: REVERSIBLE SPACE

Undoubtedly the effects of metamorphosis are more private than collective. The joy that Proust releases in us dismembers the 'us' in that through metaphor it connects words with 'fully materialized sensations' as well as memories that are personal, idiosyncratic. (*PatS*: 96) For Kristeva actually, these sensations finally result in depersonalisation, since they are nothing other than the biological drives which are the ultimate source for the renewal of language and which construct the material reservoir that grounds and embodies the subject. Joy and transubstantiation activate the thin skin of language that folds itself over the volatility of the drives, and despite the fact that Kristeva tends to use these mystical words in upward sweeps, we should not forget that their alchemical properties are as susceptible to disintegration as to psychic complexification. As we saw in Chapter 3, negativity subtends jouissance. Although she has reorientated her work to take greater account of human suffering, her fundamental view of the drives remains the same: they spell death as well as transformation for the subject, so even when a threatening noise is welcomed as revelatory event, the revelation experienced by an open system still maintains a connection with exile and estrangement. But while Kristeva doesn't therefore sentimentalise the potentialities of love and joy that she believes an encounter with the infinite resources of language may offer, she does argue that the cathartic experience that writing (and to a lesser extent, reading) is, may shield us from excessive destruction:

> In the experience of imaginative writing, due to the constant passsage between words and perceptions, one encounters the spectre of a bodily restructuring, of a revitalization which is extremely pleasurable [*juissif*] and which opens a space for the illusion of eternal life – the soul of madness ... It allows the reader to recover his/her own memory, his/her own body, and that can be a truly revitalizing experience.[22]

This phenomenon presumably is what Kristeva herself experiences when she inscribes her own mourning within a fictionalised narrative, and what the readers of Proust can enter into if they maintain an openness to his evocative metaphors.

Represented thus, the space of writing becomes synomous to Stephanie Delacour's reversible space that is at once corruptible and redemptive. The image of the restructured body takes place over a void, an empty sky; resurrection is both illusory and our saving grace. The reversible space is the most fragile indication of resistance to out and out criminality because it fully inhabits and bears responsibility for social events without ever forgetting to raise them to a higher power through the ironical if now prodigal use of metaphor. Probably more embodied than the Old Man, the (female) ambassador who guards this space as she moves between one mode of being and another is the exemplary watcher of our times. Kristeva's 'theoretical' undertaking is a risky one however, because her new psychic space is vulnerable to being reduced to a plethora of roles and images. When the writer of *Proust and the Sense of Time* claims that truth lies in analogy, she is asserting a judgement consonant with postmodernity's faith in the pre-eminence of language, or what is known as the linguistic analogy. Kristeva's unique contribution to ontologising analogy lies in her re-reading of Freudianism; in subjecting the events of Freud's texts to a revelation, if you will. To accept the primary processes of the unconscious as the zero degree of experience is for Kristeva to take their most distinctive characteristic – *motion* between or within spaces – and to make this structure pre-eminent. Henceforth the theorist will be on the look-out for any signs that will lend themselves to a reading involving movement and the renovation of space. Not surprisingly, readers of Kristeva discover such a presence everywhere. The subject is a subject-in-process, a body in motion; the lover moves between having and being the phallus, the melancholic between entombing her mother and bringing her to life in signs; the analyst precipitates the *transference* in the analysand; metaphor is a transference of meaning and sensation from one place to another, and so on. Surely this incessant interchange of qualities is indistinguishable from the dazzling play of forms that characterise the narcissists and false selves of this world. What is to prevent Kristeva's plethora of correspondences becoming if not as 'demonic' as Proust's, then as illusory and disappointing?

I do not have an escape valve for my author, doubtless because she fully embodies the dilemmas of postmodernity as much as offering a cure for its soul-death. I suspect that were she to have sought other readings of subjectivity and language, her 'reversible space' may have been conceived differently. There seems to be an anxious straining after the comforts of language and the security of intellectual analysis that is complicated by what appear to be counter-investments in states on the brink of shrugging off all meaning. This complexity gives the Kristevan psychic space an elusiveness that is finally resistant to a self-consistent form of truth and may ultimately leave at least some of her readers convinced that the strengths and limits of her interpretation of literature are actually different from the strengths and limits she brings to her practice of psychoanalysis. In short, I remain to be convinced that the imagination is as intimately associated with the drives as she would argue for I consider that as readers and writers we need the mysteriously random mutations of fiction that finally elude *all* interpretation. I maintain in fact, that our need for an exterior to give us joy is limited when we attempt to over-systematise that exterior or to fully incorporate it within language. Similarly, if transcendence is not an absolute point fixed permanently outside the system, we ought yet be able to incorporate its qualities as an exteriority within the psyche rather in the way that Newton assumed Absolute Space within a universe of perpetual movement.[23] In this admittedly anachronistic way the Absolute is neither self-sufficient nor compromised, but a space of groundedness which is 'from the outset in and for itself beside us and wants to be beside us'. Secondly and relatedly, I consider that the symptoms that appear in patient's discourses may have sources and destinations quite distinct from the Freudian universe of death and sex within which Kristeva works, although these objections would require another book and a great deal more reading before they could be adequately developed. Finally, I find her investment in women as lived forms of difference commendable, and the complexity brought to the figure of the female detective in *The Old Man and the Wolves* who is simply another variation on the figure of the female voyager after all, reminds us that she neither lionises women nor under-represents them in their desire to be thinking, loving subjects, although there are obviously more daring narratives currently being written about the feminine lived body that would reach different conclusions about subjectivity than hers.[24]

But Julia Kristeva will continue to fascinate readers and draw them into her textual universe because of the engaging way she brings together disparate discourses and grafts them into singing flesh. Her writing style is frequently seductive, lively and energetic, her personal enunciation when it occurs adding a subtle twist to the larger questions, which as we approach the end of a century that has witnessed so much upheaval, are increasingly returning to redrawing the ethics of humanism to accommodate more compassionately the essentially exiled nature of the human experience.

Selected Bibliography

JULIA KRISTEVA – PRIMARY TEXTS

Major Texts in French

Kristeva, Julia. *Étrangers à nous-mêmes*. Paris: Fayard, 1988.
——. *La Révolution du langage poétique. L'avant-garde à la fin du XIXe siècle. Lautréamont et Mallarmé*. Paris: Seuil, 1974.
——. *Le Langage, cet inconnu. Une initiation à la linguistique*. Paris: Seuil, 1981.
——. *Le Texte du roman. Approche sémiologique d'une structure discursive transformationnelle*. The Hague: Mouton, 1970.
——. *Le Vieil Homme et les loups*. Paris: Fayard, 1991.
——. *Les nouvelles maladies de l'âme*. Paris: Fayard, 1993.
——. *Les Samouraïs*. Paris: Fayard, 1990.
——. *Pouvoirs de l'horreur. Essai sur l'abjection*. Paris: Seuil, 1980.
——. *Séméiotikè. Recherches pour une sémanalyse*. Paris: Seuil, 1969.
——. 'La fonction prédicative et le sujet parlant'. *Langue, discours, société*. Eds Julia Kristeva, Jean-Claude Milner, Nicolas Ruwet. Paris: Seuil, 1975: 229–59.
——. 'Pratique signifiante et mode de production'. *La Traverseé des signes*. Eds Julia Kristeva, Madeleine Biardeau, François Cheng, Pierre Sylvain Filliozat, Michelle Loi, Daniel Sibony, Eva de Vitray-Meyerovitch. Paris: Seuil, 1975: 11–29.

Articles and Interviews in French

Enthoven, Jean Paul. 'Julia Kristeva: A quoi servent les intellectuels?' *Le Nouvel Observateur* 20 June 1977: 98–134.
Glucksman, Christine, and Jean Peytard. 'Littérature, sémiotique, marxisme'. *La Nouvelle Critique* November 1970: 28–35.
Kristeva, Julia. 'D'Ithaca à New York'. *Polylogue*. Paris: Seuil, 1977: 495–515.
——. 'Evenément et révélation'. *L'Infini* 5 (1984): 3–11.
——. 'Gloire, deuil, écriture'. *Romantisme* 18.62 (1988): 7–14.
——. 'La femme tristesse'. *L'Infini* 17 (1987): 5–9.
——. 'La littérature souveraine'. *Paris 1937–57. Créations en France*. Paris: Centre Georges Pompidou, 1981: 13–18.
——. 'La Vierge de Freud'. *L'Infini* 18 (1987): 23–30.
——. 'Le nouveau monde solitaire'. *Le Genre humain* 11 (1984–85): 207–14.
——. 'Les looks sont entrés dans Paris'. *L'Infini* 5 (1984): 14–19.
——. 'Sémanalyse et production de sens. Quelques problèmes de sémiotique littéraire à propos d'un texte de Mallarmé. *Un coup de dés'*. *Essais de Sémiotique Poétique*. Ed. A. Greimas. Paris: Librairie Larousse, 1972: 207–34.
——. 'Sophia'. *Le Nouvel Observateur* 13 (1992): 36–7.
——. 'Sujet dans le langage et pratique politique'. *Tel Quel* 58 (1974): 22–7.
Sichère, Bernard. 'Roman noir et temps présent'. *L'Infini* 37 (1992): 75–86.

Major Texts in Translation

Kristeva, Julia. *About Chinese Women*. Trans. Anita Barrows. New York: Marion Boyars, 1977.

——. *Black Sun: Depression and Melancholia*. Trans. Leon Roudiez. New York: Columbia University Press, 1989.

——. *Desire in Language*. Ed. Leon S. Roudiez. Trans. Alice Jardine, Thomas A. Gora and Leon S. Roudiez. New York: Columbia University Press, 1980.

——. *In the Beginning was Love: Psychoanalysis and Faith*. Trans. Arthur Goldhammer. New York: Columbia University Press, 1987.

——. *Language, the Unknown: An Initiation into Linguistics*. Trans. Anne M. Menke. New York: Columbia University Press, 1989.

——. *Powers of Horror: An Essay on Abjection*. Trans. Leon Roudiez. New York: Columbia University Press, 1982.

——. *Proust and the Sense of Time*. Trans. Stephen Bann. London: Faber and Faber, 1993.

——. *Revolution in Poetic Language*. Trans. Margaret Waller. New York: Columbia University Press, 1984.

——. *Strangers to Ourselves*. Trans. Leon Roudiez. New York: Columbia University Press, 1991.

——. *Tales of Love*. Trans. Leon Roudiez. New York: Columbia University Press, 1987.

——. *The Kristeva Reader*. Ed. Toril Moi. New York: Columbia University Press, 1986.

——. *The Old Man and the Wolves*. Trans. Barbara Bray. New York: Columbia University Press, 1994.

Articles and Interviews in Translation

Appignanesi, L., ed. 'Julia Kristeva in Conversation with Rosalind Coward'. *Desire*. I.C.A. Documents. London: Institute of Contemporary Arts, 1984: 22–7.

——, ed. 'Histoires d'amour: Love Stories'. *Desire*. 1984. 18–21.

Baruch, Elaine Hoffman and Perry Meisel. 'Two Interviews with Julia Kristeva'. *Partisan Review* 51 1 (1984): 120–32.

Féral, Josette. 'China, Women and the Symbolic: An Interview with Julia Kristeva'. Trans. Penny Kritzman. *Sub-Stance* 13 (1976): 9–18.

Jardine, Alice. *Discourses: Conversations in Postmodern Art and Culture*. Ed. Russell Fergusson, William Olander, Marcia Tucker and Karen Fiss. New York: New Museum of Contemporary Art and M.I.T. Press, 1990.

Kolocotroni, Vassiliki. 'Julia Kristeva'. *Textual Practice* 5 2 (1991): 157–70.

Kristeva, Julia. 'Approaching Abjection'. Trans. John Lechte. *Oxford Literary Review* 5.1 and 2 (1982): 125–49.

——. 'Ellipsis on Dread and the Specular Seduction'. Trans. Dolores Burdick. *Wide Angle* 3.2 (1979): 42–7.

——. 'Four Types of Signifying Practice'. *Semeiotexte* 1.1 (1974): 65–74.

——. 'Jackson Pollock's Milky Way: 1912–1956'. *Journal of Philosophy and the Visual Arts* (1989): 34–9.

——. 'Joyce "The Gracehopper" or the Return of Orpheus'. *James Joyce: The Augmented Ninth.* Ed. Bernard Benstock. Syracuse, New York: Syracuse University Press, 1988: 167–437.

——. 'Modern Theatre Does Not Take (a) Place'. *Sub-stance* 18/19 (1977): 131–5.

——. 'My Memory's Hyperbole'. Trans. Athena Viscusi. *The Female Autograph.* Ed. Domna Stanton. *New York Literary Forum* 12–13 (1984): 261–76.

——. 'Oscillation Between Power and Denial'. From 'Oscillation du "pouvoir" au "refus"'. With Xavière Gauthier. *Tel Quel* 58 (1974). Trans. Marilyn A. August. *New French Feminisms: an Anthology.* Ed. Elaine Marks and Isabelle de Courtivron. Brighton: Harvester, 1981: 165–7.

——. 'Phonetics, Phonology and Impulsional Bases'. Trans. Caren Greenberg. *Diacritics* 4.3 (1974): 33–7.

——. 'Postmodernism?' *Bucknell Review* 25.2 (1980): 136–41.

——. 'Say Nothing'. Trans. Salvatore Mele. *On the Beach* 3 and 4 (1984): 10–14.

——. 'Talking about *Polylogue*'. Trans. Seán Hand. *French Feminist Thought: A Reader.* Ed. Toril Moi. Oxford: Blackwell, 1987: 110–17.

——. 'The Adolescent Novel'. *Abjection, Melancholia and Love: The Work of Julia Kristeva.* Ed. J. Fletcher and A. Benjamin. London: Routledge, 1990: 8–23.

——. 'The Last Word of this Adventure'. With Louise Burchill. *On the Beach* (1984): 21–5.

——. 'The Ruin of a Poetics'. Trans. Vivienne Mylne. *Twentieth Century Studies* 7 and 8 (1972): 102–19.

——. 'The Semiotic Activity'. Trans. Stephen Heath and Christopher Prendergast. *Screen Reader 2: Cinema and Semiotics.* London: Villiers, 1981: 23–37.

——. 'The Speaking Subject'. *On Signs: A Semiotics Reader.* Ed. Marshall Blonsky. Oxford: Blackwell, 1985. 210–20.

——. 'Within the Microcosm of "the Talking Cure"'. Trans. Thomas Gora and Margaret Waller. *Interpreting Lacan.* Ed. Joseph Smith and William Kerrigan. New Haven: Yale University Press, 1983. 33–48.

——. 'Woman Can Never be Defined'. From 'La femme ce n'est jamais ça'. An interview with *psych et po* in *Tel Quel* 59 (1974). Trans. Marilyn A. August. Ed. Marks and de Courtivron. 1981: 137–41.

Kurzweil, Edith. 'An Interview with Julia Kristeva'. Trans. Bron Anderson and Margaret Waller. *Partisan Review* 53.2 (1986): 216–29.

Lipkowitz, Ina and Martha Buskirk. 'An Interview with Julia Kristeva'. *Critical texts* 3 3 (1982): 3–13.

Waller, Margaret. 'An Interview with Julia Kristeva'. Trans. Richard Macksey. *Intertextuality and Contemporary American Fiction.* Ed. Patrick O'Donnell and Robert Con Davis. Baltimore: Johns Hopkins University Press, 1989: 280–93.

Notes

INTRODUCTION

1. For information on the use of self-estrangement in Marx, see Karl Marx and Friedrich Engels, *The German Ideology* (London: Lawrence and Wishart, 1938), pp. 202–3. The quotation from Marx's *Communist Manifesto* is cited in Marshall Berman's *All That is Solid Melts Into Air: The Experience of Modernity* (New York: Simon and Schuster, 1982), p. 95.
2. In Hegel's Introduction to the *Phenomenology* and quoted by Kristeva in *Tales of Love*, trans. Leon Roudiez (New York: Columbia University Press, 1987), p. 39. Originally published as *Histoires d'amour* (Paris: Denoel, 1983).
3. *Powers of Horror: An Essay on Abjection*, trans. Leon Roudiez (New York: Columbia University Press, 1982). Originally published as *Pouvoirs de l'horreur. Essai sur l'abjection* (Paris: Seuil, 1980).
4. 'Art as technique' in *Russian Formalist Criticism: Four Essays*, trans. Lee T. Lemon and Marion J. Reis (Lincoln and London: University of Nebraska Press, 1965), p. 12.
5. Here is Roman Jakobson on the nature of the aesthetic function: 'What we have been trying to show is that art is an integral part of the social structure, a component that interacts with all the others and is itself mutable since both the domain of art and its relationship to the other constituents of the social structure are in constant dialectical flux. What we stand for is not the separation of art but the autonomy of the aesthetic function.' 'What is Poetry?', *Selected Writings, Vol. III* (The Hague: Mouton, 1981), pp. 749–50.
6. Julia Kristeva, *Desire in Language: A Semiotic Approach to Literature and Art*, trans. Thomas S. Gora, Alice Jardine and Leon S. Roudiez (New York: Columbia University Press, 1984), p. 27. A collection of essays from various sources, eight of which were originally published in *Polylogue* (Paris: Seuil, 1977). See also her comments in a recent interview with Vassiliki Kolocotroni: 'I began by using the term "poetic" in the sense used by Jakobson, that is, as a poetic language that consists of poetry but also of prose, to the extent that it is a reordering of everyday communication. I tried to enlarge the Jakobsonian notion by understanding poetic language as the inclusion of the semiotic within the symbolic.' 'Julia Kristeva Interviewed by Vassili Kolocotroni', *Textual Practice*, Vol. 5, No. 2 (Summer 1991), p. 158.
7. 'A New Type of Intellectual: the Dissident', trans. Seán Hand in Toril Moi ed., *The Kristeva Reader* (New York: Columbia University Press, 1986), p. 298. Originally published in *Tel Quel*, No. 74 (Winter 1977), pp. 3–8 as: 'Un nouveau type d'intellectuel: le dissident'.
8. In *Tales*, pp. 234–63.

9. *Black Sun: Depression and Melancholia*, trans. Leon Roudiez (New York: Columbia University Press, 1989). Originally published as *Soleil noir, dépression et mélancolie* (Paris: Gallimard, 1987).
10. Trans. Margaret Waller (New York: Columbia University Press, 1982). Originally published as *La Révolution du langage poétique. L'avant-garde à la fin du XIXe siècle. Lautréamont et Mallarmé* (Paris: Seuil, 1974).
11. *Basic Writings*, ed. David Farrell Krell (London: Routledge and Kegan Paul, 1978), 'What is Metaphysics?', pp. 95–6.
12. 'The Literary Self as Origin: the Work of Georges Poulet', in *Blindness and Insight: Essays in the Rhetoric of Contemporary Criticism* (New York: Oxford University Press, 1971), p. 80.
13. See Kristeva's preface to *Desire* where she emphasises the critical nature of her work as opposed to its literary dimensions (pp. ix–x).
14. *The Old Man and the Wolves*, trans. Barbara Bray (New York: Columbia University Press, 1994). First published as *Le vieil homme et les loups* (Paris: Fayard, 1991).
15. *Proust and the Sense of Time*, trans. Stephen Bann (London: Faber and Faber, 1993).

CHAPTER 1

1. For an examination of the borderline condition and its treatment in psychotherapy and psychoanalysis, consult Jerome Kroll, *The Challenge of the Borderline Patient: Competency in Diagnosis and Treatment* (New York: W.W. Norton & Co, 1988); and *Essential Papers on Borderline Disorders*, Michael H. Stone ed. (New York: New York University Press, 1986).
2. *Etrangers à nous-mêmes* (Paris: Fayard, 1988), p. 276. Translated as *Strangers to Ourselves* by Leon Roudiez (New York: Columbia University Press, 1991).
3. For a discussion of the relation between revelation and the event as shock, see Julia Kristeva, 'Evénement et révélation', *L'Infini*, No. 5 (1984), pp. 3–11. I will read this essay of Kristeva's in greater detail in Chapter 5.
4. For an account of Kristeva's position vis à vis Christianity, see her *In the Beginning Was Love: Psychoanalysis and Faith*, trans. Arthur Goldhammer (New York: Columbia University Press, 1987). Originally published as *Au commencement était l'amour. Psychanalyse et foi* (Paris: Hachette, 1985).
5. Beryl Schlossman, *Joyce's Catholic Comedy of Language* (Madison: University of Wisconsin Press, 1985), p. 157.
6. Ibid., p. 208.
7. From David M. Guss ed., 'Poetry is a Heavenly Crime', *The Selected Poetry of Vicente Huidobro* (New York: New Directions, 1981), pp. 209, 211.
8. From *Altazor*, Canto V, Guss ed. (1981), p. 141.
9. 'Guard rail' or *garde-fous* is the term given to the role of the formal composition of the text in restraining a complete loss of meaning. On other occasions in Kristeva the term is used to signify the part played by politics in railing off group identity from anarchy or social upheaval. See *RPL*: 209.

10. From *Altazor*, Canto III, Guss ed. (1981), p. 103.
11. Julia Kristeva, 'Postmodernism?', *Bucknell Review*, Vol. 25, No. 2 (1980), p. 140.
12. Michael Edwards, 'Writing and Redemption' in David Wood ed., *Writing the Future* (London: Routledge, 1990), p. 133.
13. Julia Kristeva, *Le texte du roman*, (The Hague: Mouton, 1979), p. 104.
14. For more detailed information on the drives, consult Chapter 3, pp. 109–13.
15. See Kristeva's explanation of this term in 'Semiotics', Moi ed. (1986), pp. 79–80.
16. Frederick G. Weiss ed., *Hegel: the Essential Writings* (New York: Harper and Row, 1974), p. 211. The term *Entäusserung* was substituted on occasion for *Entfremdung*. Marx later attempted to make a sharper distinction between the two terms, using the former to designate alienation and the latter, estrangement. See Lucio Colletti's exposition in his *Marxism and Hegel*, trans. Lawrence Garner (London: New Left Books, 1973).
17. Consult Lucio Colletti (1973), p. 58.
18. This recognition forms part of what Althusser calls the 'early Marx', and is to be found in such texts as *The German Ideology* (1938).
19. Colletti (1973), p. 177.
20. Herbert Marcuse, *Reason and Revolution: Hegel and the Rise of Social Theory* (London: Routledge and Kegan Paul, 1954), p. 283.
21. Herbert Marcuse, *One Dimensional Man* (London: Ark Paperbacks, 1986), pp. 10, 11.
22. Louis Althusser, *For Marx*, trans. Ben Brewster (London: Penguin Press, 1969), p. 226.
23. From Althusser and Balibar's *Reading Capital* in *Arthur Hirsch, The French New Left* (Boston: South End Press, 1981), p. 165.
24. Althusser, trans. Brewster (1969), p. 229.
25. On April 24, 1968 Sollers was interviewed in the communist *Lettres Français*, and described how a new revolutionary way of understanding literature subverted bourgeois decadence: 'First of all, in placing emphasis on the *text*, on its historical determinations and its mode of production; in systematically denouncing the metaphysical valorisation of the concepts of "work" and "author"; in putting into question subjectivity or so-called "objectivity", we have touched the central nerve of the social unconscious in which we live, and, in short, the distribution of symbolic property/propriety.' Cited in Patrick Combes, *La Littérature et le mouvement de Mai 68* (Paris: Seghers, 1984), p. 29, my translation. *Tel Quel's* re-reading of Marx and Lenin enabled them to redefine the determining mode of production as textual rather than economic in the classic sense of the word.
26. Kristeva's experience of exile is nicely rendered with that evocative expression of Barthes' when he first named her *l'étrangère*. See 'L'étrangère' in *Le bruissement de la langue* (Paris: Seuil, 1984), pp. 197–200. First published in *La Quinzaine littéraire*, 1970, to mark the publication of Kristeva's *Séméiotiké*.

27. Speaking of the 'autobiographical' nature of *Etrangers à nous-mêmes*, John Lechte is cautious in attributing too much of the text's investment (and origins) to personal experience: 'It is, however, not so much that Kristeva is an exile and herself a foreigner, and that *therefore* she comes to develop a theoretical perspective beyond the familiar and the same, but that in the act of theorizing foreign-ness in its various forms, she at the same time constitutes herself as a subject formed (like all of us) through foreignness.' Lechte (1990), p. 84. My view, developed more precisely in Chapter 2, is less insistent on the prioritising of 'theorizing foreign-ness' and more accommodating to the way autobiography and a representation of the personal insinuate themselves in the text 'all the same'.
28. *Papers on Metapsychology*, SE XIV, p. 139.
29. See Thomas Kuhn's *The Structure of Scientific Revolutions* (Chicago: University of Chicago Press, 1962), where Kuhn had argued that a 'revolution' occurred in the field of science when conceptual and observational categories were adjusted against a background of persistent and increasingly inexplicable novelty. Kuhn implied that what enabled a scientist to construct a new paradigm is a form of epiphany in language. For example, consult pp. 65ff.
30. 'Say Nothing'. Originally published in *Tel Quel*, No. 91 (Spring 1982), and translated by Salvatore Mele for *On the Beach*, Nos 3/4, (Summer/Autumn 1984), pp. 10–14. This reference, p. 11.
31. *Reading Kristeva: Unraveling the Double-Bind* (Bloomington: Indiana University Press, 1993).
32. First published as 'Polylogue' in *Tel Quel* 57 (Spring 1974); reprinted in *Polylogue* (Paris: Seuil, 1977), pp. 173–220. Translated in *Desire* as 'The Novel as Polylogue', pp. 159–209. This reference, p. 161.
33. Ibid., SE XVII, pp. 217–52.
34. Ibid., p. 219.
35. Ibid., p. 241.
36. Ibid., p. 226.
37. Hélène Cixous, 'Fiction and its Phantoms: a Reading of Freud's *Das Unheimliche* (the "Uncanny")', *New Literary History*, Vol. 7, No. 3 (Spring 1976), p. 531.
38. See Sigmund Freud, *The Interpretation of Dreams*, trans. James Strachey (Harmondsworth: Pelican, 1986), pp. 684–94.
39. See for instance, John Forrester, 'On Dreaming of the Future' in David Wood ed. (1990), pp. 98–105.
40. See the translated excerpt from 'Oscillation du "pouvoir" au "refus"', an interview by Xavière Gauthier first published in *Tel Quel*, No. 58 (Summer 1974) and translated as 'Oscillation from Power to Denial' by Marilyn A. August in Elaine Marks and Isabelle de Courtivron eds, *New French Feminisms: An Anthology* (Brighton: Harvester, 1981), p. 166.
41. Sylvia Plath (London: Faber, 1974), p. 130.
42. Ibid., p. 131.

43. *Les Samourais* (Paris: Fayard, 1990), p. 11. These words are actually spoken by the central character of Kristeva's novel, Joelle Cabarus, a psychoanalyst.
44. *Phenomenology of Spirit*, trans. A.V. Miller (Oxford: Clarendon Press, 1977), pp. 6–7. Hegel at this point is actually referring to the sublation of the dialectic. The object, when acted on by consciousness, results in the subject's transformation, a change which Hegel represents as cosmic in its implications. Nevertheless, there is a sense in which the transformation is effected in concert with Absolute Mind, and so has a distinctly transcendent quality about it. For a more sustained discussion of this point, see Chapters 3 and 4.
45. Proust, *Volume Three*, 'Time Regained', trans. C. K. Scott Moncrieff and Terence Kilmartin; and Andreas Major (London: Chatto and Windus, 1981), p. 899.
46. Samuel Beckett, *Proust*, in *Proust; 3 Dialogues: Samuel Beckett and Georges Duthuit* (London: John Calder, 1965), p. 70.
47. *The Space of Literature*, trans. Ann Smock (Lincoln, London: University of Nebraska, 1982), p. 33.
48. From 'Totem and Taboo', SE XIII (pp. 1–161), cited in *Tales*, p. 45.
49. From 'Mystery in Literature' in *Mallarmé: Selected Prose Poems, Essays, and Letters*, trans. Bradford Cook (Baltimore: Johns Hopkins University Press, 1956), p. 32. Margaret Waller's translation of *Revolution in Poetic Language*, quoting Mallarmé, uses the expression, 'lightning bolts' (p. 50).
50. *RLP*, p. 227. Bradford Cook's alternative translation of this passage reads: 'Then quickly, before they die away, they all exchange their brilliancies from afar; or they may touch, and steal a furtive glance' (1956), p. 33. Note also the figure in Mallarmé's 'Crisis in Verse': 'during the last twenty-five years poetry has been visited by some nameless and absolute flash of lightning'. Bradford Cook (1956), p. 41.
51. Beckett (1965), pp. 72–3.
52. Ibid., p. 74.
53. Consult, for example, Jacques Derrida's essay 'Differance' in *Speech and Phenomena and Other Essays on Husserl's Theory of Signs*, trans. David B. Allison (Evanston: Northwestern University Press, 1973), pp. 129–60. See also Paul de Man, 'Reading: (Proust)' in *Allegories of Reading: Figural Language in Rousseau, Nietzsche, Rilke and Proust* (New Haven: Yale University Press, 1979), pp. 57–78; and Kristeva's reading of Hegel in *RPL*, pp. 114–16, 195–7.
54. Kuhn (1962), p. 111.
55. 'The Agency of the Letter in the Unconscious or Reason Since Freud' in Jacques Lacan, *Ecrits: A Selection*, trans. Alan Sheridan (New York: W.W. Norton & Co, 1977), pp. 146–75. This reference, p. 174.
56. C.S. Lewis has distinguished between these two modes of perception in his autobiographical book, *Surprised by Joy: the Shape of My Early Life* (Glasgow: Collins, 1955). His account of an experience similar to Proust's is to be found on pp. 18–19 where his retelling of the 'memory of a memory' is acknowledged to be the desire of desire. Except of course that for Lewis the longing is for God as the Other.

57. Gaston Bachelard, trans. Maria Jolas (Boston: Beacon Press, 1969), p. 230.
58. For a discussion of Burke's *A Philosophical Enquiry into the Origin of Our Ideas of the Sublime and Beautiful* (1757), see W.J.T. Mitchell, *Iconology: Image, Text, Ideology* (Chicago and London: University of Chicago Press, 1986), pp. 125–9.
59. Quoted in Mitchell (1986), p. 128.
60. For an account of the mirror stage and its relation to the ideal ego, see 'The Mirror Stage as Formative of the Function of the *I* as Revealed in Psychoanalytic Experience' in Lacan (1977), p. 2, and 'The Subversion of the Subject and the Dialectic of Desire in the Freudian Unconscious' in Lacan (1977), pp. 306–7.
61. 'Subversion of the Subject', Lacan (1977), p. 295.
62. From *Seminar I*, xix, cited in Juliet Flower MacCannell, *Figuring Lacan: Criticism and the Unconscious* (Lincoln: University of Nebraska Press, 1986), p. 37.
63. See Freud, 'A Difficulty on the Path of Psycho-Analysis', SE XVII, cited in Elizabeth Grosz in *Jacques Lacan: A Feminist Introduction* (London and New York: Routledge, 1990), p. 2.
64. Lacan (1977), p. 295.
65. Ibid., p. 300.
66. See her *Proust and the Sense of Time.*
67. See the following observation from Georges Bataille: 'In practice the scrutinized sun can be identified with a mental ejaculation, foam on the lips, and an epileptic crisis.' From his essay 'Rotten Sun' in Allan Stoekl ed., *Georges Bataille: Visions of Excess. Selected Writings 1927–39*, trans. Allan Stoekl et al. (Oxford: Manchester University Press, 1985), p. 57.
68. Blanchot (1982), p. 237.
69. Bachelard (1969), p. 7.
70. 'White Mythology' in Jacques Derrida, *Margins of Philosophy*, trans. Alan Bass (Chicago: University of Chicago Press, 1982), p. 55.
71. *Of Grammatology*, trans. Gayatri Chakravorty Spivak (Baltimore: Johns Hopkins University Press, 1976), p. 70.
72. From the *Confessions*, VII, and quoted in C.S. Lewis (1955), p. 184.
73. Blanchot (1982), p. 177.
74. 'What Calls for Thinking?' in Heidegger (1978), pp. 345–67.
75. Heidegger (1978), 'Letter on Humanism' pp. 193–242, especially pp. 233–4.
76. Heidegger (1978), p. 234.
77. 'What Calls for Thinking?', Heidegger (1978), p. 351.
78. 'What is Metaphysics?', Heidegger (1978), p. 103.
79. Ibid., p. 106.
80. From H.J. Blackham, *Six Existentialist Thinkers* (London: Routledge and Kegan Paul, 1961), p. 95.
81. *Being and Time*, trans. John Macquarrie and Edward Robinson (London: SCM Press, 1962), pp. 157–62; pp. 237ff.
82. Blanchot (1982), p. 172.
83. Hegel (1977), p. 19.

84. 'The Uncanny', p. 245.
85. Madelon Sprengnether, *The Spectral Mother: Freud, Feminism and Psychoanalysis* (Ithaca: Cornell University Press, 1990), p. 232.
86. In Elaine Marks and Isabelle de Courtivron eds, *New French Feminisms: An Anthology* (Brighton: Harvester Press, 1981), pp. 245–64. 'The Laugh of the Medusa' first appeared in translation by Keith Cohen and Paula Cohen in *Signs* (Summer 1976), a revised version of the first edition which was published in *L'arc*, (1975), pp. 39–54.
87. Cixous (1981), p. 250.
88. Ibid., p. 260.
89. Ibid., p. 246.
90. Madelon Sprengnether writes in illustration: 'Thus, for instance, Alice Jardine describes Cixous as anti- or postfeminist due to the Derridean cast of her thought, while Ann Rosalind Jones regards her as obviously essentialist (*Gynesis* 20; "Writing the Body" 366). Moi sees both strains at work in *La Jeune Née*. "Fundamentally contradictory," she writes, "Cixous' theory of writing and femininity shifts back and forth from a Derridean emphasis on textuality as difference to a full-blown metaphysical account of writing as voice, presence and origin (*Sexual/Textual Politics* 119)."' These references cited in Sprengnether (1990), p. 202.
91. Hélène Cixous and Catherine Clément, *The Newly Born Woman*, trans. Betsy Wing (Minneapolis: University of Minnesota Press, 1986), p. 65.
92. Cixous in Cixous and Clément (1986), p. 79.
93. Ibid., p. 68.
94. While it would be incorrect to suggest that Cixous ignores the work of separation and death, when she does deal with it, it is as a deadly struggle. See *Angst*, trans. Jo Levy (London: John Calder, 1985).
95. Julia Kristeva, 'Within the Microcosm of "The Talking Cure"', trans. Thomas Gora and Margaret Waller, in Joseph Smith and William Kerrigan ed, *Interpreting Lacan* (New Haven: Yale University Press, 1983), p. 34.
96. Julia Kristeva, 'The Speaking Subject', in Marshall Blonsky ed., *On Signs: A Semiotics Reader* (Oxford: Blackwell, 1985), p. 214.
97. Cited in Julia Kristeva, 'Phonetics, Phonology and Impulsional Bases', trans. Caren Greenberg, in *Diacritics*, Vol. 4, No. 3 (Fall 1974), p. 35.
98. Kelly Oliver gives a deft elaboration of the relative priorities accorded to semiotic and symbolic in Kristeva's work in her *Reading Kristeva* (1993), pp. 104–5.
99. John Lechte in *Julia Kristeva* (London: Routledge, 1990), notes Kristeva's 'deepening personal commitment to analytic practice' over time, p. 6; and Paul Smith in *Discerning the Subject*, (Minneapolis: Minnesota Press, 1988) comments on what he calls the 'subjectivist impasse' into which Kristeva's work has increasingly fallen, particularly when it began to reify the semiotic as evidenced in *Powers of Horror*. Jacqueline Rose observes Kristeva's reversals from a celebration of the semiotic through a preoccupation with its obverse – abjection – to a search for a paternal ideal. See her 'Julia Kristeva; Take Two' in *Sexuality in the Field of Vision* (London: Verso, 1986), pp. 141–64. In a more critical spirit, Jennifer Stone names *Powers of Horror* as the text that shows Kristeva

taking 'leave of her feminist senses'. See Stone's 'The Horrors of Power: a Critique of Kristeva' in Francis Barker et al., eds, *The Politics of Theory, Proceedings of the Essex Conference on the Sociology of Literature July 1982* (Colchester: University of Essex Press, 1983), pp. 38–48. Finally, Alice Jardine discerns three distinct modes of Kristevan interpretation, from semanalysis in the sixties, to the semiotic/symbolic distinction in the seventies, followed by a shift to psychoanalysis in the eighties. She considers that this last shift began in 1979 with the publication of *Folle vérité* (translated by Seán Hand in Toril Moi ed., *The Kristeva Reader* (New York: Columbia University Press, 1986), pp. 216–37) where the 'true-real' (*vréel*, a compound of 'vrai', 'réel' and 'elle') came to stand for a feminine psychic space. Alice Jardine, 'Opaque Texts and Transparent Contexts: the Political Difference of Julia Kristeva' in Nancy Miller ed., *The Poetics of Gender* (New York: Columbia University Press, 1986), pp. 96–115.

CHAPTER 2

1. *The Practice of Everyday Life*, trans. Steven F. Rendall (Berkeley: University of California Press, 1984), p. 174.
2. *Unbecoming Women: Mobility, Modernity, Mechanics* (University of Minnesota Press, forthcoming).
3. Ibid.
4. 'My Memory's Hyperbole', trans. Athena Viscusi in Domna Stanton ed., *New York Literary Forum* 12–13 (1984), pp. 261–76.
5. See his essay 'Beyond the Pleasure Principle', SE XVIII, pp. 7–64.
6. See 'Oscillation' in Marks and de Courtivron eds. (1981), pp. 165–7.
7. *Discerning the Subject* (Minneapolis: Minnesota Press, 1988), p. 102.
8. Vladimir Nabokov, *The Real Life of Sebastian Knight: a Novel* (London: Weidenfeld and Nicholson, 1960), p. 192.
9. See Jane Gallop, *Feminism and Psychoanalysis: the Daughter's Seduction* (Ithaca: Cornell University Press, 1982), p. 120.
10. In 'Say Nothing', Kristeva comments: 'I could say, in paraphrasing Nabokov's famous novelistic character of Sebastian Knight: "I was a bleak woman who spoke a broken French. I am a broken woman who speaks a bleak French ...".' 'SN', p. 11.
11. 'D'Ithaca à New York', first published in *Promesse*, Nos 36–7, (Spring 1974); republished in *Polylogue* (1977), pp. 495–515. This reference, p. 495.
12. With Mallarmé, one literally becomes the die: 'the body becomes a "calm block here-below fallen from an obscure disaster" (Mallarmé)', in *RPL*, p. 132.
13. See, for instance, Toril Moi's introductory comments on pp. 272–3 to the essay 'Why the United States?' in Moi ed. (1986).
14. In Elly Bulkin, Minnie Bruce Pratt and Barbara Smith eds, *Yours in Struggle: Three Feminist Perspectives on Anti-Semitism and Racism* (Brooklyn: Long Haul Press, 1984), pp. 11–63.
15. Bulkin et al. eds (1984), p. 43.

16. Pratt's essay has been reclaimed for a more theoretically aware feminist practice by Biddy Martin and Chandra Talpade Mohanty. They claim that her narrative is actually fractured and multipositional rather than authoritative, there being 'an irreconcilable tension between ... [Pratt's] search for a secure place from which to speak, within which to act, and the awareness of the price at which secure places are bought, the awareness of the exclusions, the denials, the blindnesses on which they are predicated'. 'Feminist Politics: What's Home Got to do With It?', in Teresa de Lauretis ed., *Feminist Studies/Critical Studies* (Bloomington: Indiana University Press, 1986), p. 206. Nonetheless we can sense that Pratt is still involved in articulating a politics of place that privileges a community working for explicit social and political change.
17. 'Dreaming, Dancing, and the Changing Locations of Feminist Criticism', an in-process paper given to the 1988 Summer School of Criticism and Theory at Dartmouth (pp. 1–33). Later published in Nancy Miller, *Getting Personal: Feminist Occasions and Other Autobiographical Acts* (New York: Routledge, 1991).
18. Miller's source here is from David Grossman's book *Yellow Wind*, first published in excerpt form in the *New Yorker*, 8 February 1988.
19. Miller (1988), p. 17.
20. Ibid.
21. Elaine Showalter writes of the need to develop 'theories of women's writing, theories proved on our pulses'. See her 'Critical Cross-Dressing: Male Feminists and the Woman of the Year', in Alice Jardine and Paul Smith eds, *Men in Feminism* (New York: Methuen, 1987), p. 130. Barthes by contrast comments how 'once communication is effective ... banality becomes the heaviest of the threats which weigh upon it'. *Barthes: Critical Essays*, trans. Richard Howard (Evanston: Northwestern University Press, 1972), p. xvi.
22. 'Changing the Subject: Authorship, Writing, and the Reader' in de Lauretis ed. (1986), pp. 105–6. Miller here cites Barthes' *Sade/Fourier/Loyola*, translated by Richard Miller (New York: Hill and Wang, 1976), pp. 8–9. Barthes' sentiments delivered with reticence are reminiscent of those of Michel Foucault in 'The Discourse on Language', published as an appendix to *The Archaeology of Knowledge*, trans. A.M. Sheridan Smith (New York: Pantheon, 1972), p. 215, where he speaks of his desire to slip 'imperceptibly into this lecture'. To be 'freed from the obligation to begin' is commensurate in many respects with Barthes' autobiographical fragments.
23. Miller in de Lauretis ed. (1986), p. 112.
24. Ibid., p. 114.
25. Ibid.
26. Teresa de Lauretis is another feminist who would insist on the problematic nature of gender, regarding it as at once a representation (of desire and agency) and representation's excess; or expressed another way, as the product *and* process of representation. Since de Lauretis regards psychoanalysis as using male analytic categories to account for female psychosocial development, her enthusiasm for what lies 'elsewhere' is underwritten by the need to discover new ways of

naming 'woman'. She makes use of the 'space-off' in film theory to locate an alterity to conventional representation that is 'not represented yet implied (unseen) in them'. See her *Technologies of Gender: Essays on Theory, Film, and Fiction* (Bloomington: Indiana University Press, 1987), p. 26 and passim.

27. See *Desire*, pp. 64–91.
28. *Mallarmé: The Poems*, a bilingual edition trans. Keith Bosley (Harmondsworth: Penguin, 1977), pp. 90–1.
29. In this I follow Michèle le Doeuff who argues that philosophy is a universal discourse to which both men and women should have access. See her *Hipparchia's Choice: An Essay Concerning Women, Philosophy, Etc.*, trans. Trista Selous (Oxford: Blackwell, 1991).
30. '... je ne crée pas une femme, je fais un tableau', attributed to Matisse in Albert Skira ed., *Stéphane Mallarmé Poésies*, Illustrations de Henri Matisse (Paris: L.C.L./Gallimard, 1966).
31. This particular dismissive reading of 'beauty' receives its about turn in a much more recent reading in *BS*. See especially pp. 97–103, 206.
32. 'Seeking the Third Term: Desire, the Phallus, and the Materiality of Language' in Richard Feldstein and Judith Roof eds, *Feminism and Psychoanalysis* (Ithaca: Cornell University Press, 1989), pp. 40–64. This reference, p. 56. Note also the point that 'the primordial maternal phantasmal *objet a* serves as the material lining (*doublure*) of the subject which infers a structure (ordering) in being'. The primordial *objet a* represents Lacan's 'unary feature', the first signifier to be repressed as the unconscious.
33. Consult, for instance, Luce Irigaray, *This Sex Which is Not One*, trans. Catherine Porter (Ithaca: Cornell University Press, 1985); Hélène Cixous, 'The Laugh of the Medusa' in Marks and de Courtivron eds. (1981), pp. 245–64; Jessica Benjamin, 'The Decline of the Oedipus Complex' in John Broughton ed., *Critical Theories of Psychological Development* (New York: Plenum Press, 1987), pp. 211–44; Nancy Chodorow, *The Reproduction of Mothering: Psychoanalysis and the Sociology of Gender* (Berkeley: University of California Press, 1978); Dorothy Dinnerstein, *The Mermaid and the Minotaur: Sexual Arrangements and Human Malaise* (New York: Harper and Row, 1976); Melanie Klein, *Love, Guilt and Reparation and Other Works* (New York: Dell, 1975).
34. First published as 'le temps des femmes' in *33/34: Cahiers de recherche de sciences des textes et documents*, No. 5 (Winter 1979), pp. 5–19, translated by Alice Jardine and Harry Blake in Moi ed. (1986), pp. 188–213.
35. Quoted by Michèle Montrelay, 'Inquiry into Femininity', trans. Parveen Adams in Toril Moi ed., *French Feminist Thought: A Reader* (Oxford: Basil Blackwell, 1987), p. 227.
36. Kelly Oliver is a notable exception. While reading Kristeva critically: 'When I first began working on this project I set out to criticize Kristeva's writing from a feminist standpoint', she also recognises the value of a recuperative reading 'against the grain' of her texts. Oliver (1993), pp. 180, 17, 1.
37. Kaja Silverman is one critic who has isolated this double nature of Kristeva's thinking on women. I disagree with her diagnosis, but will

develop my own critique of Silverman in Chapter 4. Consult Kaja Silverman, *The Acoustic Mirror: The Female Voice in Psychoanalysis and Cinema* (Bloomington and Indianapolis: Indiana University Press, 1988), pp. 101ff.

38. 'Kristeva's *Soleil noir* and Postmodernity', *Cultural Critique*, No. 18 (Spring 1991), p. 116.
39. *Reading Woman: Essays in Feminist Criticism* (London: Methuen, 1986), p. 22.
40. *Desire*, p. 99.
41. According to Waller, the 'text's density and difficulty force the translator to determine at every turn whether to separate the signifier from the signified and when to privilege, in the name of clarity, the latter over the former… In some instances, such alterations had stylistic, particularly syntactic consequences: specifying antecedents, changing nouns to verbs, making passive verb forms active, breaking up and sometimes rearranging sentences, as well as inserting paragraph breaks.' *RPL*, p. ix.
42. Emile Benveniste, *Problems in General Linguistics*, trans. M.E. Meek (Coral Gables, Florida: University of Miami Press, 1971). The most pertinent essay on the 'I/You' relation is his 'Subjectivity in Language', pp. 223–30. See especially p. 229.
43. Jacobus (1986), p. 286.
44. 'The Agency of the Letter' in Lacan (1977), p. 153. Anthony Easthope, commenting on the way meaning is constructed through the elimination or absence of other possible significations, writes: 'The presence of meaning along the syntagmatic chain necessarily depends upon the absence of the Other, the rest of language, from the syntagmatic chain.' In *Poetry as Discourse* (London: Methuen, 1986), p. 37.
45. *The Haunting of Sylvia Plath* (London: Virago, 1991), p. 10.
46. See 'Oscillation' in Marks and de Courtivron eds. (1981), pp. 165–7. The following comment is illuminating: 'When a woman novelist does not reproduce a real *family* of her own, she creates an imaginary story through which she constitutes an identity: narcissism is safe, the ego becomes eclipsed after freeing itself, purging itself of reminiscences' (p. 166).
47. *The Lives and Legends of Jacques Lacan*, trans. Arthur Goldhammer (New York: Columbia University Press, 1983), p. 16.
48. Clément (1983), p. 17.
49. Ibid., p. 13.
50. Freud SE XI, p. 130.
51. Jacobus (1986), p. 165.
52. Freud SE XIV, pp. 88–9.
53. *Becoming a Heroine: Reading About Women in Novels* (Harmondsworth: Penguin 1984), p. xv.
54. Brownstein (1984), p. xx.
55. Ibid., p. xxi.
56. Kristeva herself stresses both of these aspects that pertain to the distinctiveness of the female subject when she comments to Francoise van Rossum-Guyon on the nature of the personal analysis she experienced: 'It was at once a concentration and a dissolution of "identity",

the individual image or photo standing in for the family or institution.' See 'Talking about *Polylogue*', trans. Seán Hand in Moi ed. (1987), p. 114. Originally published as 'A partir de *Polylogue*' in *Revue des sciences humaines*, Vol. XLIV, No. 168 (October–December 1977), pp. 495–501.

57. Lechte (1990), p. 184.
58. 'Reading as Construction' in Susan Suleiman and Inge Crossman eds, *The Reader in the Text: Essays on Audience and Interpretation* (Princeton: Princeton University Press, 1980), p. 67. Reader response theory is a vast field and it would be improper here not to mention at least one of its founders: Wolfgang Iser. Iser writes in *The Act of Reading* of the reader's quest for 'meaning' as being launched by an experience of the strange and unfamiliar, a voyage that I have touched on in the above attention to meaning as 'product'. The gap in meaning and intention which underlies Iser's conception of the literary text – the 'indeterminate, constitutive blank' – has affiliations with Kristeva and others, but ultimately the reader is dependent for her pleasure on the prior structures of the text and her own judging (interpretive) consciousness. See *The Act of Reading: A Theory of Aesthetic Response* (London: Routledge and Kegan Paul, 1978).
59. First published in *Critical Inquiry*, Vol. 9, No. 1 (September 1982). This edition in Moi ed. (1986), pp. 302–50.
60. See for instance, 'The Ethics of Linguistics' in *Desire*, especially pp. 28–30, where the poetic craft of Mayakovsky is discussed.
61. Cynthia Chase also makes this point in her essay 'Desire and Identification in Lacan and Kristeva'. See Feldstein and Roof eds (1989), pp. 65–83.

CHAPTER 3

1. Derrida in 'Freud and the Scene of Writing' uses the same expression, but his sense is of a 'lithography before words' that is 'nonlinguistic' and 'alogical'. See *Writing and Difference*, trans. Alan Bass (Chicago: University of Chicago Press, 1978), especially pp. 196–231. I am just as interested in describing a landscape through verbal images which would then submit, to some extent at least, to a philosophy of presence.
2. Gayatri Chakravorty Spivak, introduction to *Of Grammatology*, Jacques Derrida, trans. Gayatri Chakravorty Spivak (Baltimore: Johns Hopkins University Press, 1976), p. xli.
3. Cited by Kristeva in *RPL*, p. 248.
4. See her account of Flaubert in Schlossman, *The Orient of Style: Modernist Allegories of Conversion* (Durham: Duke University Press, 1991).
5. *Séméiotiké* (Paris: Seuil, 1969).
6. Michael Payne has observed a similar bent in Kristeva's style. See his *Reading Theory: An Introduction to Lacan, Derrida, and Kristeva* (Cambridge, Mass.: Blackwell, 1993), p. 181.
7. Derrida (1976), p. 68.

8. The wording here is on p. 69 of *RLP*. (The English translation on p. 70 of *RPL* uses 'signifying edifice'.)
9. Refer *RPL*, pp. 25–30, and consult Kristeva's footnotes 12–14 in *RPL*, pp. 239–40.
10. *Timaeus*, trans, Francis Cornford, in *RPL*, p. 239, my emphasis.
11. Consult *RPL*, p. 26. In 'Julia Kristeva et Al', Paul Smith argues that the figure of the chora acted as a transitional stage in Kristeva's progress from analysing negativity through the semiotic/symbolic 'doublet' to reifying the semiotic in *Powers of Horror*. Smith's article is critical of Kristeva's eventual capitulation to essentialism, but it is nonetheless true that the chora represents an originary stasis within the wider negativity of the semiotic. This form of positing/residual identity to my mind however, is inevitable for any discourse, no matter how anti-phenomenological. See Feldstein and Roof (1989), pp. 84–104, especially p. 96 and passim.
12. Kaja Silverman, *The Acoustic Mirror: The Female Voice in Psychoanalysis and Cinema* (Bloomington: Indiana University Press, 1988), p. 102. Also sensitive to the maternal resonances of the chora, Michael Payne suggests that the term is not merely derived from Plato, but contains the word 'chorion', 'a precise technical term ... from embryology that specifically defines the bodily site of the first signifying processes of the fetus' (Payne, 1993), p. 167.
13. Constraints of space do not permit a fuller exposition of Husserlian phenomenology, but it is important to note that Kristeva discovers the archaic pre-object in the figure of the *hyle* to which Husserl attributed the qualities of primitive material sense data. See Edmund Husserl, *Ideas: General Introduction to Pure Phenomenology*, trans. W.R. Boyce Gibson (London: Allen & Unwin, 1931), pp. 258ff. She is critical of his insistence that even within the *hyle* is to be found a rudimentary formal organisation that submits to intentionality and thus to consciousness. What interests her more are the diversity of sensory impressions comprehended by the *hyle* which she links with the primary processes that are *not* bound to the consciousness. Consult also Michael Payne on Husserl and the hyletic. See Payne (1993), pp. 170–3.
14. On Husserl's distinction between *Bedeutung* and *Sinn* (meaning), Derrida notes that: '*Meaning* [*Bedeutung*] is reserved for the content in the ideal sense of *verbal* expression, spoken language, while sense [*Sinn*] covers the whole noematic sphere right down to its nonexpressive stratum.' Derrida (1973), p. 19.
15. An example of transposition, familiar to many lay readers of Freud, is the movement of symbols from lower to upper parts of the body in cases of sexual repression. Consult *Volume 4: The Interpretation of Dreams*, trans. James Strachey (Harmondsworth: Pelican, 1986), p. 509. An example of displacement is the censorship that occurs in the dream and which 'gives no more than a distortion of the dream-wish which exists in the unconscious' (p. 417).
16. In *Desire*, p. 2. 'Ossip' Brik is mentioned in Leon Roudiez's preface.
17. See his essay on 'Qu'est-ce que la poésie?' in Tzvetan Todorov ed., *Questions de Poétique* (Paris: Seuil, 1973), p. 125. This final sentence is

omitted from the English translation in Volume 3 of the *Selected Writings* (The Hague: Mouton, 1981), pp. 749–50.

18. See particularly Kristeva's 'The Ethics of Linguistics' in *Desire*, pp. 23–35, and see also *Séméiotiké*, pp. 178–9. For a useful explication of infinity and its relation to poetic language in Kristeva, consult John Lechte (1990), pp. 91–118.
19. Freud (1986), p. 266 and passim.
20. See for example, the elisions in 'Un coup de dés'. Mallarmé also mentioned transposition in the context of rejecting realist description in favour of allusion and suggestion: 'essences are distilled and then embodied in the Idea ... This is the Ideal I would call Transposition ....' From 'Crisis in Poetry' in Bradford Cook trans. (1956), p. 40.
21. This information in Jonathan Culler, *Structuralist Poetics: Structuralism Linguistics and the Study of Literature* (London: Routledge & Kegan Paul, 1975), pp. 249–50.
22. Derrida (1973), p. 104.
23. See Freud's essay 'Totem and Taboo', SE XIII, pp. 1–161, which argues that society originates in the father's murder by his sons who then proscribe incest and commemorate the father's death with a sacred meal.
24. John Lechte reads Kristeva on Mallarmé, but only offers a partial estimation of the veracity of her reading. See Lechte (1990), p. 143. And in explaining why such a small passage of *Revolution in Poetic Language* was translated into English, Leon Roudiez, witholding judgement, remarks: 'an argument frequently based on the material shape and sound of French words would hardly be comprehensible'. Introduction, *RPL*, p. 10.
25. See his 'Les bases pulsionelles de phonation' in *Revue français de psychanalyse* (January 1970), pp. 101–36; (July 1971), pp. 543–91.
26. The game that Freud watched his grandson play was an attempt to master the fact of his mother's absence by connecting sounds with gestures that represented her presence and subsequent disappearance. Kristeva suggests that underlying this game is rejection, the binary *fort/da* pairing representing a destructive anality and a fusing orality respectively, which the infant transposes through reproducing them repeatedly on to a primitive signifying space. In so doing, through rejection he separates himself from his objects, thus establishing them as 'real and signifiable' (*RPL*, p. 123).
27. See *RPL*, p. 225 and passim.
28. Jakobson, 'Quest for the Essence of Language' in *Selected Writings*, Vol. II (The Hague: Mouton, 1971), p. 365. Jakobson is here referring to Mallarmé's essay, 'Crisis in Poetry'.
29. Julia Kristeva, 'Phonetics, Phonology and Impulsional Bases', trans. Caren Greenberg, in *Diacritics*, Vol. 4, No. 3 (Fall 1974), p. 35.
30. Irregular octosyllables, abab rhymes, caesura after the fourth line.
31. Bosley (1977), pp. 134–5.
32. The sound 'm' represents the desire for fusion that Jakobson outlined in his article 'Why "Mama" and "Papa"?' in R. Jakobson, *Selected Writings*, Vol. I (The Hague: Mouton, 1961), pp. 538–45.
33. From *Œuvres complètes*, quoted by Kristeva in *RLP*, p. 243.

34. 'Ideology and Literary Production', in Zima ed. (1981), p. 196.
35. Bosley (1977), pp. 14–15.
36. In Bradford Cook trans. (1956), p. 30.
37. See Kathy Acker (London: Pan Books, 1988), especially pp. 138–40.
38. Tzvetan Todorov, *The Conquest of America: The Question of the Other*, trans. Richard Howard (New York: Harper and Row, 1984), pp. 78ff. I am indebted to John Lechte for pointing this out to me.
39. Laplanche and Pontalis define the drives as dynamic processes 'consisting in a pressure (an energising charge, the factor of propulsion) which makes the organism orientate itself towards an aim. According to Freud, a drive has its source in a corporeal excitation (a state of tension); its aim is to suppress that state of tension which dominates its instinctual source; it is in the *object* or thanks to it, that the drive is able to reach its goal.' Cited in Marc Quaghebeur, 'Julia Kristeva, une philosophie de l'avant-garde', *Les lettres romanes*, No. 26 (1972), p. 369.
40. Alice Jardine defines the real as the 'nonhuman, at the limits of the known; it is emptiness, the scream, the zero point of death, the proximity of jouissance'. Jardine (1985), pp. 122–3.
41. 'The instincts ("vital somatic functions") provide the grounds or traces for a series of neuronal pathways traversing the body which will later mark out the pathway of impulses facilitated by the drive ... [which] is based on a corporeal mimicry of the instinct ... The drive borrows the sites, sources, and techniques of satisfaction generated by instincts to develop its own modes of (sexual) satisfaction.' In Grosz (1990), pp. 56–7.
42. Lacan, *The Four Fundamental Concepts of Psychoanalysis*, Jacques-Alain Miller ed., Alan Sheridan, trans. (London: Penguin, 1991) , p. 180 and passim.
43. Writing on the negative, Hegel notes: 'But the life of the Spirit is not the life that shrinks from death and keeps itself untouched by devastation, but rather the life that endures it and maintains itself in it ... Spirit is this power only by looking the negative in the face, and tarrying with it. This tarrying with the negative is the magical power that converts it into being.' Hegel, trans. Miller (1977), p. 19.
44. Hegel describes this process in terms of the subject who 'negates itself in indifferent, external otherness' and then 'reasserts itself as the negation of all such otherness' (= 'negating the negation'). Hegel, trans. Miller (1977), pp. 10–11.
45. Hegel, trans. Miller (1977), p. 497. In his commentary of Hegel, Robert Solomon notes that Hegel does not make a clear cut distinction between the subject of thought and substance. The self is not an autonomous entity, but instead 'cannot be intelligibly distinguished from the objects it is aware of. This subject is substance, and substance becomes subject ... when it starts to become aware of itself.' *In the Spirit of Hegel: A Study of Hegel's 'Phenomenology of Spirit'*" (New York: Oxford University Press, 1983), p. 284.
46. See *RPL* pp. 107–64 for Kristeva's understanding of rejection, and consult Payne (1993), pp. 183–94 for an illuminating reading of rejection.

47. 'Might not this *jouissance* which one experiences and knows nothing of, be that which puts us on the path of ex–istence?' Jacques Lacan in 'God and the *Jouissance* of the/Woman' in Mitchell and Rose eds (1982), p. 147.
48. Lacan, *Television* trans. Denis Hollier et al. (New York: Norton, 1990), p. 41.
49. See Kristeva, *RLP*, pp. 379–83. I have also found John Lechte helpful on this question. See Lechte (1990), pp. 114–18; 150–53, and for a detailed explanation of the infinite, see his fourth chapter in the same text.
50. Stephen Heath's article 'Difference' in *Screen*, Vol. 19, No. 4 (Winter 1978/9), pp. 50–112, deals nicely with Lacan's appropriation of the feminine as something to be seen. (See esp. pp. 51–61.)
51. 'What is bad, what is alien to the ego and what is external are, to begin with, identical.' 'Negation', SE XIX, pp. 235–6, p. 237.
52. Kristeva argues that the first instances of signified negation in children occur around 15 months which coincides with the mirror stage. It precedes or at the very least coincides with language development. From a very different perspective, Gottlob Frege has written on the qualities of negation in P. T. Geach ed., *Logical Investigations*, trans. P.T. Geach and R.H. Stoothoff (Oxford: Basil Blackwell, 1977): 'In thinking we do not produce thoughts, we *grasp* them' (p. 25). Thoughts are solidly built structures (p. 28) that cannot be dissolved by the 'chimaera' of negation: 'It must be possible to negate a false thought, and for this I need the thought: I cannot negate what is not there' (p. 37). Negation therefore recognises a positing of subject and graspable thoughts since it also contains within its grasp an affirmation.
53. See *RLP*, pp. 209–358.
54. Witness Lautréamont's opening lines: 'It is not right that everyone should read the pages which follow; only a few will be able to savour this bitter fruit with impunity'; and later, 'show me a man who is good ... But at the same time increase my strength tenfold; for at the sight of such a monster, I may die of astonishment: men have died of less.' In *'Maldoror' and 'Poems'*, trans. Paul Knight (Harmondsworth: Penguin, 1978), pp. 29, 33.
55. Hegel (1977), p. 35; *RPL*, p. 11.
56. Kristeva appeals to this figure of Bataille's several times throughout *Revolution in Poetic Language*, but the original reference is to be found in *L'Expérience intérieure, Œuvres complètes* (Paris: Gallimard, 1973), p. 220.
57. Mallarmé in Bradford Cook, trans. (1957), p. 57.
58. Jardine (1985), p. 233.
59. Blanchot (1982), p. 33.
60. Acker (1988), p. 140.
61. Gayatri Chakravorty Spivak, 'Displacement and the Discourse of Women' in Mark Krupnick ed., *Displacement: Derrida and After* (Bloomington: Indiana University Press, 1983), p. 173.
62. Kristeva, 'Ellipsis on Dread and Specular Seduction', trans. Dolores Burdick. *Wide Angle*, Vol. 3, No. 2 (1979), p. 42.

63. Mary Jacobus (1987), p. 197.
64. Kristeva, 'La femme ce n'est jamais ça' in Marks and de Courtivron eds. (1981), p. 137.
65. Grosz (1989), p. 166.
66. I think that Gayatri Chakravorty Spivak would concur with my reading of Kristeva at this point. See her article 'French Feminism in an International Frame', where she describes Kristeva as speculating about a woman's discourse 'by way of the negative' (p. 145). First published in 1981 and republished in Spivak's *In Other Worlds: Essays in Cultural Politics* (New York: Routledge, 1988), pp. 134–53.

CHAPTER 4

1. Consult Margaret Whitford, *Luce Irigaray: Philosophy in the Feminine* (London: Routledge, 1991), pp. 77ff.
2. Victor Burgin, 'Geometry and Abjection' in John Fletcher and Andrew Benjamin eds, *Abjection, Melancholia and Love: the Work of Julia Kristeva* (London: Routledge, 1990), pp. 104–23; Cynthia Chase, 'Primary Narcissism and the Giving of Figure with Hertz and de Man' in Fletcher and Benjamin eds, (1990), pp. 124–36; Barbara Creed, 'Horror and the Monstrous Feminine: an Imaginary Abjection', *Screen*, Vol. 27, No. 1 (January-February 1986), pp. 44–69; John Lechte (1990); Juliet Flower MacCannell, 'Kristeva's Horror', *Semiotica*, Vol. 62, Nos 3/4 (1986), pp. 325–55; Kelly Oliver, *Reading Kristeva: Unraveling the Double-bind* (Bloomington: Indiana University Press, 1993); Jacqueline Rose (1986); Jennifer Stone (1983).
3. See her account of abjection, motherhood and love in Grosz (1989), pp. 70ff.
4. Madelon Sprengnether (1990); Marianne Hirsch, *The Mother/Daughter Plot: Narrative, Psychoanalysis, Feminism* (Bloomington: Indiana University Press, 1989).
5. 'Julia Kristeva: Take Two', in Jacqueline Rose (1986), p. 142. This remark of Rose's is accompanied by the now notorious statement of Kristeva's in 'Stabat Mater': 'I desire the Law'; a desire which, Rose notes, was 'bound to be the ultimate effect of that earlier onslaught on the securing identity of the image, which Kristeva and the *Tel Quel* group had castigated throughout the 1970s as little more than bourgeois deceit'.
6. In some respects I am in sympathy with Kaja Silverman who argues in *The Acoustic Mirror: The Female Voice in Psychoanalysis and the Cinema* that anxiety concerning the maternal/semiotic matrix is accompanied in Kristeva's work by a romantic fantasy about the mother. This latter gesture, she claims, masks in reality a homosexual desire. While rejecting her final judgement, I do endorse the sense of ambivalence approaching that of the hysteric's towards the feminine one observes in reading Kristeva. See Silverman (Bloomington: Indiana University Press, 1988), pp. 117ff.

7. First published in *Tel Quel*, No. 57 (Spring 1974), reprinted in *Polylogue* (1977), pp. 173–220; and translated in *Desire*, pp. 159–209.
8. See further the essay 'Stabat Mater' (1976) republished in *Tales*, where Kristeva interweaves her own experience of pregnancy with a veneration of the Virgin Mary. 'Stabat Mater' will be discussed later in the chapter.
9. Kristeva may here be using the imaginary in a somewhat pejorative sense to represent the *méconaissance* of the ego. The mirror stage experience, according to Lacan, sites the ego in a 'fictional direction'. See 'The Mirror Stage', Lacan (1977), p. 2. Kristeva's later writing views the place of the imaginary more positively. See especially *Tales*.
10. See 'The Ego and the Id', SE XIX, p. 56.
11. Although at this point Kristeva is referring to the socialist East European countries, by implication her critique of their exclusion of death and time as difference may in some respects be applied to Western Europe, particularly in its most Statist pronouncements.
12. One of the emphases of feminist critical theory, particularly that writing taking its cue from psychoanalysis, has been to talk about maternity in terms of pleasure as well as reproduction. It is critical of texts that repress this pleasure. Alice Jardine discusses the American male writer who 'obsessively fears disintegration into the incestuous non-difference of the maternal space'. Jardine (1985), p. 233. Naomi Schor asks, 'What function, if any, is served by the repression of female libido within the economy of the realist text', and discovers this repression to be one of realism's 'ennabling conditions'. *Breaking the Chain: Women, Theory and French Realist Fiction* (New York: Columbia University Press, 1985), p. xi. In *The Sadeian Woman: An Exercise in Cultural History*, Angela Carter comments on how Eugenie rapes her mother with a dildo and instead of having her reach orgasm, which would confound Sade's petty libertinism and Freudian analysis of mother/daughter hatred, the writer arranges for Madame de Mistival to faint: 'Mother must never be allowed to come, and so to come alive' (London: Virago, 1979), p. 128. Kristeva has also given space to the mother's pleasure, and in *ACW* notes the daughter's socially sanctioned investment in keeping it hidden: 'That *jouissance* be forbidden to the mother: this is the demand of the father's daughter ...' (p. 32).
13. See *The Daughter's Seduction: Feminism and Psychoanalysis* (Ithaca: Cornell University Press, 1982).
14. Gallop (1982), p. 119.
15. On the mother's silence, Marianne Hirsch comments: 'The mother herself is and remains absent even to herself. The place she inhabits is vacant. Although she produces and upholds the subject, she herself remains the matrix, the other, the origin ... If the story of individual development, as Freud tells it, rests on a process of separation from the mother, then the mother's own part in that process remains absent, erased from theoretical and narrative representation.' Hirsch (1989), pp. 168–9.
16. Writing on motherhood, Irigaray for instance, chooses to represent its discourse through an imaginary conversation between mother and daughter. See 'And the One Doesn't Stir Without the Other', trans.

Hélène Vivienne Wenzel, *Signs*, Vol. 7, No. 1 (1981), pp. 60–7. Nancy Chodorow defines the mother in terms of *object relations* and describes how mothers perceive daughters as extensions of themselves. See Chodorow (1978). In *The Mother/Daughter Plot* (1989), Marianne Hirsch illustrates her text's front cover with a photograph of her *own* maternal grandmother.

17. In 'WT', Kristeva recognises the greater difficulty women have in differentiating and becoming autonomous when she draws attention to 'the connivance of the young girl with her mother, her greater difficulty than the boy in detaching herself from the mother in order to acede to the order of signs as invested by the absence and separation constitutive of the paternal function'. Moi ed. (1986), p. 204.
18. According to Elizabeth Grosz, woman is 'positioned in relation to the signifier, the phallus, which places her in the position of *being* rather than *having* (the phallus, the object of the other's desire).' Grosz (1990), p. 71.
19. See later in this chapter for a more concise definition of the terms ideal ego and ego ideal.
20. Lechte (1990), p. 178.
21. Hegel (1977), p. 7. This is so even if Hegel's intention in this figure was to privilege the activities of thought. He uses the metaphor of the sun as an affirmation of man as thinking being at home in the State, and thus a reflection of and reconciliation with the Divine. See Kristeva, *RPL*, p. 135. However, the sunburst is also a moment of estrangement that takes consciousness by surprise.
22. Mary O'Brien criticises Hegel in that she believes woman to be in actuality not abstract or particular, but in her reproductive labour, a 'living *continuity*'. The claims of paternity O'Brien argues, are negated in reproduction with the alienation of the male seed at the time of intercourse. Particularly since the intervention of birth control into reproduction and the question of choice, women are clearly involved in ethics (and theoretical discourse). See *Reproducing the World: Essays in Feminist Theory* (Boulder, CO: Westview Press, 1989), p. 188.
23. See Antonin Artaud's 'L'Automate personnel,' *Œuvres complètes*, Vol. 1, p. 179, cited in *RPL*, p. 115.
24. Kelly Oliver writes of Kristeva's double identification with her own mother and the Virgin. But Oliver stresses the 'scar' of primal repression as opposed to the more psychotic identification that I have observed here. See Oliver (1993), pp. 52–4.
25. Grosz (1989), pp. 81–2.
26. In other words, the 'famous nativity of Piero della Francesca in London, in which Simone de Beauvoir too hastily saw a feminine defeat because the mother kneeled before her barely born son…'. 'Stabat Mater', p. 246.
27. Sprengnether (1990), p. 212.
28. Angela Carter, 'Peter and the Wolf' in *Black Venus* (London: Pan Books, 1986), p. 83.
29. Ibid., p. 84.
30. 'The Psychology of Women' in Jones ed. (1949), pp. 160ff.

31. 'On Narcissism', SE XIV, p. 84. Elizabeth Grosz has also observed this relation in Freud between body and ego. See especially pp. 31–2.
32. 'The Ego and the Id', SE XIX , p. 26.
33. 'Geometry and Abjection', in Fletcher and Benjamin eds. (1990), p. 117.
34. On this point, see Juliet Flower MacCannell, 'Kristeva's Horror' in *Semiotica* (1986).
35. 'The Horrors of Power; a Critique of "Kristeva"', in Francis Barker et al. eds (1983), p. 43. Stone further remarks that Kristeva's moving constantly between horror and attraction, subject and object, is 'a Freudian paradigm for neurosis' (p. 45).
36. See the commentary on 'spaltung' offered by Laplanche and Pontalis (1973), pp. 274–9.
37. A more sympathetic reading comes from Jacqueline Rose, who in a frequently quoted passage, outlines the problematic nature of Kristeva's theory of abjection that 'arms itself with a concept of femininity as different, as something other to the culture as it is known, only to find itself face to face with or even entrenched within, the most grotesque and fully cultural stereotypes of femininity itself. Unlike some of her most virulent detractors, Kristeva knows, however, that these images are not so easily dispatched.' Rose (1986), p. 157. In search of an alternative to abjection, Madelon Sprengnether suggests that if we abandoned an originary notion of plenitude and read the mother's body as always already signifying its own difference, we would not need to see this figure as pure materiality which must be repressed or abjected. See Sprengnether (1990), p. 234.
38. 'L'expérience et la pratique' in *Polylogue* (1977), p. 107.
39. See Rose (1986), p. 159. Although Rose seems to stipulate that the affects produced by abjection are transformed through linguistic structures into effects experienced as fantasies, I have at various points throughout this thesis preferred the term affect. As I argue, the experience of separation carries a component of ambivalence and uncertainty. This undecidability supports the persistence of affects with their closer relationship to the drives, as well as effects which of course submit more fully to the symbolic.
40. Quoted in *Powers*, p. 138.
41. The pun works in French and English. The original text gives the expression, 'sans fard' (without pretence). 'Le fard' additionally means paint or makeup. See *Pouvoirs*, p. 168.
42. See *Tales*, pp. 62–9.
43. Kristeva's Other in *Tales of Love* is mediative in relation to the subject, but is itself *unmediated*.
44. See, for instance, Jessica Benjamin's 'The Decline of the Oedipus Complex' in Broughton ed. (1987), where a survey of the current literature on narcissistic disorders is included with particular reference to Christopher Lasch and Kohut.
45. Lechte (1990), p. 170.
46. Freud, 'The Ego and the Id', SE XIX, p. 31.
47. James Strachey, trans. (1922), pp. 60–70.

48. In the *Standard Edition* of Freud, this is described as the 'most primitive aspect of affective binding to an object' (SE XVIII, cited in *Tales*, p. 26); in the translation by Strachey, the relationship of identification is represented as 'the earliest expression of an emotional tie with another person.' (p. 60).
49. Freud, 'The Ego and the Id', SE XIX, p. 31, thus: 'before a child has arrived at a definite knowledge of the difference between the sexes, the lack of a penis, it does not distinguish in value between its father and its mother'.
50. 'In Conversation', Lisa Appignanesi ed. (1984), p. 23.
51. I have used Leon Roudiez' translation here in preference to Miller's, which reads 'with us, in and for itself, all along, and of its own volition'. Hegel (1977), p. 47.
52. Noreen O'Connor expresses the strange sense of meeting what we already knew somewhere else that occurs in dreams and in the analytical relationship as 'a new speaking of that which is not anticipated, not already known, but yet is felt to be that which is most familiar'. In Fletcher and Benjamin eds. (1990), p. 43.
53. Martin Heidegger, *Hegel's Concept of Experience* (New York: Harper and Row, 1970), pp. 30–1.
54. I am indebted here to Cynthia Chase: 'The critical force of Freud's allusion to an "immediate identification" (if not of Hegel's conception of immediacy) is the implication that the signifying function does not in fact take place by means of dialectical mediation or the process of annulling the particular and preserving it "beyond," at a higher level, as Lacan describes the emergence of desire through need and demand. Rather, the signifying function would not achieve mediation or sublation, since it operates through figural and material dimensions immpossible to mediate.' See 'Desire and Identification in Lacan and Kristeva' in Feldstein and Roof eds. (1989), pp. 78–9. This mode of operation is best represented, by reference to the scheme illustrated in 'SN' (1984) that links drives and representations in the form of a 'relay' between the abject mother and the Imaginary Father (p. 11).
55. *Metamorphoses*, trans. A.D. Melville (Oxford: Oxford University Press, 1987), pp. 61–6.
56. Benjamin, in Broughton ed. (1987), p. 227.
57. John Lechte also makes this observation. See Lechte (1990), pp. 171–2. For a further reading of narcissism see David Crownfield's 'The Sublimation of Narcissism in Christian Love and Faith' in Crownfield ed., *Body/Text in Julia Kristeva: Religion, Women and Psychoanalysis* (Albany: State University of New York Press, 1992), pp. 57–64.
58. SE XIV, p. 77.
59. In 'The Ego and the Id', the term 'superego' is first coined and likened to the earlier discussed ego ideal. See pp. 28–39, and the explanatory notes on pp. 7–10 by James Strachey.
60. 'On Narcissism', p. 94.
61. See Laplanche and Pontalis (1973), pp. 145, 201–2.
62. Freud, *Group Psychology and the Analysis of the Ego* (1922), p. 74.

63. *The Seminar of Jacques Lacan. Book I, Freud's Papers on Technique 1953–54.* Jacques-Alain Miller ed., trans. John Forrester (Cambridge: Cambridge University Press, 1988), p. 142.
64. Miller ed. (1988), p. 138.
65. Whitford (1991), p. 48.
66. *The Four Fundamental Concepts,* Miller ed. (1991), p. 256. Wilden has translated the *einziger Zug* ('unary feature') as 'single stroke' in this passage on love and identification.
67. Lisa Appignanesi ed. (1984), p. 20.
68. 'The subject exists because it belongs to the Other, and it is in proceeding from that symbolic belonging that causes him to be subject to love and death that he will be able to set up for himself imaginary objects of desire' (*Tales,* p. 36). Through identification, the subject is transferred to the place of the Other.
69. Judith Butler is critical of Kristeva's position on homosexuality. She takes Kristeva to task for her constant representation of female homosexuality as the 'psychotic alternative to the acceptance of paternally sanctioned laws ... [her] tactical dismissal and reduction of lesbian experience performed in the name of the law positions Kristeva within the orbit of paternal-heterosexual privilege'. See Butler, *Gender Trouble: Feminism and the Subversion of Identity* (New York: Routledge, 1990), p. 87. To an extent, Butler's critique suffers from an assumption that everytime Kristeva uses the word 'homosexuality', she means lesbianism. In the work on motherhood however, the expression is often used to indicate the close relationship that may exist between mothers and daughters, for instance.
70. She is reminiscent of those women in Freud's paper on narcissism who before 'puberty feel masculine and develop some way along masculine lines; after this trend has been cut short on their reaching female maturity, they still retain the capacity of longing for a masculine ideal – an ideal which is in fact a survival of the boyish nature they once possessed'. 'On Narcissism', p. 90.
71. Silverman (1988), p. 119.
72. See 'The Dynamics of Transference (1912), SE XII, pp. 99–108; 'Observations on Transference-love' (1915), SE XII, pp. 159–71; 'Constructions in Analysis' (1937), SE XXIII, pp. 257–69; and 'Analysis Terminable and Interminable' (1937), SE XXIII, pp. 216–53.
73. Lisa Appignanesi ed. (1984), p. 21.
74. See also Lechte (1990), pp. 182–4, 'Evenément et revélation' in *L'Infini,* No. 5 (Winter 1984), pp. 3–11, and my discussion of 'event' and 'revelation' in Chapter 5.
75. See Maria Ruegg, 'Metaphor and Metonomy: the Logic of Structuralist Rhetoric' in *Glyph,* Vol. 6 (1977), pp. 141–57, especially pp. 152–3.

CHAPTER 5

1. Tilottama Rajan has also noted this characteristic of Kristeva's earlier work. See her 'Trans-Positions of Difference: Kristeva and Post-struc-

turalism' in Kelly Oliver ed., *Ethics, Politics, and Difference in Julia Kristeva's Writing* (New York: Routledge, 1993), pp. 230–1.

2. Julia Kristeva, 'Jackson Pollock's Milky Way: 1912–1956', *Journal of Philosophy and the Visual Arts* (1989), p. 39.
3. Ewa Ziarek observes this confusion in Kristeva's representation of melancholy: 'On the one hand, melancholia is presented as a mental disorder in need of a cure, but, on the other hand, it is a state of supreme lucidity, a "hidden side of philosophy".' See her 'Kristeva and Levinas: Mourning, Ethics, and the Feminine' in Oliver ed. (1993), p. 70.
4. SE XXI, p. 70.
5. Julia Kristeva interviewed by Alice Jardine in Russell Fergusson, William Olander, Marcia Tucker, Karen Fiss eds, *Discourses: Conversations in Postmodern Art and Culture* (New York: New Museum of Contemporary Art and M.I.T. Press, 1990), p. 81. See also John Lechte's essay on the waning of affect in postmodernity, 'Kristeva's *Soleil noir* and Postmodernity', *Cultural Critique* (Spring 1991), pp. 97–121.
6. Although Kristeva maintains elsewhere that her father-figure is fully embodied, 'with all the density of his psychology, his affects, his fears', this perspective is not clearly developed in the novel. See Bernard Sichère's interview with Julia Kristeva, 'Roman noir et temps présent', *L'Infini*, No. 37 (Spring 1992), p. 81.
7. I am indebted to Ken Bragan for giving me permission to read his manuscript on psychotherapy and the psyche which suggests that spirituality needs to be grounded in the body rather than in its sublimation. Forthcoming from Routledge as *Self and Spirit in the Therapeutic Relationship*.
8. 'Une louve. Qui connaît la logique et en parle.' The translation here is my own from the French. See *LVH*: 269.
9. See her 'Julia Kristeva and her Old Man: Between Optimism and Despair', *Textual Practice*, Vol. 7, No. 1 (Spring 1993), p. 8.
10. 'Roman noir et temps présent', p. 77.
11. Ibid., p. 79.
12. Ibid., p. 81.
13. 'For Kristeva, while it may take a woman in order to *theorize* the repressed maternal in language, it is nearly impossible for a woman to be a revolutionary poet who can renovate this language ... [The different relation to language which constitutes sexual difference] seems to make Kristeva herself a paradox, an anomaly, or a "man".' Oliver (1993), p. 107.
14. 'Les Looks sont entrés dans Paris', *L'Infini*, No. 5 (Winter 1984), pp. 14–19.
15. 'Les Looks', pp. 17, 18.
16. Fergusson, Olander, Tucker, Fiss eds (1990), p. 89. My emphasis.
17. Virginia Woolf, *Moments of Being* (Grafton: Hammersmith, 1989), pp. 73, 79, 81.
18. Woolf (1989), p. 81. My emphasis.

19. See, for instance, her comments on the relationship between hallucination and the true-real in 'The True-Real', trans. Séan Hand in Moi ed. (1986).
20. 'Les Looks', p. 17.
21. 'Julia Kristeva'. Julia Kristeva interviewed by Vassiliki Kolocotroni. *Textual Practice*, Vol. 5, No. 2 (Summer 1991), p. 165.
22. 'Julia Kristeva', p. 165.
23. Peter Høeg, *Miss Smilla's Feeling For Snow*, trans. F. David (London: Flamingo, 1993), p. 38.
24. See, for instance, Iris Marion Young's use of Merleau-Ponty in 'Throwing Like a Girl: A Phenomenology of Feminine Body Comportment, Motility, and Spatiality' in Jeffner Allen and Iris Marion Young eds, *The Thinking Muse: Feminism and Modern French Philosophy* (Bloomington: Indiana University Press, 1989), pp. 51–70. Consult also Elizabeth Grosz, *Volatile Bodies: Toward a Corporeal Feminism* (Sydney: Allen and Unwin, 1994).

Index